Exploring Reli ncie

Blackwell Ancient Religions

Ancient religious practice and belief are at once fascinating and alien for twenty-first century readers. There was no Bible, no creed, no fixed set of beliefs. Rather, ancient religion was characterized by extraordinary diversity in belief and ritual.

This distance means that modern readers need a guide to ancient religious experience. Written by experts, the books in this series provide accessible introductions to this central aspect of the ancient world.

Published

Ancient Greek Divination
Sarah Iles Johnston

Magic in the Ancient Greek World
Derek Collins

Religion in the Roman Empire
James B. Rives

Ancient Greek Religion, Second Edition
Jon D. Mikalson

Ancient Egyptian Tombs: The Culture of Life and Death
Steven Snape

Forthcoming

Religion of the Roman Republic
Lora Holland

Greek and Roman Religions
Rebecca I. Denova

Exploring Religion in Ancient Egypt

Stephen Quirke

WILEY Blackwell

This edition first published 2015
© 2015 Stephen Quirke

Registered Office
John Wiley & Sons Ltd, The Atrium, Southern Gate, Chichester, West Sussex, PO19 8SQ, UK

Editorial Offices
350 Main Street, Malden, MA 02148-5020, USA
9600 Garsington Road, Oxford, OX4 2DQ, UK
The Atrium, Southern Gate, Chichester, West Sussex, PO19 8SQ, UK

For details of our global editorial offices, for customer services, and for information about
how to apply for permission to reuse the copyright material in this book please see our website
at www.wiley.com/wiley-blackwell.

The right of Stephen Quirke to be identified as the author of this work has been asserted in
accordance with the UK Copyright, Designs and Patents Act 1988.

Library of Congress Cataloging-in-Publication Data

Quirke, Stephen, author.
Exploring religion in ancient Egypt / Stephen Quirke.
    pages cm
    Includes bibliographical references and index.
    ISBN 978-1-4443-3199-8 (cloth) – ISBN 978-1-4443-3200-1 (pbk.)
1. Egypt–Religion.   I. Title.
    BL2441.3.Q575 2015
    299'.31–dc23
                                    2014017662

A catalogue record for this book is available from the British Library.

Cover image: Detail from outer sarcophagus of Khonsu, from Tomb of Sennedjem,
Luxor, c.1270 BC. Egyptian Museum Cairo/photo © Jürgen Liepe.

Set in 9.5/12pt Utopia by SPi Publisher Services, Pondicherry, India
Printed in Singapore by C.O.S. Printers Pte Ltd

1   2015

Contents

Preface

A proposal to present a new book on ancient Egyptian religion is a double challenge: first, to do justice to the vast range of existing studies across all that the topic can cover, and, then, to find the most productive ground for those interested in and actively working in those broad areas. From the foreign territory of English literature studies, the Palestinian-American writer Edward Said once delivered to an anthropological audience a frontal assault on the entire practice of anthropology (Said 1989). In the deconstructive approach of the time, every word in the title of his paper became an invitation to work with words more seriously, to appreciate how the ground of our study shifts like sand in the field of language users. His aim was not to remove the ground for research, but to pursue any enquiry fully conscious of its difficulty. Said is most famous for his longer assault on European study of the Arab World (Said 1978), where his methods and conclusions have long been both denounced and acclaimed. In that wider debate, readers sympathetic to his motivation have expressed fundamental objections to the precedence given to the literary, misgivings which I share (Ahmad 1994). Nevertheless, in his paper on anthropology, Said offers a cautionary model to follow, particularly in Egyptology, considered part of the study of human societies. Rather than taking any term for granted, I would never underestimate the weight of the baggage we bring from the twenty-first century across more than two millennia to the land and people of Kemet.

In this spirit, the first chapter begins with caution over the words we use, and may have to use, to talk about people in another time—and, for anyone outside Egypt, another space. In turning our attention to something we call ancient Egyptian religion, even the first recognition of words in a book title may imply that we have a sense roughly of where we are going and where we are. That sense of familiarity can be a powerful motor in learning, but it may also involve blocks of assumptions that need rethinking. Accordingly, the chapter identifies some core terms that cannot be left unattended in any effort at archaeological or historical understanding. The very first word that needs a warning sign is religion itself, closely followed by priest, king, and temple. For an Egyptologist, defining any of these is a problem to be explored—an active research agenda, awaiting always new study and discussion. In the battle to dislodge, or at least make visible, the embedded obstacles of vocabulary, researchers may return to different ranges of sources: first, to the evidence of the full archaeological record, rather than the selection dominant in Egyptology, where the focus has been on ancient writings and depictions; secondly, to comparative anthropology and cultural studies, and the wider circles of social and historical sciences. Many Egyptologists have advocated and worked on comparative approaches, and my aim has been to follow their example.

Chapter 1 also introduces some of the places and deities prominent in sources, and here every writer in a language foreign to the people who wrote those sources must become a translator, and apply choices, conscious or not. The names in this and any other West European language translate into Latin-based scripts such as English the written form as preserved in the ancient African script of Kemet—Egyptian hieroglyphs, and its handwritten variants. Those scripts preserve the hard and more constant edge of language sounds, called consonants in English, but not the movements between them, called vowels in English. This "consonantal writing," also known from many other scripts, is perfect for conveying the meaning of many languages, including Egyptian; alphabetic writing makes Egyptian harder, not easier, to read, because words are built on roots or sound-groups, and so, regularly, a whole group of words may sound the same (Loprieno 1996). Despite a widespread view that the alphabet is the vocation of script (countered by Harris 1986), there is no deficiency or lack in Egyptian hieroglyphs. However, the difference in script does compound the difficulties already present in translation from one language to another, multiplying the choices available to translators. Three means of translating names predominate in Egyptology, and two centuries of European-language writing on ancient Egypt leave little option other than to mingle these. The first approach is to accept previous European writings, starting from ancient Greek and Latin versions (e.g., Heliopolis, Sesostris). The second approach is to return as closely as possible to the ancient writing (e.g., Iunu, Senusret). In a third, more radical approach, indirect sources such as ancient and medieval writings in other scripts are used to estimate the ancient sound behind the writing (e.g., On, Senwosre). Throughout the book, I have attempted to follow the less-ambitious second approach, while accepting some European forms for names, particularly where the original consonantal core is not certain (so, Osiris instead of Wesir/Asetir/Isetir and Isis instead of Iset/Aset). In the aim of returning as closely as possible to the tangible evidence, I risk introducing confusion from unfamiliar versions of ancient names. The place names in particular may seem unnecessarily different: Abu for Elephantine, and for Memphis even two names, Inebhedj for the early Old Kingdom, and Mennefer from the late Old Kingdom onwards. I would ask the reader to use my choices again as an invitation to think about our distance from the world under study, and, whichever choice the reader wishes to make, to make the choice consciously and on the basis of evidence.

Chapters 3–7 test the exploratory approach of opening to wider or different ranges of sources across archaeology and comparative studies. Each chapter takes one thematic area prominent in the archaeological record and in current Egyptological writing: temple and festival, deities and the relations between them (including the Egyptological debate over the presence or absence of myths), ethics (ma'at "what is right"), healing and well-being (conceived holistically, in opposition to modern divisions such as magic and medicine), and burial customs. Before entry into this sequence of segmented areas, Chapter 2 presents the issues that unify all themes: in Kemet, what does it mean to be human, how are human life stages understood and expressed, and which spaces and times, if any, are marked as different, as more intensely sacred than others. The first part of this chapter offers more general discussion, followed by case studies where the reader can tread in greater detail in the footsteps retrieved in archaeological fieldwork. These sections sketch a threshold at which to pause and consider the full social, material, and historical context for all the evidence for the themes in Chapters 3–7. At the end of Chapter 7, I briefly return to the question of unity and segmentation, toward a future collaborative approach for a more holistic understanding of past people along the Saharan Nile.

CHAPTER 1

Belief without a Book

⊐⊐⊐⊐⊐

Word Worlds: Ancient and Modern

Religion?

In this book, I seek to address those questions of life in ancient Egypt that most speakers of modern European languages might place under the word *religion*. More neutrally, the core question could be rephrased as: how did inhabitants of Egypt in ancient times express their places in the worlds of Nile and Sahara and their relation to one another, to other peoples, and to the forces and features of life? The terms *religion*, from Latin, and *philosophy*, from Greek, can be used for these topics, but both belong firmly within European histories and therefore carry associations that may fail or obscure attempts to understand non-European settings. The French writer Jacques Derrida has emphasized the specifically West European weight of the word and concept *religion* (Derrida 1998). If we replace *religion* with the word *belief*, we find the same risks of imposing alien ways of thinking on other peoples (Davies 2011). Today, the declaration "I believe in One God" defines the speaker as *not* believing that there are many gods, as holding one belief and not another. Such affirmations place belief in a system of choices, where personal *faith* may be built on the rock of one Holy Book, as with the Torah of Judaism, Christian Bible, and Quran of Islam. Before and outside the idea of the sacred book, *faith* and *belief* may not be matters of choice between opposing systems. Whereas religions of the book refer explicitly to other options of believing or disbelieving, a human group may instead express itself without reference to any contemporary or earlier other society or way of expression.

An analogy might be drawn with literacy. A part-literate society deploys writing in different ways to a fully literate society; in part literacy, then, our clearest analogy would be not reading-and-writing literacy, the norm in richer countries, but computer literacy, still variably extended through social lives. Today, religion occupies a

Exploring Religion in Ancient Egypt, First Edition. Stephen Quirke.
© 2015 Stephen Quirke. Published 2015 by John Wiley & Sons, Ltd.

part in a society, even in a deeply religious society, because the religion expresses itself in relation to other religions and other beliefs such as agnosticism or atheism, denoting them, for example, as superstition, paganism, or apostasy. Most sources for ancient Egyptian society correspond instead to a single expression of being in the world: the expression applies across not a part, but the whole, of social life—much as reading–writing literacy may cover most of West European or East Asian society.

After 525 BC, long-term foreign rule brings different belief systems into the Nile Valley more emphatically than before. Achaemenid Iranian rule (525–404, 343–332 BC) introduced Zoroastrian ideas as well as some larger Jewish communities into Egypt; Macedonian Hellenistic rule (323–30 BC) then installed the Greek. When Egypt became a province of the Roman Empire after 30 BC, the pace of Hellenization increased, accompanied strongly from the third century AD by conversion to Christianity, the state religion from AD 313. With these changes, the final millennium of *ancient Egyptian religion* seems to involve a mixed environment structurally closer to the present world of differing belief systems (see papers in Clarysse et al., 1998).

By contrast, in the history of Egypt from the first writing (3100 BC) to the beginning of Achaemenid Iranian rule (525 BC), only once was a different choice expressed as the new and now sole option: years 5–17 in the reign of King Akhenaten. For those dozen years, old expressions of a divine Hidden One (in Egyptian *Amun*) were physically erased in word and image, and all images of the king were directed to a new formulation expressed in image as a sun sphere (in Egyptian *Aten*) extending the hieroglyph *ankh*, "life," to the nose of the king, and in words as "Ra Horus-of-the-Horizon, rejoicing in the horizon, in his name as Light which is in the *aten*" (Figure 1.1). The next generation restored the earlier system (Figure 1.2) and eventually dismantled the monuments of Akhenaten; later king lists omitted the names of those who had made offerings to the creator in the formula "Ra Horus/Ruler-of-the-Horizon, rejoicing in the horizon, in his name as Light which is in the *aten*."

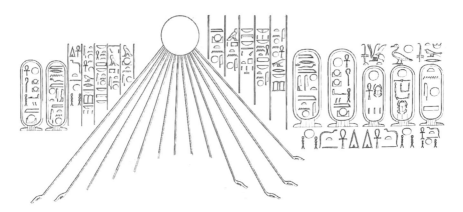

Figure 1.1   Visualizing the creator as sun disk with two kingly names, as formulated in the reign of King Akhenaten, North Tombs of high officials, Akhetaten, about 1350 BC. From Richard Lepsius (ed.), *Denkmäler aus Aegypten und Aethiopien*, Berlin 1849–1859, vol.3, pl.99.

Figure 1.2   The creator expressed in animal–human form sailing over the defeated force of chaos, depicted as giant snake, tomb of King Sety I, Valley of the Kings, Waset, about 1290 BC. © Gianluca Miniaci.

Egyptologists have emphasized this reign as a breakthrough in the history of religions, as the first visible example of monotheism or of belief, and as the exception that illustrates what was *ancient Egyptian religion* for the rest of this 2500-year span (Assmann 2001). The Akhenaten rupture may be of particular fascination for twenty-first-century readers also because they can more easily understand it as a choice in belief, confirming the modern meaning of religion. For other periods, without that apparent choice, the words *belief, faith,* and *religion* may stand in the way of an attempt to understand the lives and self-expression of past people.

Modern study of ancient worlds

The words for the object of study are not the only obstacles: the words for, and practices of, the study itself raise equally serious barriers. Over the past 200 years, distinct university disciplines were developed for study of societies. Despite efforts at interdisciplinary research, a university might separate the department of archaeology to study past societies, anthropology for contemporary small-scale societies, sociology for contemporary large-scale societies, history for written documents, and art history for visual sources. Much as past and present producers in different materials adopt forms and technologies from one another, each discipline has developed productive methods and approaches that other disciplines can then take up for study of their own main area. To take two prominent examples,

ethnoarchaeologists developed anthropological applications to interpret archaeological evidence, and the mid-twentieth-century *Annales* historians adopted
quantitative measures from sociology.

Both the separation of disciplines and their reconnection in new fields such as
cultural studies can help generate fresh insights in understanding the world we
inhabit. Egyptology occupies a curious position within this academic landscape,
somewhere between archaeology and history. Taken literally, the combination of
French or English *Egypt(e)* with Greek *logos*, "word," might be expected to desig-
nate a holistic *study of Egypt*. Yet, already from its early use in the nineteenth century, it was taken for granted that *Egyptology* never meant all *Egyptian studies*—that
would have covered land, fauna, flora, and people of all ages, in short, the full range
found in the monumental *Description of Egypt* published out of the French
Expedition of 1798–1801 (Godlewska 1995). Instead, the word narrowly denotes
study of the Egyptian past through the ancient Egyptian language as preserved in
hieroglyphic inscriptions on monuments, together with any associated finds. The
latest version of the language, Coptic, is still used in Christian liturgy in Egypt and
is often added to Egyptological study area. Any reader enquiring after *ancient Egypt*
needs to be aware that, in university departments, Egyptologists generally train to
read Egyptian writing, not to undertake archaeological fieldwork, or study visual
arts, or even comparative or historical linguistics. The discipline developed, not as
an area study, but as the philological recovery and study of ancient writings—less
Egyptology *study of Egypt*, than Egyptiology *study of ancient Egyptian*. If the reader
does not know this, she or he may have false expectations over what we can pres-
ently know, and the very name of the discipline can become an obstacle to understanding the past. The same risks are run with the rest of our vocabulary, as with
modern categories *religion, philosophy*, and indeed *economy, society*, and *nation*;
each writer and reader must make their own decisions on which terms can be used
and how, and few are likely to make great impact on how, collectively, any one term
will continue being used in any group. For our choices, individual and collective,
some awareness of the history of use can still be useful. In the case of *ancient
Egyptian religion*, the recovery of available evidence may be distorted as much by
the term Egyptology, as by the category *religion*.

Three hurdles

From the experience of preparing a workshop in Berlin on *animal cults* in ancient
Egypt, the Egyptologist Martin Fitzenreiter identified several major failings in
Egyptology, with substantial impact on the modern question of religion in ancient
Egypt (Fitzenreiter 2004): *eurocentrism, overemphasis on written sources, and lack
of theoretical reflection.*

Eurocentrism

Egyptians today speak Arabic, and people of different cultural backgrounds around
the world express strong interest in the ancient past of Egypt. Yet, early twenty-
first-century Egyptology remains overwhelmingly a European-language study in
institutions of European form: research university and, to a lesser extent, museum.

Eurocentrism makes this condition seem natural, assuming lack of interest by non-European peoples in their own histories (Said 1978; Colla 2007). Internal factors contributed to the emergence of West European studies of the Egyptian past, ahead of Egyptian Arabic and Ottoman Turkish, in the mid-nineteenth century (Mitchell 1988). Current gaps between Arabic-language and European-language production follow most directly from European overseas intervention. Anglo-French control of Egyptian finances after the construction of the Suez Canal opened the way to British invasion of Egypt (1882), with military occupation down to 1952 (Al-Sayyid Marsot 1985; Cole 2000). London-dictated budgets, laws, and university fees and structures, along with Anglo-French agreements on museum directorship and antiquities inspectorate, ensured that Egyptology neither supported Egyptian professionals nor published in Arabic (Reid 2002).

Already from the 1820s, the first people to be called Egyptologists were as European as that word itself. It was they who defined as primary target of study the script area of ancient Egyptian hieroglyphic script. That script first became accessible in print publication in French through Jean-François Champollion (1824 Précis, following his announcement in the 1822 Letter to M. Dacier). Inside and outside the discipline, we forget that he was taught Egyptian language (Coptic) by an Egyptian Christian in Paris, Father Hanna Chiftigi (Louca 2006, 89–116), and that numerous Arabic studies on ancient Egypt were written before print by Egyptian and other Arab world geographer–historians such as Makrizi and Abd al-Latif of Baghdad, drawing in part on earlier Muslim scholars such as Dhu al-Nun (El Daly 2004). The endemic historical amnesia maintained by Egyptologists led the contemporary feminist Egyptian writer Nawal El Saadawi to accuse them of cultural genocide (El Saadawi 1997, 169).

Overemphasis on writing
Since the Champollion 1820s publications, Egyptology has remained predominantly a study of ancient writings in the Egyptian language. In the history of ancient Greek and Roman archaeology, written evidence also tended to receive most attention (Morris 1994). As there, philological focus on particular writings separated Egyptology from archaeological fieldwork practice and theory (Giddy 1999). With relatively few exceptions, Egyptologists worked on monumental temples and tombs and failed to apply the advances in prehistoric archaeology to settlement sites, resulting in chronic gaps and distortions throughout our knowledge of the ancient society (Moreno Garcia 2009).

When Eurocentric philological Egyptology adopted as its object of study the language area of ancient Egyptian, they might have defined ancient Egypt as one speech community, tangible in space and time through ancient manuscript and inscription. For emergent nations of nineteenth-century and above all early twentieth-century history, language area may have provided an implicit natural definition as the earliest nation-state. However, in Egyptological practice, script took precedence over language. Although Egyptian is still today written in a Greek-based alphabet, Coptic, and although Coptic is taught in many Egyptology departments, Egyptologists keep the ancient hieroglyphic script as the hallmark of their area of study. Their choice builds on intermittent precedents in Greek, Latin,

Renaissance, and later European writings, where hieroglyphs epitomized enigmatic, mystical forces of symbolism. Definition by hieroglyphic script delineates a time–space block *ancient Egypt* as the span 3100 BC–AD 400, in Nile Valley and Delta, from Aswan to the Mediterranean. The block has been expanded to cover prehistoric material culture in the lower Nile Valley, where it is considered ancestral to ancient Egypt, and to adjacent areas where ancient Egyptian script is found— eastern and western Egyptian deserts, Nubia to the south in the Nile Valley and adjacent deserts, and Sinai to the east, with more limited distribution of hieroglyphic inscriptions across southwest Asia and Mediterranean islands and coasts.

In general, a linguistic definition of ancient Egypt provides a clear criterion and so a clear object of study. The focus on writing has brought remarkable advances, particularly in the privileged domain of literary studies (Loprieno 1996). Yet the discipline has become too easily isolated and lost the advantages of comparative and interdisciplinary study, with surprisingly limited engagement even with the disciplines of linguistics and history. Written sources often interweave with figurative art and can only be understood in architectural context, and philological Egyptologists have often included study of visual arts. Nevertheless, despite remarkable studies within Egyptology, no developed contribution can be found within art history, perhaps the result of too little sustained contact with art historians.

The extent of disciplinary isolation can be exaggerated, and the problem is not confined to Egyptology (archaeology and ancient history Sauer 2004; and anthropology Gosden 1999). Although Egyptology and archaeology tend to practice mutual exclusion, some archaeological expeditions in Egypt have introduced current archaeological theory into Nile Valley fieldwork (Wendrich 2010). The inclusion of prehistoric Egypt into many Egyptological departments and conferences has allowed greater contact with archaeology and anthropology (Wengrow 2006). In some countries, there are also strong links between Egyptology and religious studies (West Germany after World War II, the Netherlands, where Egyptology sometimes belongs within theology departments).

If these links all tend to remain within Eurocentric philosophical frames, that itself is a general problem in interdisciplinarity. From its service in colonialism, anthropology developed the strongest self-critical debate, with insights of great potential for the future of Egyptology and archaeology (Asad 1973; Fabian 1983, 2007). Self-critique holds the power to return beyond the disciplines to their more humane motivation, a description of a society where we seek to understand rather than to control another, aware that understanding only avoids control when resistance is possible from the other side. In his 1940 *Theses on the Philosophy of History*, Walter Benjamin warned that even the dead are not safe from lethal impositions of the present (translation Benjamin 1968 [1940]). The moment of danger does not pass. If we aim to hear, as well as study, past people of Egypt during its centuries with written evidence in Egyptian scripts, the most secure path may be within comparative social sciences, incorporating the advances in understanding provided from philology. In this approach, the study of *religious* practice or ideas about life can start as an open source-grounded effort to recognize what members of that society marked as distinctive and how—whether or not that corresponds to *religion* within our own understanding of societies.

Egyptologists prioritize written sources in their own writing about *ancient Egyptian religion*, perhaps because their questions and assumptions over *religion* require narrative evidence. Despite the anticlerical Republicanism of early nineteenth-century philologists including Champollion, the first question in religious studies of ancient Egypt came to be, did they believe in One God (monotheism) or many (polytheism)? In answering this anachronistic question, the researcher would extract from collections of written sources the evidence for or against monotheism. Fitzenreiter emphasizes how, whether consciously or not, the models for the approach were scripture and theological commentary as developed in and for monotheistic religions of the book. In prominent sources, ancient writings combine with images are strongly framed by monumental architecture, the principal home of inscriptions and images from ancient Egypt. However, art and architecture did not provide ready verbal answers to such questions as the creation of the world, or the relation to divinity. Instead, these answers were sought in narratives of deities, in manuals for rites, or in hymns and prayers. The work of Jan Assmann stands out for the way he questions what religion means in the context of ancient Egypt and for his close attention to the specific context of each piece of writing and to changing contexts over time. Relatively few studies have started from a wider context as in landscape archaeology, but this aspect is receiving more study now (Effland and Effland 2010; Jeffreys 2010). Similarly, few general accounts of ancient Egyptian religion start from settlement evidence, outside the monumental frame. Nor, where monuments form part of the living landscape, have we yet considered the impact in practice of a monument or inscription on what might be called, following the historian–sociologist Michel de Certeau, the *daily invention* of each social life (de Certeau 1980).

Reflection

Despite a professed love of word, the philological focus has been on detail rather than holistic picture. Philologists have left intact a received picture of ancient Egypt, by their unreflective use of generalized concepts and categories such as society, economy, and religion. For describing any other society, particularly outside the European frame, our vocabulary for cultural and material practices may be inappropriate. Even our most general categories turn out to be unexpectedly recent: Timothy Mitchell has charted the extraordinarily late (mid-twentieth-century) development of the contemporary meaning of *economy* in European-language use (Mitchell 2002). General terms for dimensions such as economic, political, religious, and social may be useful filters for sifting and analyzing evidence. Yet they continually merge and overlap in practice, and the way we use each term in the set must affect our understanding of each of the others and of the whole set. Our approach will differ according to whether we adopt society or culture or ethnic group as the label for the totality, however porous and impermanent we consider it. If we do not define our terms, or reconsider our categories, we are likely simply to reproduce the dominant ideas of our place and time. This problem, raised by Marxist historians (de Ste Croix 1989), should be of concern to all interested in studying any society, because those dominant ideas may not apply automatically to our particular field of study.

An ancient Egyptian definition of religion? The composition the King as Priest of the Sun

For the dimension of *religion*, over the past fifty years, Jan Assmann has worked most prolifically to define our terms explicitly in a West German theological and literary frame. From eight sources connected with kingship and its writings, Assmann reconstructed a remarkable ancient Egyptian written composition, with no ancient title, called by him *The King as Priest of the Sun*. One key passage states why the creator sun-god Ra installed the *nswt*, "king," on earth (Assmann 2001, 3–6):

> the Sun-god installed the king on the earth of the living, for ever and eternity,
> to judge between people and to satisfy the gods,
> to create what is Right, to annihilate what is Evil,
> giving offerings to the gods, voice-offerings to the blessed dead.

Assmann interprets the first two lines as a broad definition of religion, as ethics and justice: the king must make possible *ma'at*, "what is right," the just and ethical behavior among humans, underpinned by law, *to judge between people*. The next two lines would then respond to a narrow definition of religion as ritual: the king must ensure that offerings were made to satisfy deities and the blessed dead. By using this source to illustrate his broad and narrow definitions of religion, Assmann anchors the Egyptological argument firmly in ancient writing.

The power of the research by Assmann comes not least from his unsurpassed knowledge of the written sources and sensitivity to their architectural and historical context. Yet here, the limitations of the definition from writing can also be seen, both in the restricted circle of sources for this ancient articulation and in the openness of writing to different analysis. In other ancient Egyptian written sources, particularly the literary genre of *Teachings*, the concept of *just and ethical behavior*, includes care for the deities, and the dead (see Chapter 5). Therefore, the division between ethics and cult, central to religious movements such as Reformation Christianity, may not apply in any clear-cut fashion to that ancient Egyptian definition of kingship. In another evident limitation, the *Teachings* describe ethical precepts as given by father to son: even within a conceptual frame of the nuclear family, they leave unanswered how a father might have advised a daughter and a mother a son or daughter and how sisters and brothers spoke. Feminism and gender studies introduce fresh questions and prospects for research.

Accordingly, in place of a theological focus on the most developed expressions of *religious thought*, Fitzenreiter prefers an anthropological focus in order to consider more broadly religious practice, as social activity, out of which *religion* might emerge as a collective longer-term presence, as religious institutions. This approach allows him to suspend certain Eurocentric assumptions, such as the centrality of a written tradition, or the monotheism versus polytheism debate (as in Hornung 1996), extensively discussed in Egyptology, with reference both to the definition of the word *netjer* (used in Christian writing in its Coptic form *noute* as the translation for Greek *theos*, "God") and to the dozen years when King Akhenaten focussed worship and offerings exclusively on one deity. According to Fitzenreiter, a shift away from word focus to practice allows greater attention to recurrent and prominent phenomena marginalized in previous histories of Egyptian religion, such as ancestor cult and divination, oracles, and the phenomena studied under the heading of *animal cults*.

Using written sources in context

Eurocentrism, logocentrism, and disciplinary isolation are not overturned in one step, and the challenge from Fitzenreiter cannot be met until more studies of broader ranges of sources have been undertaken, from archaeological survey and fieldwork and from new material cultural studies. If the focus on written sources seems set to continue, research can at least be set on the most productive footing possible, following Assmann to seek greatest possible awareness of partiality and context. In one of the main disciplinary divisions, of archaeology from history, a misreading on either side has tended to reinforce mutually a lack of trust and interest between those studying pasts. History may tend to privilege written above material context, without discussion, while archaeology may eject all written sources as *elite*, without defining *elite* (a problem in sociology also, see Scott 2008, 27).

In place of this standoff, a material primacy could be acknowledged, within which writing provides one more indirect approach to peoples in the past, one with the power of human speech (Morris 2000). All writings may be biased to a particular view, but archaeology can help in identifying and analyzing bias, because it offers a context for each manuscript and inscription. Regularly, this context is not direct or primary, as most written material survives only in second, third, or fourth hand places of deposition or inscription. Still, even secondary or tertiary context, precisely observed, allows modern readers to assess the social location of words, much as an anthropologist in direct observation has an opportunity to assess the social location of their participant in conversation.

In the end, the danger with writing bias lies in our usage: we fail too often to observe precise social context, and we exclude other evidence, as if written and spoken words provide a direct guide to the society of the speaker. Implicitly, we assume a society free of contradictions and complexities, one which we could simply read in words. Yet, if we omit the written evidence, we might still impose modern categories and thinking on the past. Beyond any message or communication, the enormous potential of ancient writings is in their linguistic content: they give words to the world in a language that is not the language of the modern writer and reader. The words may prove to be from an *elite*, but even where the linguistic evidence can be made so simple, the vocabulary is not directly that of a twenty-first-century global *elite* that writes and reads studies of the past. As long as we treat writings as just a subset in the range of evidence, their vocabulary and syntax can help to create a different, less Eurocentric introduction to their society.

Language and politics

In both written and spoken forms, language can act as a medium for expressing or effecting change or continuity in a society. According to one understanding of language, words do not merely label phenomena in a fixed reality, but rather they are one of the means by which humans model and construct social life. In social and historical context, there are collective forces around individual speakers. For appreciating and analyzing those forces in words, we might adopt from the Russian literary theorist Mikhail Bakhtin the concepts of unified language/centralizing monoglossia as against different dialects/centrifugal heteroglossia (Hirschkop 1999). There is a danger that our interpretation might become one-dimensional, pitting heteroglossia as heroic resistance against monoglossia as the epic voice of a tyrant. Against this, the complementary linguistics of the Italian political writer Antonio Gramsci can keep open to historical enquiry the precise measure and impact of monoglossia and heteroglossia in each context (Ives 2004).

The two extremes of the European twentieth century underpin these two writers. In Russia, Bakhtin had to live through the lethal effects of a unified official vocabulary and speech during the Stalin years of terror before and after the World War II, including mock trials, mass-scale executions, and mass sentencing to labor camps. For Bakhtin, the singular sober voice (monoglossia) carried a literal death sentence, even if, unlike his communist cowriters and friends Valentin Voloshinov and Piotr Medvedev, he survived horrendous hardship to teach in university in the Soviet Union. Conversely, Gramsci saw disunity in speech as a fundamental reason for the fragmented resistance that allowed Mussolini to take power in 1920s Italy, leading to an alliance with 1930s Germany under Hitler. Broken by ten years in Fascist prison, Gramsci did not live to witness the Nazi concentration camps, but his prison notebooks, smuggled to Moscow after his death, preserve his incomplete explorations of the problems of language in human society. Gramsci studied linguistics at university, and his insights may encourage those in archaeology working on even the more *elite* written sources from part-literate societies.

According to the linguistic school in which Gramsci was trained, all speech contains evidence of contradictory workings, allowing us to see how some social expression acquires the force of prestige, almost forcing others to model their own expression on that of the center. Gramsci recognized how those dominating a society are best placed to express their place in the world and to apply its expression to maintaining that place. By contrast, only a fraction of resources for articulating and sharing beyond local horizons would be available to those whose lives are dominated by manual labor. To describe and analyze the more fragmented reflections among manual laborers, Gramsci subversively used the label *folklore* (Crehan 2002). These concepts of unifying versus fragmented, and of prestige in expression, may be productive for Egyptologists. They can help to account for changes over time in the ancient Egyptian written evidence, as well as giving a framework for assessing the social position of any particular verbal expression from the past. The social understanding of language provides crucial justification for including written sources prominently within the archaeological study of the past.

Applying critical theory to Egyptology

With the conceptual tools of mono-/heteroglossia and prestige, from Bakhtin and Gramsci, the written evidence can remain an essential part of the range of evidence for the particular society/societies in ancient Egypt, provided that it is decentered from its status as core. The subject of study *ancient Egypt* might still be defined as the area of the language community *ancient Egyptian speakers*, if only as a provisional device to commence study. From the introduction of the hieroglyphic script around 3100 BC to the start of Achaemenid Iranian rule in 525 BC, ancient Egyptian is the main language attested in the area from First Cataract to Mediterranean. Accordingly, dominant script and language have formed together one of the criteria for defining my time–space focus as that time span and area. The geographical limit is reinforced by the fusion of the hieroglyphic script with *ancient Egyptian art*, a specific manner of figurative expression. The far larger scope of material culture without writing or depiction further broadly confirms the language area: the same archaeological map emerges from study of the major production industries, pottery and textiles.

In time, the boundary might be drawn later or earlier: during the early first millennium, material culture shifts with the introduction of iron production, and in the opposite direction, the script art fusion remains strong as late as the second–third centuries AD, when some of the best-preserved ancient Egyptian temples were built and some of the most informative ancient Egyptian temple manuscripts were copied. Against these earlier or later alternatives, the major justification for 525 BC as an end point is the change in script/language use. As a unitary and integral social field, *ancient Egyptian religion* ends at the point when the Achaemenid court and administration introduce into the Nile Valley a government using Aramaic script and language, and Zoroastrian beliefs. Even if the new script/language/beliefs exist alongside the ancient Egyptian and even if such coexistence finds New Kingdom antecedents, a new long-term history begins at this point. Coincidentally, or perhaps from the first formal observation, Johann Joachim Winckelmann had inferred the same break in his massively influential 1764 history of ancient art, where he proposed just two periods of ancient Egyptian visual production, pre-Achaemenid and Achaemenid, to Roman.

As ancient writing is my own research focus within the evidence spectrum, doubtless, it remains too central throughout this volume. This introduction is intended to keep the reader fully aware of the bias. Alongside visual arts and architecture, the range of material culture and the less tangible yield of modern extensive archaeological fieldwork remain to be explored. Only a joint staff could muster expertise to cover all the possible domains, and a full history of religious practice would need new multidisciplinary research. Within these constraints, a philologist introduces the terrain, noting separate and joint limitations and potential of each in its range of source types. In the distance, the impossible ideal of a total history remains a powerful frame of interpretation and motivation. In a society, those with greatest economic resources may be directing the material form and content of production, as well as the ideas that influence all parts of the society. Research can target these dominant structures and their impact and assess the scope for filling some of the gaps in our knowledge, for example, the religious practices of fragmented dominated groups, including the bulk of the population in ancient agriculture and animal husbandry, or groups less visible in written and visual source material, by their age, gender, type of work, or ethnicity.

Future

Writing after the January 25, 2011 revolution, new directions may emerge in the study of the past within Egypt, and Arabic may rejoin European languages as a leading research medium. However much we hope for this, much needs to be learned from the lack of change in exactly this area after the 1952 revolution, despite the pan-Arabism and pan-Africanism promoted by Gamal Abdel Nasser into the 1960s (Hassan 2007). The early twenty-first century is being seen as shifting the global centers to South and East Asia; the implications of this for Eurocentric academic studies, including anthropology and archaeology, remain uncertain. A shift in centers of prestige could create new scope for non-European studies, including here Arabic studies of Egyptian evidence, whether or not divided into the same time blocks as now. On the other hand, Eurocentrism may be replaced not by Egyptocentric or Afrocentric study, but by absence of study and thought, amounting to a gap in being human, a failing that is denounced in Islam by the Arabic word *jahaliya*, "ignorance." The better future lies in the hands not of established Egyptologists but of a new generation of thinkers particularly in Africa, including Egyptian Egyptologists and extending broadly across reflective and creative worlds.

Elementals and Sources

Landscape forces and resources

The unique setting of Egypt combines two extremes, expressed in the ancient Egyptian names Kemet, "Black Land," for the fertile Nile Valley and Delta and Deshret, "Red Land," for the Sahara desert with its mountains, flats, and sand seas of shifting dunes. The valley supports abundant plant and animal life; desert cliffs and mountains contain quarries of hard and soft stones, mines of precious metals, and routes to other lands. The Kemet–Deshret dividing line became sharp as today by 3000–2500 BC, when the climate changed to the hyperarid phase that still guarantees almost zero rainfall across northeast Africa between central Sudan and Nile Delta (Wengrow 2006). With the onset of hyperaridity, the river floodplain became far more closed as a social field. The extent of closure can be exaggerated, as in the

Egyptological myth of a uniquely isolated ancient Egypt. In practice, the isolation seems more relative, within dominant patterns of movement for most inhabitants; desert borderlines are always open for crossing, but desert oases never support the same level of population as the river valley, and agricultural settlements might have interacted only sporadically with desert nomads. Until the regulation of the river in the nineteenth–twentieth centuries (Tvedt 2003), the Black Land would be separated from the Red anew in a tense drama every summer, at the unpredictable rising of the river. Summer rains in Ethiopian highlands would swell the river, first detectable in Egypt at the First Cataract, around mid-July, when water pools on Elephantine may have gurgled in anticipation and the waters began to muddy. August and September marked full flood, as low-lying land in the river plain filled slowly or torrentially, until any higher ground stood as islands within a vast elongated lake penned in by desert at either side (Butzer 1974). By November, most floodwaters had spilled out into the Mediterranean, leaving behind a blanket of fertile black silt.

These annual convulsions would have radically different impact on human populations of the Black and Red Lands, depending on their way of life. A trading nomad, a shepherd, and a settled farmer each needed to react at varying speed, to secure collective or individual resources. Those living above the highest predicted flood level might have most time, if a flood surge hit that year, and nomads might have the option to move away entirely for the season of danger. Medieval and early modern Nile levels demonstrate how utterly impossible it would be in any one year to predict the height of the coming flood (Seidlmayer 2001). Too high a flood would create a destructive surge, sometimes inflicting high death tolls on people and animals; the deluge in 1821 was strong enough to sweep away temple ruins at Qau al-Kabir (Belzoni 1835). Too low a flood would leave insufficient water and silt for the farmer, and famine might follow; at different periods, ancient and medieval, Egyptian written sources indicate repeat low floods and devastating famines. Under this lethal annual tension, the flood attracted greater reverence than the river itself. From ancient Egyptian written sources, no name for the Nile is known—it is simply *iteru*, "the river" (the modern word Nile from Greek *Neilos* possibly derives from the plural *na iteru*, "the rivers," the Delta branches). In contrast, the Egyptian word Ha'py, "Nile flood," is a divine principle; Ha'py was depicted as a bearded man with heavy-hanging breasts, delivering the abundant food and drink that the flood made possible (Figure 1.3).

Once the Nile flood subsided, again, different opportunities would arise for trading, for herding, and for farming, where a season of sowing could follow and the crop be ready in time for a summer harvest. A detailed history of irrigation cannot be written, until we have an archaeology of the countryside, but in very general terms, increasing numbers of dykes and canals eventually allowed for a second crop and harvest (by 1250 BC?). The floodplain divides into segments, each comprising a basin, into which floodwater flows and overflows away from the main river course and then back around to the river. As a result, irrigation is a relatively local matter, against earlier theories that river control contributed to the creation of

Figure 1.3   The Nile flood (Egyptian *Ha'py*) in dual form as two men with pendant breasts, tying together Upper and Lower Egypt. Inscribed block from the palace of King Merenptah at Mennefer, about 1225 BC. From W. Petrie, *Memphis I*, London 1909.

a centralized state (Wittfogel thesis of *Hydraulic* Oriental Despotism, refuted by Butzer 1974). The ancient agricultural annual cycle disappeared in the nineteenth century AD, when river dams allowed far greater control of water, with year-round irrigation. For ancient times, the interactions between larger and smaller settlements, between town and country, and between different social groups within the settlements remain largely unknown.

Town and countryside

Archaeological sources for the countryside are sparse, but by 4000 BC, agriculture and animal husbandry are visible in the settlements and cemeteries along the desert edge in Upper Egypt. The annual river flood has removed most of the evidence for the lives of past people, who must have lived in greatest number within easiest reach of fresh water, so in the floodplain area. If they lived anywhere the flood reached in later centuries, their homes lie buried along with their fields within the floodplain under accumulated meters of annual silt deposits. If they lived on the higher ground *islands* above the flood limit, the same ground is most often still settled land, and so their homes remain today beneath modern cities and towns, awaiting future archaeological investigation with more sensitive techniques. The desert edge alongside the fields preserves ancient housing much more accessibly, and some of the best-known excavations of ancient towns have been along the Saharan fringe of the Nile valley (Middle Kingdom Lahun, New Kingdom Amarna) (Figure 1.4).

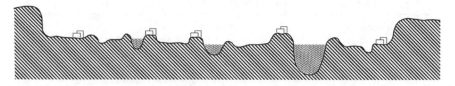

Figure 1.4 Section of the Nile floodplain in Middle Egypt, where the Bahr Yussef, a lateral Nile branch, runs roughly parallel with the main river. © Wolfram Grajetzki *after Kessler 1990.*

By 3200 BC, larger settlements formed at Nekhen and Nubet in southern Upper Egypt, later historic centers (Trigger 1983). Already, the Nile Valley would have offered at least two different experiences of town life: the high-ground *island* within the flood plain, where inhabitants became islanders during the autumn flood months, and the desert margin, where the island of life would be formed on one side by the permanent presence of the Sahara and on the other by the temporary intrusion of the Nile. When we now consider how the inhabitants of ancient Nile Valley and Delta experienced and expressed their lives, we are already facing a wider range of life experience than implied by our term *the ancient Egyptians*. In addition to differences in life chances according to age and gender and by 3200 BC also social class, there are the varying ecologies among the urban, rural, and desert based, with different seasons and spaces. Even within a unit we might assume to be relatively homogeneous, the farming village, historians of more recent rural Egypt warn us against our assumptions on the life of the *fallahin* (the Arabic word for *farmers*):

> Egypt's peasantry were not a homogeneous mass. At the beginning of the nineteenth century, village society comprised economic strata ranging from 'large' landholders of 50 feddan or more, to smallhold fallahin and the landless. (Cuno 1988, 133)

For assessing ancient expressions on our place as humans in our world, different answers might be expected for every one of the social groups implied by our words *village, town, countryside,* and *desert*.

Time–space blocks: ancient egypt as a chain of ecologies

From the geography of Egypt, the diversity of experience across the Black Land can be set at the level of ecology or lifestyle. Ecological unit then becomes the critical factor in an open definition of *religion* provided by Gramsci:

> the problem of religion understood not in the confessional sense but in a secular sense as unit of faith between a conception of the world and a corresponding norm of conduct (though why call this unit of faith "religion" rather than "ideology" or just "politics"). (Gramsci, ed. Gerratana, Quaderni del Carcere II, 1975, 1378)

Table 1.1   Time–space blocks of ancient Egypt

Region (with modern cities)	Ecology
Southernmost Upper Egypt (Aswan to Luxor)	Narrow floodplain, sandstone cliffs/desert
Northern Upper Egypt (Luxor to Asyut)	Broad floodplain, limestone cliffs/desert
Middle Egypt (Asyut to Beni Suef)	Broad floodplain, Nile branch, limestone cliffs/desert
Fayoum	Nile branch outflow basin forming *oasis* W of Nile
Northernmost Valley (Cairo)	Narrow floodplain, limestone cliffs/desert
Western Delta fringe and Wadi Natrun	Floodplain margin, desert flats, natron/salt deposits
Central Delta plain	Extensive floodplain, sandhills, northern marshes
East Delta fringe and Wadi Tumilat	Floodplain margin, desert flats, herding terrain

Again following Gramsci, we might define *regions* in terms of their relations with one another, in a chain of *adjacent different ecologies*. This approach suggests eight units within the Nile Valley and Delta from First Cataract to Mediterranean (Table 1.1 and Map 1.1).

Rather than this multiple identity, ancient written and visual sources emphasize the duality of Egypt on varying models: *Shema'*, Upper Egypt, and *Ta-Mehu*, Lower Egypt; *idebwy*, the Two Riverbanks; or *Deshret*, Red Land, and *Kemet*, Black Land. A small number of second-millennium BC written sources confirm the different status of regions 1–2 as *tep-res*, "head of the south," divided at Waset (modern Luxor), or as *Khen-Nekhen*, "Hinterland (?) of Nekhen"—Nekhen being a town in the center of region 1 (Quirke 2009–2010). For the Red Land, the western desert has well-trodden trade roads and the major oases of Dakhla, Kharga, Bahriya, Farafra, and, farther west, Siwa, while the eastern desert has roads to quarries and across to the Red Sea, notably through the Wadi Hammamat parting from Qift/Koptos or Qena, and farther south from Nekheb (Friedman 1999). It is uncertain how far Egyptian language dominated those desert areas. From the second millennium BC, its term for Egyptians was *remetj-en-Kemet*, "people of the Black Land," perhaps not excluding the Red Land but rather as the home to the overwhelming majority of the settled population. Different readers may choose different numbers of regions to test evidence and assertions in this book—the eight ecological regions of the Black Land, or just the six forming the core Valley and Delta, or, instead, the 10 regions, adding the western oases and eastern trade routes. The important point is less an exact number of regions than the plural regional characters and lifestyles to consider beyond the general headings *Egypt* and Kemet.

The time of kemet: dynasties and periods

For time divisions within the third to first millennia BC, Egyptologists use a framework of 30 or 31 *dinastiai*, "groupings of rulers," from a history in Greek by the third-century BC Egyptian writer Manetho. His work is preserved mainly in early

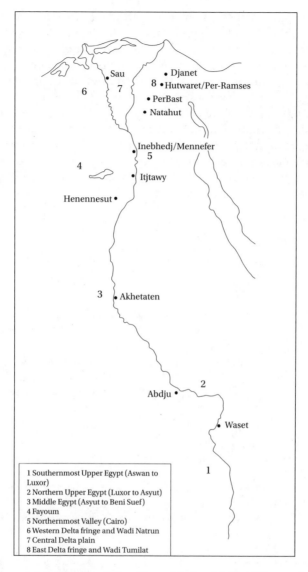

Map 1.1 The regions of Egypt as defined by arable floodplain, with central cities of 3000–525 BC. © Wolfram Grajetzki.

medieval Greek and Armenian summaries, sometimes contradicting each other (Waddell 1940). Each dynasty is identified by city, perhaps because Manetho considered the city deity to protect those born there. That already indicates a difference between his conceptions of time and those of more recent historians. Some groupings can be confirmed from sources dating to the particular rulers, and some comprise members of one family, as in the European concept of dynasty. However, many groupings do not start or stop with a new family, and some may derive from ancient revisions of sources (Malek 1982) or literary devices in earlier records of the past. In one version of Manetho, "the Seventh Dynasty is seventy kings of Memphis, who ruled seventy days" (Waddell 1940, 56–57); the numerical alliteration seems to be a literary means of expressing the end of an era. As a further complication, Egyptologists employ dynasty numbers selectively and variably; most consistently used are 1–6, 11–12, 18–20, 26, and 28–30. Broader, often more manageable divisions can be constructed on the criterion of political unity versus disunity, giving Old, Middle, and New *Kingdoms* and Late Period, separated by First, Second, and Third Intermediate Periods. The centers of power and production can also be used to construct a sequence more closely anchored in the land and the archaeological record. The summary in Table 1.2 includes concordance with dynasties; year dates before 664 BC are all rough estimates and the place-names cited in the form known from the particular period.

Table 1.2   The time of ancient Egypt

Period	Years BC	Dynasties	Regional centers
Early Dynastic	3000–2700	1–2	Abdju-Inebhedj
Old Kingdom			
Early	2700–2500	3 to early 4	Inebhedj only?
Late	2500–2200	Late 4–6	Abdju-Inebhedj/Mennefer
First Intermediate Period (division)			
	2200–2050	7/8–9/10 to early 11	Waset-Henennesut-Mennefer
Middle Kingdom			
Early	2050–1850	Late 11 to mid-12	Waset-Mennefer (from 1950 Itjtawy)
Late	1850–1700	Late 12 to mid-13	Waset-Abdju-Itjtawy-Hutwaret
Second Intermediate Period (division)			
	1700–1550	Late 13 to 15 to 17	Waset-Hutwaret
New Kingdom			
I	1550–1350	Early/mid-18	Waset-Mennefer-Perunefer
II	1350–1325	Late 18	Akhetaten-Mennefer?
III	1325–1200	End 18–late 19	Waset-Mennefer-Perunefer/ PerRamses
IV	1200–1050	End 19–20	Waset-Mennefer-Natahut
Libyan (united)	1050–850	21 to mid-22	Waset-Mennefer-PerBast-Djanet
Third Intermediate Period (Libyan, divided)			
	850–725	22 to 23 to 24	Waset-Mennefer-PerBast-Sau regions
Napata/Kushite	725–664	25/Assyrian invasions	*As TIP but under Napata, 671–664 Ashur*
Saite	664–525	26	Waset-Mennefer-Sau
Achaemenid	525–404	27	*As Saite but under Persepolis/Susa*
Late Dynastic	404–343	28 to 29 to 30	Waset-Mennefer-Sau-Tjebnetjer-Djedet
Achaemenid	343–332	31	*As Saite but under Persepolis/Susa*

Figure 1.5 The *sepat*, "provinces," Neit south and Neit north, depicted as kneeling Nile flood figures, bringing the abundance of water and food offerings, amounting to *power* (*was* scepter) and *life* (looped *ankh* hieroglyph). Red Chapel of the joint sovereigns Hatshepsut and Thutmes III, about 1475 BC, temple of Amun-Ra, Karnak.
© Gianluca Miniaci.

Greater detail combined with national coverage can be obtained from a series of ancient written sources, which preserve a conceptual geography of Egypt in thirty-nine *sepat*, "districts" or "provinces," from Aswan to Delta shore (Figure 1.5 and Table 1.3: often Egyptologists cite 42 *sepat*, but this number is only found in some Ptolemaic Period sources; see Helck 1974). From at least the Eighteenth Dynasty, on formalized measuring rods offered at temples or placed in the burial equipment of senior officials, the *sepat* are tabulated and aligned with subdivisions of the cubit, a standard length measure at 52.5 cm (Schlott-Schwab 1981). This eternal chart sets all centers at the same level, without historical variables of changing population size, political significance, or cultural production. Nevertheless, when considering the sources on which we build any image of *ancient Egypt*, it is worth checking their chronological and geographical distribution against this ancient ideal tabulation, because the larger number of units allows more detailed assessment and highlights just how fragmentary the source base remains.

Preservation: geological and historical factors

The list of provinces illustrates the massive gaps across Middle and Lower Egypt in preservation of temple walls, one of the main sources for inscriptions and depictions in modern accounts of ancient Egyptian religion. If we add the temples

Table 1.3　The *sepat*, "religious provinces," of ancient Egypt

Upper Egypt

Name of *sepat* with (modern usage) number	Town	Name of deity	Extent of preservation of temples	
			Pre-332	Ptolemaic/ Roman
1. Land of the bow	Abu	Khnum		Blocks, foundations
		Satet	Reconstructed	
2. Throne of horus	Edfu	Horus	Gateway	Intact main temple
3. Nekhen	Nekhen	Horus	Foundations	
	Nekheb	Nekhbet, Sobek	Foundations	
4. Waset	Waset	Amun	Substantial	
		Mut	Blocks, foundations	
		Khons	Intact	
		Ipet		Intact
5. Twin gods	Gebtyu	Min, Isis	Foundations	
6. Iq (crocodile form)	Iunet	Hathor		Intact
7. Bat	Hutsekhem	Hathor? Bat?		Blocks
8. Tawer	Abdju	Osiris	Foundations	
9. Khentmin	Ipu	Min	Under town?	
10. Wadjyt	Tjebu	Nemty		Nile destroyed 1821
11. Seth (?)	Shas-hotep	Khnum	*Not located*	
12. Iatfet	Per Nemty	Nemty	*Not located*	
13. Nedjfet fore	Saut	Wepwawet, Anubis	*Not located*	
14. Nedjfet rear	Qesy	Hathor	*Not located*	
15. Wenet	Khemenu	Thoth	Gateway	Blocks, foundations
16. Mahedj	Hebenu	Horus	*Not located*	
17. Input	Saka	Bata, Anubis?	*Not located*	
18. Nemty	Hutnesut	Nemtywy?		Blocks, foundations
19. Wabwy (?)	Sepermeru	Igay?	*Not located*	
20. Naret fore	Hutnennesut	Heryshef	Blocks, foundations	
21. Naret rear	Shenakhen/ Semenuhor	Khnum/Horus	*Not located*	
22. Medenyt	Tepihu	Hathor	*Not located*	
Fayoum	Shedyt	Sobek, Horus	Blocks (site overbuilt in the 1990s)	

Table 1.3 (*Cont'd*)

Lower Egypt

Name of *sepat* with (modern usage) number	Town	Name of deity	Extent of preservation of temples	
			Pre-332	Ptolemaic/Roman
1. Inebuhedj	Mennefer	Ptah	*Not located, under village?*	
2. (Name unknown)	Khem	Khentykhem	*Not preserved*	
3. Imentet	Hutihyt	Sekhmet-Hathor	*Not preserved*	
4. Neit south	Djeqa'per	Sobek	*Not located*	
5. Neit north	Sau	Neit	*Not preserved*	
6. Khasu	Perwadjyt	Wadjyt	Limited remains	
7. Wa'mhu west	Besyt?		*Not located*	
8. Wa'mhu east	Peratum	Atum	Limited remains	
9. 'Andjety	Djedu	Osiris	*Not preserved*	
10. Kemwer	Hutherib	Khentkhety	Blocks	
11. Hesbu	[Tell Moqdam]	?	*Not preserved*	
12. Tjebnetjer	Tjebnetjer	Inheret-Shu	*Not preserved*	
13. Heqa 'andju	Iunu	Ra/Atum	Enclosure, blocks, obelisk	
14. Iabty	Benu?/Tjaru	Horus	*Not identified/preserved*	
15. Heb? Djehuty?	?	Thoth?	*Not identified*	
16. Hatmehyt	Djedet	Banebdjedet	Granite shrine	

First attested as sepat *in reign of Hatshepsut, circa 1450* BC:

17. Behdet	Iunamun	Amun	Foundations	

First as one sepat *in reign of Sety I, circa 1300* BC; *as two under Napatan rule, Dynasty 25, circa 700* BC:

18. Imet fore	(Per-)Bast	Bast	Blocks, foundations	
19. Imet north	Imet	Wadjyt	Blocks, foundations	

Attested as sepat *under Napatan rule, first in lists of* sepat *in Ptolemaic inscriptions:*

20. Sopdu	Persopdu	Sopdu	*Not preserved*	

constructed for the eternal cult of rulers during their reign, including the pyramid complexes of the Old and Middle Kingdom, a similar pattern emerges. The best-preserved structures are all sandstone monuments in southern Upper Egypt, with the exception of the limestone monuments of the pyramid complexes and associated cemeteries from Fayoum to Giza, and buried temples at Abdju.

In this architectural geography, natural history combines with human intervention. Geology gave Egyptian builders two main stones, coarser sandstone and finer limestone. From central Sudan to as far north as southern Upper Egypt, the Nile

Valley is bordered by sandstone desert and quarries; from Waset/Thebes to the Delta, so for most of the Egyptian Nile Valley, the surrounding desert cliffs and their quarries are limestone. As builders would use blocks from nearby quarries for the bulk of any stone construction, most stone temples from southern Upper Egypt are of sandstone, the northern outpost being the late Ptolemaic and early Roman Period temple of Hathor at Dendera, while stone temples from Waset/Thebes to the Mediterranean are otherwise of limestone. Recycling was common practice at many if not most periods, but the Romans introduced a new method of recycling limestone: it can be burned to obtain lime, essential for the plaster used to cement a new civic architecture. At the end of the fourth century AD, Christianity became the exclusive official religion of the Roman Empire: the temples, already without institutional funding since the third century AD, suddenly became sites for a vast industrial enterprise, lime burning. The effort required for dismantling monuments must have been as great as the effort in their original construction, so this is no local village-level iconoclasm, but a massive expression of national or state will. At a number of sites where limestone monuments once stood, limekilns have been unearthed, some dated by coins to the late fourth to fifth centuries AD (Petrie 1890).

In sum, the ancient architecture survives in Egypt in three specific circumstances:

Structure too large to dismantle (the largest pyramids, though these too are in variable condition, and not one preserves its original outer casing intact)

Structure covered by sand during major periods of ancient to modern dismantling (pyramid complexes and surrounding cemeteries of Old and New Kingdom at Saqqara, kingship temples at Abdju)

Structure built of sandstone (temples of New Kingdom at Waset/Thebes and of Ptolemaic and Roman Period in Lower Nubia, Kom Ombo, Edfu, Esna, Waset/Thebes, and Dendera)

The resulting absence of evidence for entire regions, across Middle as well as Lower Egypt, is compounded by the loss of the very core to ancient Egyptian religious writing, the temples at Iunu/Heliopolis and Mennefer/Memphis. On the basis of scattered but repeated writings, these were arguably the two greatest sacred enclosures in the country. For Iunu, some information has been gained from sporadic excavations on the vast site; the base of a structure might be identified as remains of an extraordinary artificial mound that elevated the main precincts for the worship of Ra', the sun (Contardi 2009). For Mennefer, the site remains a mystery; visitors are often shown a low temple site as the temple of Ptah, but its inscriptions and depictions indicate that it was for the cult of King Ramses II, and it seems to face west toward the original Ptah temple, perhaps buried below a renowned medieval village Mit Rahina (Malek 1992). The Ptah temple has a name unique in form, Hut-ka-Ptah, *domain of the ka-spirit of Ptah*, perhaps the origin of the Greek Aigyptos, in turn the source of West European names for the country including English Egypt. Here, it seems, there once flourished a sacred precinct so central to Egypt that it became its very name; yet we do not know why the shrine should, unlike any other sacred place in Egypt, be identified as for the ka-spirit of a deity, rather than directly for the deity itself, and we have no information on the form or plan of this Hut-ka of Ptah (Figure 1.6).

(a)

(b)

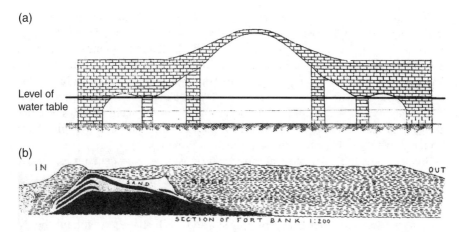

Figure 1.6 The High Mound of Iunu, as recorded by two early twentieth-century AD archaeologists: (a) E. Schiaparelli, redrawn after F. Contardi, *Il Naos di Sethi I da Eliopoli. Un monument per il culto del dio Sole*, Milan 2009, p.14 (b) W. Petrie, *Heliopolis, Kafr Ammar, Shurafa*, London 1912.

Even with those gaps, the climate, geology, and history of Egypt have preserved a quantity and scale of ancient monument with few parallels across the world. Moreover, there are substantial compensations for the gaps in the architectural record, in the wide range of manuscript sources and the smaller sculpture and inscription available. Egyptologists have privileged the written evidence, supported by visual arts, across these three source types—the architectural monument, sculpture in three and two dimensions, and the manuscript. From written and visual evidence around material monumental remains, we can identify sacred architecture as primarily a space for making offerings, with three types of recipient: *netjeru*, "deities"; *nesyu*, "kings"; and *akhu*, "the effective/good dead." Yet is this ancient Egyptian religion, or rather, what part of ancient life in the Nile Valley are we choosing to see here? And what are we omitting?

Beyond written sources: mudbrick architecture

Gramsci commented that "every religion ... is in reality a plurality of distinct and often contradictory religions" (Gramsci 1975, 1397). We might start, then, not from a modern sense of religion, with buildings and books, but set out instead on a comparative quest for how other groups of humans have historically marked out parts of living as intensive or separate, so in our terms as *sacred*. If we turn from geography, with its spatial analyses, to the historical periods, for analysis by time phase, we might draft a rather different list of architectural sources by date. Here, we might consider not the most visible, but the least tangible, where archaeological techniques and questions have both retrieved immeasurably more sheer data and generated most substantial new understanding of how different groups of humans live or have lived. From the evidence of the smallest recorded units, through every scale of structure and settlement, we could restore attention to less central and less well-preserved temples such as the mudbrick structure uncovered near Badari at the border of Upper and Middle Egypt (Chapter 3). Here, the greatest advance in Nile Valley archaeology has been outside the Egyptological mainstream, from research into predynastic Egypt and into Sudanese and Egyptian Nubia to the south (Edwards). The record within the time–space of *ancient Egypt* remains less intensively developed, despite the important analyses of recent decades (Lehner 2010). A list of excavated sites from which plans of small-scale house units have been published could start from a draft such as Table 1.4.

Greater geographical–historical range can be gained from cemeteries, always taking into account the different chances of preservation and, often overlooked, the variations in funeral and burial customs. Burial practice varied far more than the view, common even among Egyptologists, that ancient Egyptians *took everything with them*; even richer groups only stocked tomb chambers with full-house inventories at only two points in Egyptian history, the period around unification, circa 3000 BC, and the period of greatest military presence in western Asia, circa 1450–1300 BC. Changing funeral and burial customs dramatically affect the selected edition of life made available to us as burial equipment (Chapter 7). At some

Table 1.4   Some key published settlement sites in Egyptian archaeology

Date BC	Upper Egypt S	Upper Egypt N	Middle Egypt	Oases	Fayoum	Lower Egypt
4000–3500		Badari			Fayoum	Merimda, Maadi
3500–3000	Adaima Nekhen	Badari (Naqada)				
3000–2400	Nekhen Abu					Giza Abusir Dahshur
2400–2000	Abu	Abdju		Balat		Mendes Kom al-Hisn
2000–1600	Abu	Wahsut Waset		Balat	Lahun Qasr al-Sagha	Abu Ghalib Hutwaret Lisht Mennefer
1600–1450	Abu	Deir al-Ballas				Hutwaret Mennefer
1450–1100	Abu	Malkata Waset Deir al-Madina	Akhetaten		Madinat al-Ghurab	Qantir Mennefer
1100–650	Abu	Madinat Habu	Khemenu			Mennefer
650–525	Abu	Madinat Habu				(Naukratis)

periods, a small selection of goods was placed with richer men and women, as if to sustain them on one final journey, rather than to stock them for eternity. More often, the burials of younger women and of infants would receive greater protection in the form of amulets and jewelry, as if for puberty or childbirth rites they did not live long enough to see (Dubiel 2008). In addition to the variations over time, substantial differences may be expected to nuance, adjust, or overturn the generally top-down normative picture within each period. With improved knowledge of the history of burial rites, a researcher can explore cemetery excavation records as another always-mediated *mirror of life*.

Across different sites, we might look less for monumental or written assertions of activity and first for more direct material traces of actions. Votive deposits provide the primary sources for offerings, and studies of these have begun to bridge the gap with a more broadly defined archaeology of religion (Pinch 1993). Similarly, food and drink, or their containers, and floral remains would provide the essential evidence that the banquets depicted in chapels did take place. Archaeological floral and faunal deposits place in context the visual and written sources for rites of daily and festival offerings and celebrations. Some activities may only be accessible to us in written and visual form, such as the words and gestures of hymns among other ancient performance and practice. Finally, ethnoarchaeology looks to descriptions of living societies to shed light on archaeological material. Direct comparison with other societies can risk doubling the heap of assumptions we make about other societies, but an indirect or heuristic comparative anthropology can provide fresh material from one society for rethinking assumptions about another. The decolonization of archaeology in general and of Egyptology in particular should advance the same aim, of multiplying the number of approaches to ancient material, beyond current Euro-American monopoly on production of knowledge.

Ancient practice and modern prejudice in distinguishing elite *and* popular religion

One of the most deeply rooted modern assumptions pervading accounts of *ancient Egyptian religion* is the opposition between official cult and personalized practice. Such distinctions have impact as a mechanism for legitimating *our own* practice and demoting those *of others*. In the history of religions with a founder figure (so including Buddhism, Christianity, Islam, Judaism), later reforming movements express the need to return to the first generation when the founder was alive, in order to recapture the purity of a pristine initial form of practice. These movements identify any intervening developments as deviation but may in turn be denounced as deviating from the original intentions or mission of the founder. In western European history, the sixteenth-century AD Reformation and then Counter-Reformation provide dramatic examples of this violent religious history. A Muslim parallel to Luther or Calvin might be the eighteenth-century AD Wahhabi movement in Arabian Islam.

The vocabulary used against religious opponents within a founded religion includes charges on the one side of superstition, magic, or witchcraft and on the other of an empty official cult or ritual devoid of sincerity. Perhaps the motivation for attack and counterattack lies in a political and/or psychological need to know who is sincere in their religious practice and who is not. Sincerity and purity tend to be located by modern society outside institutions and their buildings, which may be seen as corrupted and commercialized. In any particular historical context, there may be strong evidence for the accusations against the institutions and strong need for reform. However, there may also be human limits to the ability to identify sincerity and falsehood in others and therefore powerful human drives to institutionalize the sincerity/falsehood division by new forms of religious practice in explicit rejection of others.

In considering practices in other societies, in particular in other times, modern writers struggle to set aside ingrained thinking. The European oppositional approach seems set already by the time of eighteenth-century Enlightenment perceptions of initiated *elite*, manipulative priesthood, and gullible populace. On this model, Egyptologists have asked whether a popular religion existed outside the monumental temples, implicitly equating temple with church or mosque or synagogue. Later twentieth-century Egyptologists recognized these assumptions and so considered instead whether the official cult might not be a small part of a religious world that included *practical religion* with practices that included ancestor worship, divination, and oracles. However, the practice/cult division remains caught on modern binaries of *elite*/popular, initiated/ignorant, and ritual/prayer, none of which may apply. The central topics of ancestor worship, divination, and oracles require fuller attention to wider ranges of sources, but all appear also within the written and visual sources for kingship and the highest officials of the royal court. Most of the material consigned by Egyptologists to categories of, formerly, magic or superstition or, currently, practical religion could be placed without social bias under the heading of *healing*. In the verbal, visual, and material struggle for good health, there is no evidence that a king or courtier turned to any forms or forces different to those invoked among any other visible sector of society. Deities protecting birth, maternity, infancy, and health appear in the same form on amulets found at all levels of society in the archaeological record (Chapter 6).

In a related, equally persistent fallacy, a *religion of the poor* might be identified whenever and wherever inexpensive, often organic materials, sometimes in forms requiring little time or skill, are used for offerings, instead of visibly skillfully produced or inscribed materials—as if the rich make the things they use. The offering of a lump of mud tells us nothing automatically about the social status of the offerer; a particular offering practice might, instead, require that the person in need, or in gratitude, must fashion an offering with their own hands, in which case the rich adult and poor infant may produce similar material results. More sensitive recording of archaeological contexts can be followed by a more open comparison of contexts, with a conscious self-critique to identify as much as possible of the bias each of us brings to drawing a picture of the past: implicitly, the picture will have to become a collaborative and open-ended venture.

Suspending assumptions

In order to avoid the automatic attribution of any form or material to a particular point on a presumed social scale, we might recast these assumptions as questions for new research. Age and gender categories are among the more destabilizing frameworks both in a society and in analysis of that society for instituting continual processes of change within the body of the person/group and for disrupting the tendency of description to produce a static image of the society described. Useful models could be sought here from fields where the assumptions may be least active, for example, in predynastic studies (Hendrickx, Huyge and Wendrich 2010) and Sudan archaeology (Edwards 2005).

Within the written record in the ancient Egyptian language, clues to at least the explicit construction of identity at birth and puberty could be sought in the wide social spectrum documented in personal names. Whereas wealthier levels of society are the more visible in the material record in general, the legal and administrative records from the third to first millennia include manual labor in at least as great numbers, even if still not in proportion to the overall population (written records attest to a high proportion of the highest officials, against only a fraction of the overall population, but the total number of names recorded will be in the low thousands for both less and more wealthy). In very general terms, in each period, no great difference can be found between social classes in the patterns of naming children. For example, in lists of stone haulers from Lahun, circa 1800 BC, many men are named after the king whose burial and cult complex were at Lahun, Senusret II, in the same manner found for high officials of the same period (e.g., Collier and Quirke 2006, 49–53, UC32170, 32184). The connection between hometown and its cult and personal name can be confirmed from other sources. Other worker name lists show a similar preponderance of individuals named after the local god, so placed under their protection. From the same period as the Lahun lists, a legal document from Waset names runaways in southern Upper Egypt town by town, and here again, repeatedly, men from a particular place are named after the main deity of that place (Hayes 1955). Generalizing across the three millennia, the local anchoring of the personal name in local temple cult is an extremely significant finding for the study of the relation between different sectors of society in relation to deities, for it indicates a single social field, with emphasis on king and on local deity—without the class division introduced in studies of *popular* or *practical religion*. This finding justifies closer examination of the written and visual record for the *netjer niuty*, "city deity," of the main towns of ancient Egypt (Assmann 2001, 17–27).

Netjeru deities: *names and forms*

Across the regional map of Egypt, as preserved from scattered inscriptions, certain names appear twice or more as principal deities of a town or *sepat*, whereas others appear only once. From the depictions of different periods, we also obtain an impression of the visual forms most often associated with the names (Table 1.5). Table 1.5 is not intended to present a pantheon of all Egyptian deities. Instead, it

Table 1.5   *Netjeru*, "deities," in the *sepat*, "religious provinces"

1. Attested as principal deity in more than one *sepat*	
Name of deity	Main form
Amun	Man wearing double falcon plume, ram with down-curling horns
Anubis	Jackal/jackal-headed man
Atum	Man wearing double crown
Hathor	Woman with cow horns and sun disk, cow/cow-headed woman
Horus	Falcon/falcon-headed man with double crown
Isis	Woman wearing throne hieroglyph (*Isis*)
Khnum	Ram with horizontal horns/ram-headed man
Min	Man with erect phallus, wrapped body, raised arm holding a *flail*
Neit	Woman wearing red crown or crossed lines on oval
Nemty	Falcon on boat/falcon-headed man, *Seth animal*
Osiris	Man, wrapped body, wearing ostrich plumes headdress
Sobek	Crocodile/crocodile-headed man
Thoth	Ibis/ibis-headed man, baboon
Wadjyt	Rearing cobra, lion-headed woman, woman with cobra and sun disk
2. Attested as principal deity in one *sepat*	
Bast	Lion-headed woman, cat
Bat	Human face with cow horns, on plinth
Heryshef	Ram with horizontal horns/ram-headed man
Igay	*Rare*
Khentkhety	Falcon/falcon-headed man, crocodile
Khentykhem	Falcon/falcon-headed man
Mont	Falcon/falcon-headed man with double falcon plume
Nekhbet	Vulture/woman with vulture headdress
Ptah	Man with wrapped body wearing skullcap
Satet	Woman wearing tall horns and plume headdress
Seth	*Seth animal*/*Seth animal*-headed man
Soped	Man with long beard, double plume headdress
Wepwawet	Jackal, jackal-headed man

summarizes the main forms for just the main deities listed for the 39 *sepat* that constitute the conceptual geography of ancient Egypt. Other deities are equally frequently attested, as partner to main deities or main deity in other towns: Sekhmet appears in cult centers of Ptah, depicted most often as a lion-headed woman; Mut has her own temple, south of the Amun precinct at Karnak, and is depicted as a woman or lion-headed woman wearing a vulture headdress and double crown. Even within its limits, though, the list demonstrates two fundamental features of the ancient Egyptian depiction of deities: a name could be given more than one form, and the same form may be used for more than one name. Correlation of even these names with just their principal forms should, then, be enough to convey the dominant principles behind ancient Egyptian depictions of deities—teaching us how to read the visual form and how not to.

Evolutionary readings of ancient images

Nineteenth- and early twentieth-century commentators interpreted ancient depictions as idolatry, animal worship, and fetishism. Wallis Budge summarized the work of a generation of Egyptological colleagues at the British Museum under the title *From Fetish to God in Ancient Egypt* (Budge 1934). By the time this was published in the 1930s, it must have seemed dated to researchers in other fields; the philosopher Ernst Cassirer was then already redefining his more synchronic approach to *symbolic forms* (see Chapter 4). Earlier histories of Egyptian religion confidently ascribe object forms to a prehistory in which people supposedly worshipped objects or emblems as fetishes; according to this view, people became more sophisticated and worshipped animals instead, until, by early historic times, they were worshipping human forms. This evolutionary history allowed early Egyptologists to read the various forms of deities as an amalgam of different phases in a history of depiction, where human, human–animal, animal, and object stood in a hierarchy on the road toward a single anthropomorphic deity or, in more agnostic or atheistic readings, no deity at all. Yet no such evolution appears in the attested sequence of depictions over time. Following the fourth-millennium BC patterns of depiction, a radical reformulation of depiction accompanies the introduction of writing shortly before 3000 BC. In the new system of depiction, alongside the introduction of hieroglyphic script, the forms of images follow the same principles of composition as the hieroglyphs; or, to put it the other way round, hieroglyphs are small images constructed on the same principles and proportions as large figures. In this new world of expression and communication, art and script are fused (Fischer 1986). From the sparse Early Dynastic sources, all four options for depicting a deity seem already available—human, animal headed, animal, and object (Figure 1.7). Far from being an evolutionary sequence, the four image types are a series of contemporary options for depicting what is not known, according to the information to be conveyed and the requirements of the composition.

Compositional considerations may account for the recurrent choice between depicting a named deity as an animal and as an animal-headed human. None of the names listed earlier was depicted only as an animal or only as an animal-headed human, nor are there any examples where more ancient sources show only animal form, more recent only animal headed. Presumably, then, the body/head choices offer complementary means of visualizing the being or force evoked in the same name throughout the history of this religion art. At a simple level, the compositional principle may have been rhythm and harmony, whereby artists resisted radically different forms within a line of deities, particularly where the king stands or walks or sits among them. Also on the simplest, pragmatic level, a human body might most fluently serve a composition where a named deity would need to sit on a throne or to hold a scepter. Other artistic principles could have generated different results, with, for example, birds holding tall scepters or quadrupeds seated on chairs; such choices are found within ancient Egyptian sources, on manuscript visual descriptions of a world turned upside down (as in the so-called Satirical Papyrus of Turin, from Waset, about 1250 BC, Omlin 1973). The preference for animal-headed human bodies must

(a)   (bi)   (bii)

(c)

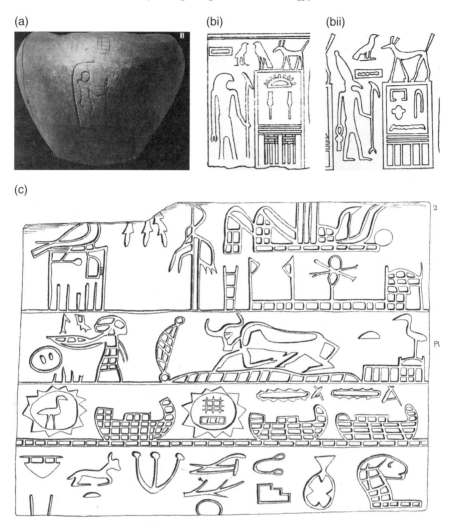

Figure 1.7   Synchronized differences: different depictions of deities as human, animal headed, animal, and object within the period 3100–2900 BC: (a) stone bowl inscribed with image of a deity as a standing wrapped man in a shrine, identified by the aforementioned three single-consonant hieroglyphs as the god Ptah (Semenuhor cemeteries, tomb 231, about 3100 BC); (b) two forms of one deity on a single seal impression, (i) falcon and falcon headed, generally identified as Horus, and (ii) mixed (?) animal and human with the same head, generally identified as Seth (images reconstructed from mud seal impressions found in tombs of late Second Dynasty kings, Abdju); (c) deities depicted through living animals and distinct objects, (i) wild (?) bull in an oval enclosure (second register) and (ii) emblem with crossed arrows in a rectilinear enclosure (first register) (wood label with name of King Aha, found in tombs of First Dynasty kings, Abdju). From (a) W. Petrie, *Tarkhan I*, London 1913 and (b) and (c) W. Petrie, *The Royal Tombs of the Earliest Dynasties II*, London 1901.

Figure 1.8   Limestone stela with two images, cow and adult woman, both with cow horns and sun disk, jointly identified in the hieroglyphic inscription between the two hearing ears of the deity as *Hathor, lady of the sycamore*. From Mennefer, about 1300 BC. W. Petrie, *Memphis I*, British School of Archaeology in Egypt, London, pl.28.

be recognized as specific decisions within a particular conception of, and desire for, harmony—not as some *natural* or inevitable device in a system of visual rules. Comparison of the frequent depiction of the same named deities in whole animal form generally confirms that this is not an attempt to show a different kind of divine nature, but a choice guided by the aim of the composition. A named deity may be depicted as a falcon or hippopotamus particularly in scenes where difference is emphasized either among the deities (as in Late Period and later *catalogues* of deities) or between deity and worshipper (as on New Kingdom and later votive stelae). Entirely animal forms are also more common where a deity is depicted alone, as in votive sculpture. However, in some instances, a visual composition includes other principles of duality or symmetry, where different shapes are juxtaposed without any such spatial logic (Figure 1.8). In such cases, the plural, perhaps even antisingular, image can be recognized as one strategy to communicate a multifaceted divine presence, using visual means where a hymn might deploy combinations or sequences of names or phrases to delineate the elusive deity. On present evidence, a supposed historical evolution from animal to human form seems implausible, as it cannot be seen at work in the choices of creative producers at any period.

Ancient and modern multiplication of forms of netjeru

Late Period and later bronze figures of deities can create an impression of endless variety, particularly where the individual images accumulate in temple deposits or, even more, are assembled from different sites in modern collections. In ancient times, the number of different forms within a single group may not have been so overwhelming, and each form seems to have had tight localized meanings, lost wherever exact provenance has not been recorded. The bronze figurines were common in early modern collections of Egyptian antiquities in Europe, reinforcing biblical and Roman prejudice against ancient Egypt as home to animal worship. However, the form of the figurine need not be an ancient statement identifying a named deity. Frequently, for example, cat figurines are inscribed with invocations asking the goddess Bast to give life to a named person, and the museum label will then identify the cat as Bast. As the inscriptions do not explicitly identify form and name, it would be more accurate to interpret them as evidence that the cat could convey some feature essential to Bast. In other words, no ancient Egyptian deity *is* an animal or a bird, but instead, the animal or bird world could be used to convey some quality considered divine.

The closest to *animal cult*, in the sense of worship of a living animal, would be the extraordinary status of the sacred bull of Ra at Iunu, Ptah at Mennefer, and Mont at Armant (see Chapter 2, Section The separateness of the human). Only one sacred bull was alive at any one time, the next being sought immediately on the death of the old; the exceptional role of these three bulls is reflected in the unique special name for each—Menwer for the bull of Ra, Hep/Apis for Ptah, and Bekhu for Mont. The sacred bull lived in a special enclosure, as the *herald* of the god, and at death was buried in a stone sarcophagus like a king or high official. The unexplained and remarkable care for the three bulls did not stop, but nor did it seem to foster, the new practice after 700 BC of embalming literally millions of birds and animals for burial in substantial, apparently state-funded catacombs (Figure 2.2). The later embalming of species perhaps reflects instead the meeting of two phenomena: spread in embalming techniques in the first millennium BC to a wider social and geographical range and the use of certain species to denote qualities of *netjeru*. Rarely, a living species might denote a quality only found with one name, separate from all other named divine forces, as in the case of the ibis, only deployed for images of Thoth. Far more often, a particular animal or bird might depict a quality found with several separate names, as the falcon might be a form appropriate for depicting Ra, Horus, and Mont or the lioness for Sekhmet or Wadjyt.

Visual forms as poetic metaphors

As with any language, the elements in this visual repertoire gain their meaning from the ranges and contexts of their use, often most clearly seen at the point where they are not used. The lion-headed woman form may not automatically evoke any *eye of Ra* (force sent out in fury from the creator), because not all images named *eye of Ra* take that form. On the other hand, fury more broadly may be a core idea in the lion metaphor. In reading visual and verbal together, modern readers may find it easiest to consider each visual(–verbal) composition not as *art*, but as *poetry*—as Ogden Goelet recommends us to read ancient Egyptian afterlife literature in the same frame of mind we might bring to surrealist poetry (Goelet 1994). By taking each visual form as a metaphor to decode, we may come closer to the aims of the composer. The surviving range of written sources, literary and others, can help to interpret the visual forms, minimizing the associations we might think *natural* for each form. For example, the cow form can more plausibly be identified with maternal love, because the hieroglyphic writing of the verb *ames*, "to care for," ends with the hieroglyph of a cow turning to lick the calf at her udder. Before this interpretation begins, archaeological fieldwork and survey provide the context of material culture and ecology for each period, essential to any understanding of the words and images.

Rare compositions combine different forms in an emphatic demonstration of multiple faces of a deity. In one striking example, four forms of a goddess, perhaps Hathor, are combined in a single statue from perhaps the mid-first millennium BC as cow, rearing cobra, lion-headed woman, and woman with sun disk and cow horns (Louvre E26023). The four forms create an exceptional impression specifically on the number four, separating this quadruple divine force from others. Such combinations are not frequent at any period, especially on the scale of that substantial stone image, perhaps intended to act as cult image at a place where offerings would be made to the goddess. In some instances, Hathor is depicted as the maternal cow, providing milk for the king, eternally effective as a statue in offering chapels; the best-preserved example is from the temple of Hatshepsut as king, at Waset, and others include one in a cemetery chapel at Iunyt (Downes 1974; Figure 1.9). Late Period images of the creator adopt a different strategy for a similar effect, adding to one body elements from several different species, sometimes with two or more heads, as a visual statement on the plurality of creative force within the one creator.

Fission and fusion in names of netjeru

The combinations indicate different possibilities for constructing imagery and developing name: whereas the quadruple Hathor statue opens a single name to subsets, fissioning into several *deities*, the creator images merge the multiple into a single, opening the possibilities of fusions. Both directions are frequently found across the two and a half thousand years and can be understood perhaps most easily as changes in focus. In a sense, each deity name identifies for us what an ancient group wished to mark out, or experienced as marked out, as divine; even at any one period, the areas demarcated as separate, by the strategy of naming, might overlap. Over time, the singular impact of an area or force might come to be considered multiple, and each of the multiple parts might be considered sufficiently separate to receive offerings, sometimes under different forms. Horus might be visualized as Horus the Child and then as Horus the Child of a particular place; in specific context, an image of a child deity might be intended to refer to only that localized presence of a divine force. Some contexts might require a succession of different expressions of one divine force; in the embalming rituals, four forms of Anubis may correspond to the four cardinal points or to four duties required in the physical operation. Claude

Figure 1.9   The statue of Hathor and King Amenhotep II, as found in the rock-cut chapel beside the temples of Hatshepsut and Thutmes III, overlain by the later monastery Deir al-Bahari, on the West Bank at Waset. The statue is now in the Egyptian Museum, Cairo; the photograph shows the statue in its original location, just after it was uncovered. E. Naville, *Deir el Bahri I*, Egypt Exploration Fund, London, 1895, pl.27.

Traunecker has noted the impact of architecture on the historical process of fissioning: a particular architectural feature, such as a symmetrically sited chapel or a slot in a sequence of symmetrically arranged wall registers, might create a space for new use of a divine quality as a full name (Traunecker 1997). By this *wall theology*, from Isis the good sister, the quality of good sister (in Late Egyptian *Tasenetnefret*) might separate off to provide the harmonious rhythm of wall scenes or temple chapels, where *Tasenetnefret* might stand as an independent deity receiving offerings of her own, a separately acknowledged divine quality to which people of that time and place decided to give space and in some instances offerings.

   Equally, over time, two areas might be fused to a composite form (*syncretism*), as in the dominant New Kingdom combination Amun-Ra, where the expression of universal power as *imen*, "hidden" (Amun), combines with the expression of universal power as the source of light and heat *ra'*, "sun" (Ra), leaving three possible areas to celebrate: Amun, Ra, and Amun-Ra. Rather than puzzling over the decision to leave all three as options, we might understand each occurrence as a choice by one ancient inscriber or composer to focus on one or other or both of the sources of universal power.

Ancient descriptions of netjeru: *hymns and narratives*

For understanding the shared features as well as the separate identities of *netjeru*, Egyptologists have explored three types of ancient writing: hymns, descriptive treatises, and narratives. In hymns, the reciter defines the *netjer(et)* in sets of actions or qualities, where hymns to each named deity can be compared, to cata-logue features as shared or unique to one name. Hymns to Osiris and to the sun-god as creator have received most attention. Sometimes, the regular frame of praise is expanded to include more explicit references to relations between *netjeru* (see Chapter 4, stela of Amenmes). Treatises with descriptions of religious geography bring together deities in statements of action more often. Among the treatises, the passage of the sun through the sky of the world and underworld, core motif in tombs of New Kingdom rulers, and the dramatic depiction of the world on ceiling compositions in the tomb of Sety I and in the unique tomb-shrine for the god Osiris behind the temple for the king at Abdju/Abydos may be counted. More difficult to place architecturally, a loose block of basalt inscribed in the period of Napatan rule over Egypt preserves accounts of the creation and of the establishment of kingship at Mennefer/Memphis (Shabako Stone). In general, modern researchers draw on narrative sources, where *netjeru* are more clearly described in action together. Yet longer tales of deities are so rare that Egyptologists have had to rely in part on ancient Greek and Latin versions, above all the account by Plutarch of the Osiris myth. In 1975, Jan Assmann proposed a radical rethink, arguing that there were no myths, in the sense of narratives about deities, before the New Kingdom. As will be discussed in Chapter 4, in the subsequent debate, Susanne Bickel proposed to widen the definition of *myth* beyond narration, while Joachim Quack has observed how *telling the story* of a deity is a form of worship and that the primary goal of the ancient Egyptian sources is to praise—hence the dominance of hymns and the relatively rare use of long tales.

Some Egyptologists have doubted that a *religion* could have *gods* without narra-tives to teach each new generation who and what the gods are. Yet if, following Gramsci, *religion* concerns the connection between human behavior and the con-ception of human life, then the ethics can be grounded in individual episodes, with no privileged or prior role for a chronological sequence of episodes. Even from an anachronistic position, the religions of the book do not need to be, and in fact are not, taught from a narrative of birth to death of the founder, but instead, begin from the main precepts for behavior put forward by the founder. These ethical precepts can certainly be placed in the life narrative of the religion founder, as in annual festivals evoking Genesis and Exodus, birth and death of Christ, and the life-trans-forming journey of Muhammed. Yet, precisely the annual rhythm of the religions shows that each episode carries meaning for the faithful through the link to the teachings of the founder, rather than as a didactic story where you start each time at birth and finish at death. Any overall story can be built up over time, but need not be fully present at any one moment. Moreover, in teaching practice, ethical advice and the guiding content of sermons and sayings take precedence over biographical story lines. For each festival, ritual, and other social action, the immediate relations of the act in their divine dimension would be a stronger starting point than a longer story—which might never have been needed until, in Plutarch, a Greek tradition of narrative met the ancient Egyptian motifs. Whether or not we call the relations between *netjeru,* "myth," when they are expressed outside narrative form, is a decision for the reader: given general current English usage, though, *myth* may be another word that confuses when applied to a society that did not primarily narrate its divine world. These sources are explored in Chapter 4.

Instituting sacred space: the question of priesthood

The monumental scale of well-preserved temple architecture and sculpture encouraged later generations to a caricature of ancient Egypt as a land ruled by priests and superstition. However, the temples in question were not designed for crowds to hear sermons or readings, but more as containers for safely defusing the encounter between offerer and deity. As offering place, the sacred architecture required stocking with goods and staffing with personnel to keep the place clean and the offerings flowing each day and at festivals. In this sense, there is no clergy, only a *temple staff* (Egyptian *wenut*). Against the image of a separate priestly caste, written sources indicate that most staff served by monthly rota. Anyone with a temple position might serve a maximum of three months in a year but quite possibly less. The rest of the time, presumably, they worked outside the temple, explaining why men with temple positions often also bear administrative titles—a reminder too that ancient work was not a 9–5, 365-day commitment. As will be discussed in Chapter 3, there was no one word for *priest*: the English word is used for a series of ancient Egyptian titles, which presumably reflected different responsibilities but are difficult to separate in practice—*god's servant, god's father,* and *pure.* Perhaps, the ancient word closest to our term *priest* is the *nesut,* "king," who must be initiated into sacred knowledge of the workings of life. However, little detail is yet known on the Egyptian term for such *initiation (bes),* leaving much to be discovered, as considered in that chapter. With neither priest nor king, the ancient Egyptian landscape is marked by institutions we also struggle to understand in our efforts to classify: the House of Life, the House of Gold, and the holders of the title Bearer of the Festival Roll at the palace and temple. The entire framework seems at odds with all the assumptions we bring to the study of the sacred in the past.

Checklist on assumptions

At the close of these discussions, a reader might compile a short vocabulary for key words where regular English usage renders the term difficult or impossible to apply to the study of ancient Egypt and use this to check the content of the chapters to come. The following words might figure on the list, but each reader will have their own warning vocabulary:

Cosmos (and cosmology)
Dynasty

King (and kingship)
Magic
Myth
Priest
Temple
Tomb

The words will continue to circulate, and most recur in most chapters. The more a reader remains conscious of problems in using them to describe other worlds, the better the chances of a dialogue with those worlds.

CHAPTER 2

Finding the Sacred
in Space and Time

⌐⌐⌐⌐

Holiness: Absolute or Relative

In a comparative study on sacred landscapes, the anthropologist Jane Hubert reflects: "Not every stone or plot of earth can be treated with the same degree of respect. Does this mean that there are *degrees* of sacredness? Or is it, again, merely limitations in the understanding of the cultures and languages concerned?" (Hubert 1994, 18). On these lines, we might ask whether people in Egypt 3000–525 would live their lives in constant appreciation of all matter and being as infused with divinity. Or is such extensive sanctity a projection from more recent European traditions? Anthropology of religion charts the wide range of ways in which different human groups conceive of time and space, including the time and space of the body. Twenty-first-century citizens may separate out categories of time and space, each divided into ordinary and special, for example, between daily life and carnival days or between unmarked space and separated, sacred, or forbidden space. Space–time segments can frame our lives with greatest impact where we would not use the term religion. In contemporary urban societies, the most heavily marked space might be a mental asylum or a prison, where physical separation is reinforced by both interior policing and an external collective act of forgetting.

Against the patterns in secular cityscapes, other societies might, in theory, avoid separating out any time or space at all and instead consider all lived experience as sacred. In such a view, sacredness would be a permanent quality of earth, air, and all materials from water and rock to animal and human bodies. Archaeological sources, including writings and depictions, offer limited but still useful evidence for any attempt to identify the main approaches to sacredness in ancient Egypt. Writings on the earth god Geb or sky goddess Nut might imply that the earth itself was considered a sacred material on which we walk and the air a sacred material wrapped around us. If the names and roles of these deities suggest a world where everything is sacred, we then need to ask whether ancient individuals felt conscious

Exploring Religion in Ancient Egypt, First Edition. Stephen Quirke.
© 2015 Stephen Quirke. Published 2015 by John Wiley & Sons, Ltd.

of that sacredness throughout their day and night. In this chapter, while bearing in mind the possibility of evenly sacred world, I examine evidence that some times and spaces were marked as more sacred than others.

The human body

Humans on the world: separation versus continuity

In traditional European-language division between culture and nature, human impact on the environment is contrasted with a world without humans. Anthropologists and historians have explored other ways in which different societies might think about, or express, the relations between humans in the world. In one radical review, Eduardo Viveiros de Castro identifies outside European tradition a widespread insistence on the continuity between all that exists. Only his term for this, *perspectivism*, seems still caught in other European traditions, where art, philosophy, and politics all maintained a belief in the individualized *point of view* of an all-seeing individual eye (introduction and critique Ramos 2012). Nevertheless, his writing takes most direct aim at the European instinct to classify and so to reduce all being to categories, starting with animate and inanimate.

In contrast to Viveiros de Castro, Philippe Descola finds differences between human groups around the world in the way they relate the group member to others and to what European science would classify as nonhuman (Descola 2005). He considers varying expressions of physical exterior and *interiority* of beings or, perhaps more neutrally, the tangible externals and intangible other qualities. The logical product of these two options would be a quartet of possible combinations, where, at each encounter with any other physical being, the thinking individual might consider that other as having:

1. Similar physicality, similar interiority	2. Similar physicality, different interiority
3. Different physicality, similar interiority	4. Different physicality, different interiority

The quartet is intended not to straightjacket peoples by descriptive labels for their views, but instead as possible ways to see, or to think, around the variety of recorded accounts from groups across the world. For this rethinking, Descola finds new uses for terms that have been defined in more than one way in previous generations, and gives examples, geographical distribution and definition for each:

1. Totemism: Other beings are considered to have similar external and internal properties; some Australian groups identify a knowledge-man with an animal species (not an individual), which can assist him and, when damaged, can hurt him; other Australian groups identify their sub-groups with species.
2. Naturalism: The physical construction is considered similar, but ethical and moral properties differ; in a European scientific approach, everything *animal* has similar bodily properties, distinguishing them from everything vegetable and mineral, but the human alone has such features of subjectivity as conscience and free will.

3. Animism: Differences in external appearance conceal underlying shared *interiority*; what may seem different species, such as human and jaguar, are kin, as among Amazonian groups in South America.
4. Analogism: Both exterior and interiority are different, in a great plurality of species that allows for an equally vast web of analogies; west African groups express the human body as a hybrid fusion of elements, for example, the Samo (Burkina) human as comprising body of flesh from mother, blood from father, breath (from blood of the heart), *nyìni* essence (from blood of the body) generating heat and sweat, mental personality (understanding, memory, and imagination, may be reincarnation of that of an ancestor), *double* (immortal essence unique to each individual, traced in the shadow, also characteristic of plants, animals, and some inanimate materials such as clay and iron), *individual destiny* (determining the lifespan), and name.

The fourfold classification may be disputed, both in the differences between terms and in the number of categories. Dominant features in this account reside within the European philosophical traditions that Viveiros de Castro seeks to escape: the distinction between physical exterior and *interiority* of beings seems to recast a European dichotomy body–mind and the logical quartet as a philosophical device derives from Aristotle in fourth-century BC Greek writing, via the twentieth-century French writing of Greimas. Although Descola does not claim to describe all human societies in this tight frame, the danger of the Aristotelian quartet is that it induces such totalizing descriptions in reading and application. Nevertheless, the exploration by Descola provides fertile ground for considering how we understand the evidence from ancient Egypt. As ethnographers have recorded such varied expressions of being human in the world, where would ancient Egypt be placed? Or, perhaps more productively, which of these relations to others can shed most light on our fragmentary record?

The separateness of the human in Egypt 3000–525 BC

The anthropological summaries prompt us to consider how relations between human and animal were expressed in Egypt 3000–525 BC. The evidence for special treatment of animals alongside humans seems strongest at the outer limits of this time span. For the period leading up to state formation, perhaps 3200 BC, current excavations at Nekhen have revealed an unparalleled range of animal burials, including the most formidable creatures outside the agricultural and pastoral circle: African wild bull, large feline (leopard?), elephant, and hippopotamus. The significance of the astonishing assemblage remains uncertain. However, as Nekhen is a major center of kingship in the late fourth to third millennia BC, the animal burials might collectively demonstrate the variety of creation under the power of the ruler (Friedman, Van Neer and Linseele, 2011, Figure 2.1).

After 700 BC, so at the other end of the period studied here, certain species of animals and birds begin to be embalmed, wrapped, and deposited in mass burials on a spectacular and unprecedented scale. Although these mummified species are among the most familiar and popular sights in modern museum displays, we know extraordinarily little about the history and social setting of this religious practice. Possibly,

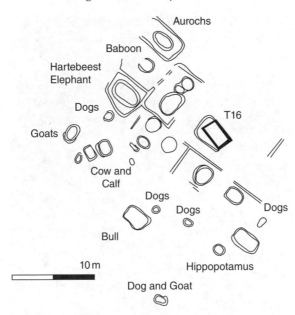

Figure 2.1   The animal burials around Tomb 16, at site H6, Nekhen. Drawing by Wolfram Grajetzki after the preliminary report by Friedman, RF, W. Van Neer, and V. Linseele, 2011. The *elite* Predynastic cemetery at Hierakonpolis: 2009–2010 update, in Friedman, R.F. & Fiske, P.N. (eds.), *Egypt at its Origins 3. Orientalia Lovaniensia Analecta* 205. Peeters, Leuven, 157–191. Drawing © Wolfram Grajetzki.

species were identified as emblems of the powers in solar creation and renewal, for rituals of the solar New Year which required an immortalized presence, so a mummified (eternally alive) rather than a living (mortal, to die) example. Innumerable votive inscriptions and later manuscript documents attest to the devotion of individuals in dedicating the mummified creature. Yet the construction of catacombs and temples to house them and maintain cult for them seems to be an operation on a grander scale, equal to the building of great temples for deities in the same periods. On this scale, the operative ancient Egyptian institution is kingship; many inscriptions and images indeed attest to the central role of kings in founding and maintaining estates and buildings for cult of divine animals (Kessler 1989). New research is needed into how and why the practice of mummifying such large numbers of animals and birds began and whether it continued uninterrupted over the following eight centuries into the early first millennium AD. Within that time span, at least at some periods, the mass mummification of species involved a cull: X-rays of mummified cats in different collections show that the individuals were mainly very young, most often with neck wrung, and in these instances, the provision of a mummified animal for a ritual or festival was evidently the overriding concern, not any devotion to the individual animal in the manner of a modern, or ancient, pet (Figure 2.2).

Two special cases emphasize the central role of the bull in particular throughout Egyptian history: at Iunu/Heliopolis, the creator sun-god Ra could be approached

Figure 2.2 Rock-cut catacombs for burials of mummified animals and birds, northern cemeteries of Mennefer (Saqqara), first millennium BC. Excavation photograph, © Egypt Exploration Society.

through a bull in the role of *herald* (the Egyptian word is *wehemu*), called Menwer (in Greek Mnevis), and similarly at Mennefer/Memphis, the creative force Ptah had a *herald* bull named Hep (in Greek Apis). These special cults were closely tied to kingship, with a *race of the Hep* among kingship rituals from the third millennium BC. At least from the time of Amenhotep III (after 1400 BC), Hep bulls were buried in massive hard-stone sarcophagi, like kings, at first separately, after Ramses II (from 1290 BC), grouped along great corridors, at Saqqara. The *herald* bulls may have served as a model for the later practices of mass animal and bird mummification. However, unlike those, the Hep and Menwer remained individual animals, rather than special treatment of large numbers of a species, and with a more specific link to the creator-gods they served as *heralds*, Ptah and Ra.

Different beings sharing space: pets, people, and the food chain
Careful excavation of settlements has revealed how animals could share living space with humans, breaking down our division between rural farming environment and urban life in at least some townscapes (see section "Were All Creatures

Held Sacred at Abu?"). Yet cemetery patterns show only occasional burials of animals among humans, confirming written evidence for a strong distinction between *remetj*, "people," and other creatures. Rare exceptions to this pattern include the sarcophagus of a cat and mummified bodies of dogs. In cemeteries associated with kingship, mummified bodies of monkeys and even a gazelle are recorded. The practice of assigning personal names to individuals may also help to reveal lines of demarcation between some creatures and others. In addition to humans and deities (*netjeru*), personal names are found for dogs and, more rarely, cattle; a few instances are found where a cat is named, but the name is always *cat*. This written evidence for naming practice does not map neatly onto the range of pictorial evidence for pets; anonymous monkeys as well as named dogs are found from third- and second-millennium depictions (Figure 2.3).

For the king, there are also depictions of accompanying lion, with name. However, the king seems to be a separate category of being: from 3000 to 1100 BC, burials of kings are out of all proportion to others, and second-millennium BC word lists separate *nesyu*, "kings," from *netjeru*, "deities," and *remetj*, "people" (Gardiner 1947). These and other writings divide people into three groups, apparently on the principle of concentric circles around the king: an innermost circle of bodyguard and closest courtiers is called the *henmemet*, written with sun disk and rays, and so often translated *sun people*; the middle circle, still close to the king, is *p'at*, often translated *nobility* or *elite*; and the rest of humanity is *rekhyt*, often translated *populace*. Animals and plants are absent from this section of word lists, but the prominence of animals and birds in the iconography of deities warns us against assuming the separation of human from animal, just on the basis of that one genre of writing.

From about 1950 BC, one funerary composition on the divine personification, Grain, categorizes living beings according to their sustenance or place of sustenance. The words are set in the mouth of Shu, the divine force of the light and air between sun and created world:

> Falcons live on birds,
> Jackals on trails,
> Swine on rocky ground,
> Hippopotami on marshes,
> People on Grain,
> Crocodiles on fish,
> Fish on the waters, that are from the Nile Flood,
> As commanded by Atum.
> I lead them, I cause them to live by this my mouth,
> (being) the Life that is in their nostrils.
> ...
> I cause to live the geese and snakes who are on the back of Geb (the earth),
> For I am indeed the Life under Nut (the sky).
> (from Coffin Text 80, Bickel 1994, 132–133)

Here, people are anchored in agriculture, depending on the grain from which the staples bread and beer are produced. A desert nomad woman or a Nile fisherman

Figure 2.3 Limestone sarcophagus for a cat named Tamiyt, inscribed with the same words used to obtain eternal life for humans, commissioned by the high priest of Ptah Djehutymes, son of King Amenhotep III, about 1375 BC. Drawing © Wolfram Grajetzki.

might foreground other features. The poem does not set out to categorize all being, but rather, it offers analogies between different species and their sources of food, all circling around the floodplain at the center of the world of this poet. All depend on a divine life principle that supports all beings under the sky and over the earth.

The sanctity of the human: bodily integrity

Ancient Egyptian treatment of the body suggests a general concern to keep the human being whole as a separate unit. Here, the contrast with other periods and practices can clarify what is distinctive here. In some earlier burials of 4000–3000 BC, sometimes, body parts are absent, replaced with animal body parts or pottery vases (Wengrow 2006, 118). In perhaps the most striking example, the place of the head is taken by an ostrich egg, finely incised with animal figures. Substitution of nonhuman material for body parts in burial was never common, and it may not occur after 3000 BC. For Egypt 3000–525 BC, although patterns of burial do vary greatly (Chapter 7), the body seems mostly an ideal unit to be preserved whole. Some slight confirmation comes from the written evidence: in one literary composition, known from a single papyrus of about 1550 BC, a wise man objects when a king wishes to experiment on a living man, being held in captivity, "not to people!" (Papyrus Westcar, Lichtheim 1973, 219). At the other end of the time range, in the late first millennium BC, another attitude to the human body may be at work, when cremation was introduced into Egypt by settlers from Greece. As with the predynastic Egyptian evidence, the difference with ancient Egyptian practice may be significant, indicating for the periods between prehistory and Hellenism an extreme anxiety to preserve the whole physical body (Figure 2.4).

Certain bodily conditions, including contagious diseases, would have brought tangible or visible impact on the lives of others and their response. For ancient Egypt, there is a range of limited evidence for different social treatment of individuals with such conditions (Fischer-Elfert 2005). From 1500 to 525 BC survive a great number of votive stelae from offering places, small inscribed stones with depictions of one or more individuals, offerings, and deities. Out of perhaps over a thousand, a single votive stela of 1350 BC shows a regular offering scene, only that here the

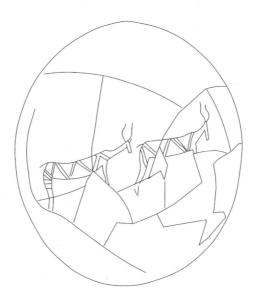

Figure 2.4   Ostrich egg, incised with drawing of two deer and lain in place of the head, in tomb 1480, Naqada: from the 1894–1895 excavations directed by W. Petrie, now Ashmolean Museum 1895.990. Drawing © Wolfram Grajetzki.

principal figure is a man with one shriveled leg, supporting himself on a walking stick. His condition has been identified by modern medics as symptom of polio, and his stela seems to imply that his condition was no bar to integration into society (Figure 2.5).

Conditions such as epilepsy could present other challenges to social order on another unpredictable timescale. From written sources, Hans-Werner Fischer-Elfert has identified a case where seizures apparently prevent a man from helping to carry an image in procession at festivals (at Waset, 1250 BC); he has to be excluded from this important communal activity, but seems not to suffer any other negative effect in social life. Besides congenital conditions (where physical capability is different from birth), Fischer-Elfert considers the effect of bodily change during adult life, where a person would no longer be able to perform their social tasks, either

Figure 2.5   Limestone stela from Akhetaten, with depiction of a man named Reme, with leg shriveled, perhaps by polio, at a table of offerings, together with two companions identified in the inscriptions as his wife Timia and "her son" Ptahemheb. About 1350 BC. Now in the Ny Carlsberg Glyptotek, Copenhagen. Drawing © Wolfram Grajetzki.

temporarily or permanently and either by physical inability, as in ageing or injury, or by cultural prohibition. If visible wholeness was required to enter the most sacred spaces, someone with symptoms of skin loss or change might be forced from office. A literary letter (from Hiba, 900–700 BC) describes the repeated expulsion of a man who served in a local temple; from his lament, his exile to desert oases, and his extreme emphasis on wishing good health for the friend or patron receiving the letter, the man might be a temple staff member forced from office after developing a contagious skin condition such as leprosy. The literary sources help to raise questions for archaeological recording on future excavation of cemeteries, our most direct physical encounter with past lives.

Separation and inclusion in burial-places

Individuals with severe skin conditions such as leprosy have not been recorded from cemeteries in Egypt 3000–525 BC, but the absence might merely reflect the rarity, even at Saharan desert edges, of ground conditions dry enough to preserve skin, compounded by very limited publication of larger populations. However, it remains possible that the ancient society excluded from its afterlife space any body with visible decay, because it insisted on the integrity of the body to its surface. In the most spectacular exception, the body of King Ramses V bears lesions typical of smallpox, a disease which would have been contagious enough to have killed his embalmers too (Fischer-Elfert 2005). However, the king may have been considered a different species: written and rarer pictorial sources emphasize that the king is born as a seed of the creator-god, implanted in a woman, and so not physically human (Berlev 2000). There is no similar written or visual source with direct comment on how ancient Egyptian society at different periods and places understood the processes of birth and growth for (other) human beings.

Returning to the primary evidence, the bodies themselves, cemeteries show little evidence for different treatment of individuals where the skeleton implies visible physical difference. At Rifa in Middle Egypt, one tomb (1900 BC) included burials of two men, called Nakhtankh and Khnumnakht; the spine of Khnumnakht was irregular (from kyphoscoliosis according to medical analysis in 1908 and the 1970s), but there was no difference in external appearance after wrapping or in other features of burial equipment, including the three small statuettes inscribed for the men (David 2007).

Difference in childbirth and early infancy may have been considered divinely marked, as documented from two examples at different periods in the first millennium BC. At Beni Hasan, about 900 BC, an infant died of extreme brittle bone disease, where the bones would have broken at any move, and was buried in a unique small coffin adorned with the double plume and sun disk associated at that time with the god of the afterlife, Osiris (Dawson and Gray 1968, 13–14). In the second instance, in baboon catacombs at Tuna, somewhere within the time range 600–100 BC, one human infant burial showed anencephaly, a condition where part of the brain is not developed, causing death before or at birth (Geoffroy Saint-Hilaire 1822, 1826). At the neck was found an amulet in the form of a small baboon figurine, a form regularly used to depict Thoth, god of wisdom and of the region of

Tuna. The infant may have been buried among the mummified baboons, echoing their appearance and evoking Thoth himself, and therefore to be placed with them in terrain sacred to Thoth. The present location of body and figurine is unknown, and the early report on the find is vague, but the account is still a precious indication of one ancient treatment of a physical difference that would have been lethal at birth.

Ideal and divinity in depicting human bodies

Rare written and pictorial sources mark some bodily differences against a general background of depicting all individuals regardless of age as youthful. That general mode of depiction perhaps corresponds to the Egyptian word *nefer*, "beautiful," specifically the extending of the body to a taut physical ideal of youth after puberty (cf. Berlev 2000). On this principle, even prepubescent children appear as adults: the difference in age is marked, not by the different bodily proportions of children in growth, but instead by smaller scale, nudity, and a sidelock of hair. For later stages in life, the marks of prosperous maturity (belly folds) and of old age (wrinkles, white hair) are rare in formal depictions (cf. Sweeney 2006).

Perhaps the most numerous exceptions are depictions of adults with shorter body, flatter skull, and bandy legs, for whom the written sources give the Egyptian word *nemi* translated as *dwarf* (Dasen 1993). Archaeological evidence for inclusion of dwarves in royal court life goes back to the turn of the fourth to third millennia BC. Beside the tombs of two First Dynasty kings at Abdju, Semerkhet and Qa'a (about 2900 BC), skeletal remains were identified as of dwarves among the courtiers buried there. In the double row of courtier tombs around the burial chambers for King Semerkhet, two contained bones identified as of dwarves, and one of these was marked with name-stones inscribed with an image of a dwarf and the name Neferit in hieroglyphs (Figure 2.6). Written and pictorial sources suggest integration into social and economic life, as well as reverence for the dwarf as powerful liminal force among humans. The form and name *nemi* is used in some later sources for Ptah, god of metalwork and craft creation at Mennefer/Memphis. Several depictions show dwarves as goldsmiths or in the treasury, and there are votive dwarf figurines of both sexes around 3000 and 1800 BC. The features emphasized on figures suggest that sometimes the dwarf may have been revered specifically for the combination of child-stature body with a face lined with marks as in old age. The same body proportions and bandy legs are a regular feature of images of a divine force with leonine face, named Aha in second-millennium BC sources and Bes in the first millennium BC–AD (see following text, Infant burials in houses).

Reverence for physical difference is a theme in Chapter 25 of the Teaching of Amenemipet, a literary composition known from early to mid-first-millennium BC copies:

> Do not mock the blind, or torment the dwarf,
> Do not inflict hardship on the lame.
> Do not torment one who is in the hand of the god,
> Or become angry with him for his slips.
> People are clay and straw—god is the builder.

Figure 2.6   Limestone stela inscribed with depiction and name of the dwarf Neferit, from subsidiary burial M at the tomb of the First Dynasty king Semerkhet, Abdju, about 3000 BC. W. Petrie, *Royal Tombs of the First Dynasty*, Egypt Exploration Fund, London, 1900, pl.60.

The need for such teaching can be seen in other sources. Around 2400 BC, several chapels of officials have depictions of a puberty game or ritual where boys shackle and vilify a *traveler* or nomad, depicted in one example as a hunchbacked man (Fischer-Elfert 2005). In this moment, the visibly different body becomes an object of othering to mark the passage from boyhood to manhood. However, the scene does not show how the shackled man was treated outside the ostensibly cruel game; the rite could imply criticism of the cruelty of the children, as something they have to grow out of, rather than approval (Figure 2.7).

Off and on the body

In Egypt 3000–525 BC, according to the preserved depictions and excavated burials, the human body as a unit served as a core for ornamentation, by adding jewelry and, particularly around the eyes, paint; among the richer, this would apply to all regardless of gender or age. More rarely, the bodily surface was permanently altered by practices such as tattoo or scarification. At some periods, again breaching any ideal of absolute bodily wholeness, items of jewelry involved incision into the body: earrings and piercings for them are found after 1800 BC, for men and women (figurine Bourriau 1988, 124). More substantial reel-like ear studs are found 1300–1000 BC, progressively expanded to fill the lobes. By contrast, and unlike neighboring regions and other periods (such as Neolithic Gebel Moya, Upper Nubia), nose rings, nose plugs, and lip studs are not attested in Egypt. Preserved remains and depictions in some tombs of court officials (about 2400 BC) indicate a widespread, though not universal, practice of circumcision for men, but not for women (Feucht 2003). Written sources do not comment on the ritual significance or hygienic intention of the practice, and it is not known whether it was confined to the richer in society. There is also no social history yet for the methods for controlling natural growth of body hair and toe/fingernails: elaborate versions of tweezers and scissorlike utensils occur in some of the richest burials in 1400–1300 BC, but it is not clear how widespread such attention to the body may have been across the society and over other periods. Grooming at all periods might

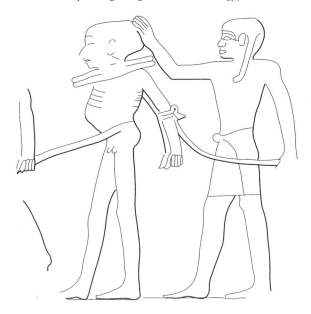

Figure 2.7 Scene of ritual insult of a shackled hunchbacked man, on limestone wall blocks of the tomb chapel of the high official Khentika Ikhekhi, cemetery of Inebhedj (Saqqara), about 2300 BC. Drawing © Wolfram Grajetzki.

focus on hairdressing, both the cutting of hair and the addition of headgear including wigs. Preserved from richer burials in the period 1450–1000 BC, wigs for both men and women are highly elaborate, with some examples of special mounts and boxes to maintain them. For the rich, the arranging of hair would itself become a ceremony, again for both genders, though most famously celebrated in scenes of hairstyling with hairpins for the women closest to the king, from 2000 BC. Different utensils appear to highlight this in different periods: where we might think of hair scissors, equipment of 2000–1700 BC focussed on hairpins, and that of 1500–1300 BC on adding combs, often with figured handpieces, recalling fourth-millennium BC grooming arts (Ashton 2013). Razors of different forms are prominent in cosmetic equipment for the richer, both men and women (flint in the third and early second millennium BC and copper alloy later); a literary composition of about 1850 BC includes the barber among occupations for life. Ancient depictions tend to align grooming and cosmetic equipment with women (Robins 1993). Yet both men and women are depicted with eye paint, ornate wigs, and jewelry, and in the archaeology of cemeteries, items such as mirrors are found in the burials of men, and children, as well as of women (Lilyquist 1979, 83–93, Figure 2.8a–c).

Haircutting could also be the primary device for marking specific times and spaces as sacred: many images of men show them shaven, not because they hold a full-time occupation as priest, but because the shaven head is appropriate to sacred space. Not all markers of distinction were visible: grooming also required scented oil and fat, which were preserved in distinctive small containers, varying in form and material over time, and found across a wider social range. Nor were all these markers derived from human intervention in bodily appearance. On a small number of statues of men, the sculptor has indicated the effects of age in balding, and accompanying inscriptions identify these individuals as the *balding/aged men* (Egyptian *isy*) of Hathor, goddess of beauty and sensuality (Clère 1995). This example shows that grooming or the lack of grooming might be related to a divine name or being—that human physical change might be seen as divine in some way. The special status *isy* seems to denote the transitional state, balding, not the condition of being bald; as with the Nile flood Ha'py, the divine is visible not in permanence or stability, but in the process of change.

The beginnings and ends of human life
The balding men of Hathor introduce the dimension of human lifespan into the social concept of the sacred. In the archaeological record of ancient Egyptian cemeteries, the bodies of men, women, and children all seem to be treated as integral units to be preserved whole, even when the items placed with them might vary according to status, gender, and age. Yet, in this generalized 3000–525 BC picture, where does this shared treatment begin and end in each human life? Was it considered as necessary to keep whole the fetus, infant, child, as well as the most elderly? Again, anthropology and sociology warn against assuming that all societies treat their youngest and oldest as core members of a society. Today, acute legal ethical debates arise over the point at which human life may begin and end. In urban centers across several industrialized nations, the most elderly often leave their homes to receive full-time care in special buildings. For ancient Egypt in its many periods and regions, general answers on life attitudes are hazardous. The archaeology of settlements in Egypt has been too limited to identify any separate spaces that might have been assigned to very young or very old. Too few larger cemeteries have been sufficiently carefully excavated and published to reach conclusions over the absence of infants and most elderly. The limited cemetery statistics have been used to establish average life expectancy, from twenties to forties, but any results need to allow for the possibility that these cemeteries may not include the youngest or oldest in a society. Cemeteries specially for the more elderly are not known to me, but there are examples of separate burial for the very young. One cemetery at Deir al-Madina (Waset, 1500–1400 BC) housed mainly child burials, with some distinctive offerings (Meskell 1999, 161–168). Moreover, throughout the second millennium BC, infant burials occur in houses at settlement sites (Pilgrim 1996, see following section); this could explain why only one child less than a year old was among the 93 individuals in one better-documented cemetery at Saqqara (late second millennium BC, Bentley 1999). This may be a distinctive feature of *ancient Egypt*, as later sites offer different results; in the cemetery at Kellis in Dakhla Oasis, almost 100 of 700 burials from the early first millennium AD are fetal or infant burials (Tocheri 2005).

(a)

(b)

(c)

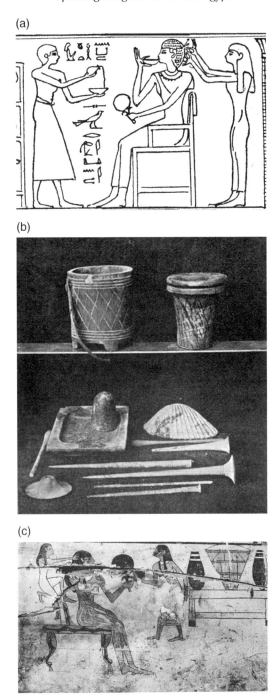

Figure 2.8   (a) Scene depicting a woman using hairpins to arrange the hair of the king's wife Kawit, carved on the limestone sarcophagus of Kawit, Waset, about 2000 BC, now

Infant burials in houses

At settlement sites of the period 2000–1700 BC, burials of infants of less than two years old have been found in houses, the bodies placed in regular boxes rather than specially made coffins and accompanied by small items such as beads, amulets (including seal-amulets), or pottery, sometimes a small vessel with spout for feeding a baby. No ancient writing provides comment on the reasons for burying infants within a house; from archaeological finds in other ancient societies, the practice may reflect a need either to keep family members within the house, for their protection, or to keep them content, for the peace of the family (Scott 1999; for attitudes to the dead, see further Chapter 7). The burials do not reveal whether the society drew the line around human life at conception or birth. In one house on Abu island, at the border of Egypt with Nubia, at levels dated 1950–1900 BC, the body of a baby six to twelve months old was found buried beside the platform for grinding flour (Pilgrim 1996, 34–36, House 25a, see section Houses at Abu 1800 BC). In depictions, grinding is shown done by women, and the burial place for the child may have been chosen for the link between the women, their work, and the child, for protection for the living or dead, or mutual. This speculation may provide questions for future researchers into infant burial practice and location. Any link may have been indirect or general, as the burial seems to have taken place when that house was already abandoned. Infant burial within houses seems a recurrent feature in second-millennium BC settlements in Egypt. According to carefully documented excavations, sometimes these house burials occurred while the house was in use, sometimes an abandoned house became burial places for infants, as in the case of the Abu house (Pilgrim 1996, 36 n.84).

Attitudes to the period between conception and birth are also difficult to identify from other parts of the archaeological, including the written, record. Burials of fetuses in the tomb of King Tutankhamun indicate reverence, but as with the body of King Saptah, bodies physically connected with kingship may have been given different treatment. The Egyptologist Dimitri Meeks has identified the ancient Egyptian word *bes* as a term for the infant from before to just after birth. In the first millennium BC, the word became the regular name for a particular divine force, with leonine face, identified in earlier depictions as *Aha*, "fighter." Depictions of Aha/Bes in two and three dimensions present a body either lionlike or human and, where human, with long limbs or with dwarf proportions. The form/force may be female but is most often male, with lion tail, sometimes disproportionately long. From depictions over amulets, seals, and furniture, at least some sectors of society

---

Figure 2.8   (*Cont'd*)   Egyptian Museum Cairo, E. Naville, *Deir el-Bahri* I, Egypt Exploration Fund, London, 1895; (b) group of ivory hairpins among other items of cosmetic equipment placed in the burial of the lady of the house Seneb, about 1850 BC, cemeteries near modern Beni Hasan, Garstang 1907, 113–114; (c) scene depicting a woman arranging the hair of a woman, painted on the wooden coffin, from cemeteries of Inerty (at modern Gebelein), about 2000 BC, now Egyptian Museum Berlin, G. Steindorff, *Grabfunde II. Das Grab des Sebek-o, ein Grabfund aus Gebelein*, W. Spemann, Berlin 1902, pl.5.

Figure 2.9   The hippopotamus–lion image variously named Reret, Ipy or Taweret, here in northern sky constellations, painted on the ceiling of the burial chamber of King Sety I, Valley of the Kings, Waset, about 1285 BC. © Gianluca Miniaci.

would have been permeated by this motif of the infant and perhaps particularly the infant dead at or shortly after birth—perhaps the majority of births in any land of high infant mortality. Alongside, a second figure is equally prominent: a hippo-potamus standing on hind legs, belly protruding as in pregnancy, often with lion-like legs and ears and crocodile-like back ridge. Earlier inscriptions name the figure Ipet or Ipy, sometimes Reret, "the Sow," while later she can be named Weret or Taweret, "the great one." Her image dominates part of the northern sky constella-tions, in depictions from the fifteenth-century BC onward, as if protection of the infant shared the same struggle as all material existence. Together, Aha/Bes and Ipy/Taweret dominate the iconography of birth and bodily protection in second- and first-millennium BC Egypt (Figure 2.9).

Ancient views of conception and the substance of the human

At present, it remains difficult to assess materially the way or ways in which ancient Egyptian society conceived of human life, starting from conception itself. Histories of medicine now tend to start later, from views among ancient Greek writing (Glenister 1964), including the view that a fetus was entirely developed from the semen deposited in a female body (Empedocles of Agrigentum, fifth century BC; Galen in Alexandria), as well as the view that both man and woman contributed to the substance of a fetus (Aristotle, fourth century BC). Manuals for healing from the previous fifteen hundred years do not provide direct ancient Egyptian com-ment on conception, though several shed light on treatment of mother and child at birth. The earliest is a three-page series of pregnancy treatments and birth prognoses from about 1800 BC, found at Lahun (see following text); rather than the word *khered*, "child," a prognosis refers to "the one she will give birth to" (UC32057, col.3, 2). Other sources refer to the child in the womb, though it is still not clear from precisely which point of pregnancy a *child* is thought to be present. A papyrus roll from about 1400 BC preserves a series of protective incantations including one "to be spoken over the two bricks" supporting the mother at birth (Roth and Roehrig 2002). The speaker asks the personification Meskhenet, "birth brick," to "make the ka of this child who is in the womb of this woman" and asserts "I have made a divine decree of Geb that he make the ka" (Berlin 3027, col.5, l.10–col.6, l.1). Another in the same series aims to repel any negative force "from the head, from the brow, from any limb formed by Khnum for this child born of his mother" (col.1, l.8–9). The earth god Geb and the clay-molding god Khnum appear more often in written sources relating to the birth and protection of the king but seem to be invoked in these passages as forces fashioning all human body and life. These second-millennium BC manuals may reflect the richest circles, where the view of humanity may have been modeled on still earlier views of the king as a seed of the sun-god present from conception, with a physical body fashioned by Khnum as a potter fashions clay into a vase (Bickel 1994, 202–203 comparing Pyramid Text 324, for King Teti, about 2300 BC).

Social and historical context may also separate off the single instance where richer humans are given a different origin to other people, a desert quarry inscription dated about 2000 BC, when the kingship of Egypt was disputed between Waset in the south and Hutnennesut in the north. According to that inscription, the leading social group of governors and their kin come from the tears of the creator, while less wealthy groups are from his urine. This startling division in human origins is without parallel in Egyptian sources; it might be a rare glimpse of *elite* views, or it might reflect the harsher worldview of that social group, or a part of it, only at a moment of conflict and extreme stress, with competition over selection for rule.

Human being: components or aspects?

In addition to their information on ancient technical understanding of anatomy, healing manuals can be usefully analyzed for ancient general vocabularies of human bodily existence, as explored also from the funerary literature by Rune Nyord (2009). From the written sources, special words are known for aspects or elements of the individual, as often emphasized in modern summaries on ancient Egyptian afterlife: words translated body (*khat*), limbs (*haw* and *awt*), name (*ren*), shadow (*shut*), and heart (more awkwardly for us the two words *ib* and *haty*), as well as three terms often translated as spirit or soul (*akh, ba, ka*). Rather than combining these into an ahistorical ancient individual, all of these need to be set in context, including date and immediate compositional context. Ancient religious writings sometimes provide their own combinations; these might be taken as proof that each must be different in essence, but most human languages allow for synonyms and overlaps—consider the wide range of uses of English *soul* and *spirit*. Moreover, some sources reflect rituals of embalming, where the body might be more likely to be listed as a series of separate parts. On a block from the tomb chapel for the overseer of fields Amenemhat (Waset, about 1250 BC), each of the four *children of Horus*, guardians of the internal organs, brings one part or aspect of the person—heart, *ba*-soul, *ka*-energy, and image or body. Although the scene helps to identify four primary features of the human in this period, the number four is the number of *Horus children*, not a catalogue of the human (Taylor 2001, 14–16).

Depiction of separate items does not necessarily imply a claim that these are dissected autonomous parts of the person. Another type of religious composition aligns each in a series of anatomical parts with a named deity, to ensure the divinity of the combined body; the same approach is found in literary compositions (and outside Egypt in the Biblical Song of Solomon). These list only physical body parts, omitting three types of term often found in Egyptological descriptions of the ancient Egyptian concept of the human, the intangible or invisible forces such as *ba* or *ka*; summarizing terms such as image or body; and generalizing terms such as *limbs* (*ha'w*, *'awt*) or the *wekhedu*. The lists of parts show how the physical body could be catalogued and then each part expressed as a divine dimension (Quack 1995). Assmann has documented how the same body part could be aligned with different deities: the nose could be Wepwawet (jackal) or Thoth (ibis). Clearly, then, the literal association of a body part with a deity was not the important point; rather, the lists establish a general principle that the human body is divine, or made divine, through the rituals of healing, including the ultimate healing process, embalming for eternal life.

Concepts of ageing

Beyond the social and thematic limits of the written record, the broader totality of material culture and context could deliver more findings in the future. For such broader understanding, anthropology offers examples in comparison, where one human society might give standard views on the development of the body over its lifespan. Maurice Bloch has summarized how the Zafimaniry in Madagascar consider the body to calcify over time until it becomes coral-like, to be incorporated into the houses of wisdom as an ancestral bodily presence (Bloch 1998). Within the world of ancient Egyptian writings, such texture of life is captured for youth in the recurrence of the term *wadj*, "verdant," "fresh" in writings; in hieroglyphic script, this is written with a flowering papyrus stem and is also the regular scepter held by goddesses in formal depictions of offerings. For the latest stages of the ageing process, another vegetal metaphor is used, *isy*, "brittle," written with a triple-leaf branch, as if the person dries out over life like a plant, rather than becoming stone or mineral. This shift from fresh to dry may be the metaphor applied in script, but it is not clear whether it was the dominant concept of human living or how far it reached across different social groups and times. Future research might develop means of testing this plant metaphor across the rest of the material cultural evidence. In one pattern of burial during the period 1850–1700 BC (Chapter 7), the deceased was equipped with faience figurines, in forms also found deposited at temples, apparently as votive offerings. The best known of these faience figures include animals from the desert-to-marsh margins of settled life: wild cat, gerbil, lion, and hippopotamus. However, this burial equipment as often included plant forms, particularly gourds such as cucumbers. Possibly, this attention to the plant world might relate to an underlying conception of life force. The importance of the lotus flower and bud in visual arts, including architecture throughout the three millennia, might also be considered in this light. However, depictions and descriptions of the lotus emphasize a human animal quality, the sense of smell. Other written evidence also points away from the fresh–dry plant analogy. The literary Teaching of Ptahhotep (perhaps 1950 BC, copies known as late as 600 BC) opens with a lament over physical decay with more focus on the human body, more animal than plant in our terms. The lament is then countered by praise of the wisdom and experience offered by the elderly: "no-one is born wise" (Chapter 5).

Shared naming practices, distinct names

Social recognition of the human individual can take form at specific moments or rites of naming. Here, it is easier to find evidence for kingship than for humanity. The main written source for naming practices is a literary narrative on the birth of kings to the creator-god (Papyrus Westcar, perhaps 1550 BC). The main visual source is, again, on the divine birth of the king, a narrative cycle of scenes, first found in the temple for Hatshepsut as king (1475 BC, Robins 1993, 46–47, 82–83). There may be echoes of practice beyond kingship, in the content of names of other people, as most of these names have direct expressive meaning in the ancient Egyptian language: many invoke the blessings of the gods or family, and some seem to capture the cries of relief and joy at a safe birth (Vernus 1986, 125–126): "Abundance of the Nile flood!," "May the Gold (Hathor) protect her!," "May she/he live!," "May she/he be well!," "She/he is for me!," "A son for me!," "Health to me!," "What peace!," "My heart is cleansed (joyful)," "As my name lives!," and "May she/he be well for me!." Although perhaps not universal, the giving of a second name is found across the three millennia and is the dominant naming pattern in some periods. As with the single name, it is not certain when a person received the second name. In the century around 1800 BC, official documents list individuals by two columns of names, with the mark *it is his name* (i.e., *no second name*) for the minority with only one name; the double column demonstrates that two names would have been the norm at this period. The second column tends to give shorter names, as if the first gave the fuller, more formal one. One list of workers from Lahun in this period has only the second column of short names filled in, with a mark perhaps for *child* quickly scrawled on each line of the first column (Collier and Quirke 2006, 55–56, UC32130). Evidently, these children were old enough to be working, but had not yet received their second name: perhaps, then, the child received the first name at or near the moment of birth and the second at puberty.

Rites of passage at body-changes

That solitary work list shows how slight our evidence is still, for such crucial life passages as naming and puberty rituals. Anthropologist Arnold van Gennep used the term *rites of passage* for special rituals and by which different societies may mark transition from one phase of life to the next. As moments of risk and instability, depictions of these are rare in the world of ancient Egyptian depictions, where a perfect harmony is projected into eternity for each owner of a *menu*, "enduring monument." Birth, puberty, and marriage are strikingly absent from most offering-chapel scenes; only the funerals appear, as part of the mission to overcome death and be born into a perfect afterlife. We cannot be sure, on this visual and written evidence, how prominent puberty and marriage rites might have been—an unexpected gap for such a widely known ancient society. The wider archaeological record is essential especially on these life questions.

Female body cycles

For the social framing of changes in the female body, archaeology provides a pattern of material evidence from the period 2200 to 2000 BC, in the better-recorded excavation of cemeteries north of Qau. Distinctive leg and hand amulets are found at the ankle and wrist particularly in burials of younger women, around teenage years: most are of red carnelian (Dubiel 2008). The material and the age and gender of the wearers together suggest that these amulets offered protection through menarchy, when the disruptive and powerful force of menstrual blood first announced the change of the girl into a woman able to give birth. In the burials, the amulets perhaps promised the possibility of becoming a mother in the afterlife, for a girl who had not yet reached puberty when she died. We cannot be sure that such amulets were made for and worn by the living as well as the dead, until there are finds of the same kind of amulets at places other than burials—at sites such as settlements or more secret places in the landscape—or until new research investigates traces of wear on the amulets before they were placed in the tomb. Nevertheless, the forms and material demonstrate ancient attention to individuals who needed support through a bodily change in their lives (Figure 2.10a and b).

Another, more opaque red stone is associated with menstrual blood in a short formula copied on funerary papyri from 1400 BC to the Roman Period:

> Formula for a *tiyet*-amulet of red jasper placed at the neck of this transfigured one:
> You have your blood, Isis,
> You have your changing powers (*akhu*), Isis!
> The healing amulet (*wedjat*) is the protection of this great one,
> Guarding against his injurer.

Again, the phrasing may have been adapted for the special context of embalming, burial, and eternal cult of the dead. Nevertheless, the first lines marrying blood and power may capture an ancient recital of words by and for a woman in her adult monthly cycle. From 1350 BC on, examples of the *tiyet* are known in material form, as amulets in red jasper or carnelian or the artificial paste faience, again often in red. The motif itself is found already at the end of the fourth millennium BC. The *tiyet* has a form similar to the *ankh*, "life," but with side loops downward rather than short horizontal arms; plausibly, both were originally lengths of cloth which were looped and loosely tied. Where the *ankh* became the general symbol of life, the *tiyet* had a closer connection with women and notably with the great healing

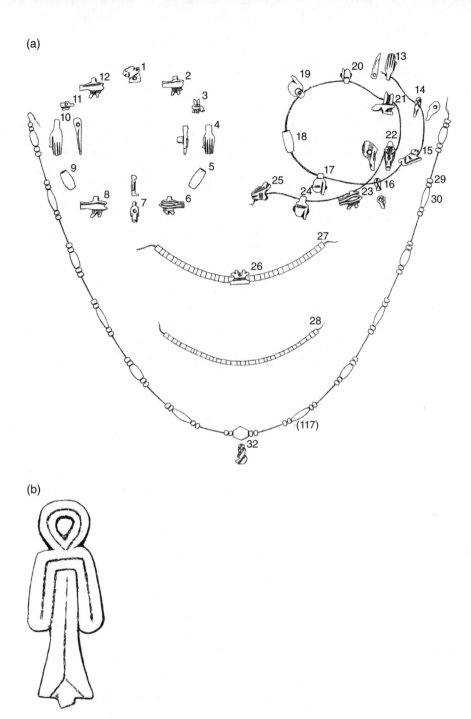

Figure 2.10 Protective material: (a) hands of red carnelian among strings of amulets (nos. 4, 10, 13), as found on a burial near modern Dishasha, late Old Kingdom, about 2200 BC. W. Petrie, *Deshasheh*, London: Exploration Fund, 1898; (b) tiyet or *Isis knot* amulet, unusually in bronze, from burial of a *pure-priest* of Isis, Saiset, at Abdju, Eighteenth Dynasty. © Petrie Museum of Egyptian Archaeology, UCL.

goddess Isis. It may, as Westendorf argued, evoke general use of cloth at menstruation, or specific bandaging in extremes, above all at birth (Westendorf 1965).

Similar uncertainty surrounds the age frame for other gendered items to be worn, as found in the archaeological record both as separate material items and in depictions. Cowrie-shell girdles are found in burials of wealthier women in 1900–1750 BC and again in 900–600 BC; they are depicted on faience fertility figurines of the earlier period, always worn by young women, who are often tattooed (cf. Morris 2011). The shell may, then, have evoked, and perhaps protected, the young woman, perhaps specifically her ability to give birth. The questions then arise whether the girdle was worn as part of a puberty ritual, just once or cyclically (monthly or annually?), or until a first childbirth, and whether girdles would be found only in wealthier households or more widely throughout the society.

Hints of male puberty rituals

In comparison with the special amulet forms attested for some periods in burials of young women, the puberty of young men seems less visible in the cemetery and settlement record, either of artifact form or of marked spaces or times of practice. If practiced, male rites seem less material. Clues may be found instead in some unusual depictions and suggestive phrases in writings. An offering-chapel block from about 2400 BC shows among athletic wrestling and acrobatic dances by boys and girls a man wearing a lion mask and holding a unique staff with hand-shaped end uppermost. The lion mask evokes the Aha/Bes images associated with childbirth. Perhaps the core concern of that motif is not, after all, specifically birth, but the points of transition in life: at birth, from inside to outside the body of the mother, and at puberty, from boy to man. An Egyptian term equivalent to life phase is *kheper*, "transformation"; in Nile–Sahara context, an immediate example or model would be the snake shedding its skin, a motif found in other writings (Figure 2.11).

For the boy, both birth and puberty involve a cut, and ritualized cutting may also be central to Aha/Bes and other figures otherwise associated with birth. Passages in life descriptions, healing manuscripts, and mortuary rituals refer to *tying the headband* in relation to youth; possibly, this alludes to rites of circumcision or to a band worn to mark the young man at or immediately after circumcision. The sidelock of hair that marked childhood is directly linked to knotting and tying in a composition known from two coffins of about 1850 BC and then numerous later papyri (*Coffin Text 640 = Book of the Dead chapter 50*, Quirke 2013):

> A knot is tied behind me, in the sky, of the earth, by Ra,
> On the day of fastening the knot against the inert forces at the feet,
> On that day of cutting the side-lock (of hair).

In the following lines, Ra is followed by the embodiment of disorder, Seth, and the sky goddess, Nut, in tying the knot. The passage was to be recited to enable the deceased to win eternal life, and the wording may have been adapted to that

Figure 2.11 Depiction of man wearing a lion mask, tomb-chapel wall block, 2400 BC, probably from cemetery of Inebhedj (Saqqara), now British Museum. Drawing © Wolfram Grajetzki.

context, the funeral and then the cult of the dead. However, it may still preserve a kernel or echo from otherwise lost rites marking life changes in the male body.

Throughout the questions of gendered life difference, in the bodily distinction of times, the written and visual record may give more clues than answers. Yet these can help to focus research attention on the wider material and archaeological record of distribution of materials, as evidence for their social use.

Living human geography: case-studies

Sacredness around the human—visible and invisible

Religious landscapes are not immediately transparent surfaces. Sacredness of space might be private or, in some circumstances, deliberately concealed. The invisible sacred space is well documented from more recent histories. In seventeenth to eighteenth-century Ireland and Scotland, British law permitted only Anglican Christianity, and Catholic services had to be held in secret at rural *Mass stones* or *Mass rocks*. Some would be identifiable archaeologically, but in many cases, oral tradition becomes the only guide to past treatment of a location as sacred, as at Derrynagalliagh:

> fragments of a small cross, now placed against a ditch, traditionally indicate the location. Local people say the residents of Bethlehem and Doonis, etc., in Co Westmeath crossed the Inny estuary of Lough Ree by boat to attend Mass at this site. (http://www.longfordgenealogy.com/history/h2.html consulted 3.12.2011, cf. Te Brake 2011, 236–237)

Ethnographic accounts of ritual have similarly served as warnings of how much in a human performance cannot survive in an archaeological record (Insoll 2004). Such descriptions indicate the need for caution in reading any past landscape as sacred or not.

Few Egyptian landscapes have been explored archaeologically to an extent that would allow us to reconstruct a life pattern in a particular place. How did people in their place experience the hours from waking to sleep on any particular day? Three archaeological case-studies show the range of evidence available for answering these questions.

Case Study 1. A desert-edge shrine near Badari   One rural shrine is located on the desert edge of fields near Badari, below the high desert cliffs. Here, 1920s teams uncovered remains of a temple dated around 1600–1500 BC, over traces of an earlier temple on a different alignment, perhaps 2200–1800 BC, in turn built on top of fourth- to third-millennium settlement debris (Brunton 1927, 18–21, pl.7 *spur 3*, pl.22–23). Farther south, the expedition documented dozens of 2200–1500 BC burials (Brunton 1930). There is no record of any contemporary houses of valley dwellers who might have built and used the temple; future archaeological work might help to fill this gap. In the meantime, the burials and temple remains at least allow a material glimpse of life in this particular land-scape at specific times (Figure 2.12).

Around 1550 BC, kings from Waset were fighting to expel their rivals from Hutwaret/Tell el-Daba in the north. The temple built in that century had an enclo-sure wall 30 meters east to west and 17 meters north to south and some 1.7 meters thick. Like its predecessor, the temple had walls of mud mixed with sand and some white stones and floors of mud-plastered brick; there was no sign that stone blocks had been used at any point. The entrance may have been from the west side, and a corridor ran around the shrine area, where the main focus of cult seems to have changed; the earlier temple had a single shrine, whereas later there was a double shrine. The excavation director Guy Brunton speculated that a local cult for a force of disorder—the regional ferryman god Nemty or the more famous Seth—had been twinned after 1600 BC with a balancing cult of Horus, god of order. This is certainly one possible interpretation, as twinning for balance in temple architecture is found for the voracious god Sobek, depicted as a crocodile (Nubyt/Kom Ombo and Shedyt/Madinat al-Fayoum). Modern perennial irrigation and canal extensions have transformed farming life, including the exact location of the edge of the fields and the extent of any marsh pools. When the temple stood, it may have overlooked pools teeming with bird and fish life, in landscapes long since drained for agricul-ture. There would still have been larger, more dangerous animals in the river and its marshy desert-edge *backwaters*. In the nineteenth century AD, crocodiles were still being hunted in Egypt, but the more powerful and violent creature would have been the hippopotamus, still a bigger killer in Africa than either lion or crocodile. A votive stela from the main town of the province, just to the south, shows the mayor of Tjebu Hatiay adoring Seth in the form of a hippopotamus in the marshes (Figure 2.13).

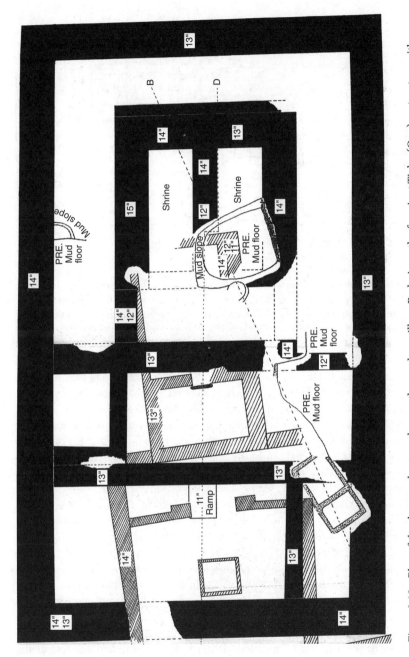

Figure 2.12 Plan of the desert-edge temple near the modern village Badari, north of ancient Tjebu (Qau); a structure with thicker walls was built perhaps by 1500 BC over an earlier shrine of different alignment (Brunton 1930). © Petrie Museum of Egyptian Archaeology, UCL.

Figure 2.13 Limestone stela depicting the regional governor Hatiay in adoration of Seth, depicted as a hippopotamus, found in the cemeteries at the regional town Tjebu (Qau), now Egyptian Museum Cairo JE47637 (Brunton 1930). © Petrie Museum of Egyptian Archaeology, UCL.

The main second temple finds were small glazed objects of varying forms: faience tubes and disks, a rounded shell type perhaps derived from the earlier cowry girdles, blue glass disk bead, and a glazed steatite scarab with stylized motif, possibly floral (Brunton 1930, pl.11, pl.19 no.54). Beside these, Brunton recorded two amulet types: (1) a crowned standing goddess or queen, with one arm to breast, and (2) the mixed form of the childbirth protectress variously called Ipy, Reret, and Taweret, a hippopotamus body standing upright on slender lion hind legs, with crocodile-like *tail* along the back. The presence of blue- and green-glazed goddess and childbirth amulets and the absence of other colors among the beads seem significant. Blue- and green-glazed materials predominate at shrines to Hathor, goddess of fertility and sensuality (Pinch 1993). The Badari temple material is too scant to identify the shrine as to a goddess, though the dual shrine layout would not exclude the possibility: at Qift, the main temple has a double axis, with one sanctuary for Min, god of male potency, complemented by a second for Isis, the healing goddess. If this was a shrine to another divine force, it might still have attracted those who needed to invoke protective powers for pregnancy or birth.

The women closest to the Badari temple
The person or persons who deposited, or perhaps dropped, the amulets at the Badari desert-edge temple may have lived alongside or may have come up from the fields toward the desert. They may have come at a time when the land as a whole

awaited the new flood or new sowing season, or at a time of more individual personal need. A few burials nearby date to the century when the rebuilt temple would have been in use. One young woman was found untouched under the robbed bodies of an adult woman and girl of about twelve, originally placed all together in a single wood coffin (burial 3712):

> On the head were many thick plaits. On the fingers were shell rings, the gold mounted scarab, and the uninscribed amethyst scarab. The body was covered with a profusion of beads, some of them certainly of Predynastic and Old Kingdom date. Strung with them were eighteen other scarabs and scaraboids. ... Strips of bone veneer or inlay with concentric circles showed that there had been a trinket box; and with them was a little *kohl*-pot ... of some very decayed material, with a lid of bright blue glaze. (Brunton 1930, 8)

The burial populates the temple landscape with these three women of different ages. They may be the closest we can come at present to considering how much of the space and time felt distinctive, sacred, to them and others approaching or passing the place. The pottery and jewelry in that burial are all types known within Egypt and of Egyptian materials. Finds at sites a little farther south provide a useful reminder that ancient populations could be diverse. Pottery typical of Nubian east desert nomadic groups was found at a campsite and in single or grouped circular huts (Brunton 1930, 3). One burial in this area belongs to the same Nubian desert tradition, with gazelle skull and horns (3918). More than one language may have been heard around the shrine at Badari, with more than one social expression of human life and afterlife.

Case Study 2. Identifying sacredness on Abu: from house to landscape   At its southern boundary, Egypt meets Lower Nubia across the granite rock outcrops that interrupt the flow of the Nile, its First Cataract. The earliest main town known in the area stood at the southern end of an island named Abu in Egyptian and Elephantine in Greek, facing east across the river to the ancient mainland town Sunet, "trade," under modern Aswan. The distinctive regional landscape includes quarries for hard stone on both sides of the river, with narrow tracts of fields hemmed in by sandstone cliffs and deserts. Grander tombs were cut in the western mainland cliffs for local governors, but there were also cemeteries of the third and second millennia on the West Bank and on Abu island itself. However, for once in Egyptian archaeology, the tombs are less well known than the island houses of the living, carefully recorded by German and Swiss expeditions since the 1950s. This town on Abu includes the only Egyptian temple site excavated from prehistoric to Roman Period. By 3000 BC, walls had been built to mark off a group of three massive rocks, perhaps at a pool where the first gurgling of the coming flood would echo each July. Around 2300 BC, the rock outcrop was fronted on the east by massive mudbrick walls forming a forecourt roughly 5 × 8 meters. At its center stood a 1 meter square structure of solid brick; from adjacent postholes, this could have formed a sheltered podium for an image on carrying chair, a type known from the third to first millennium and connected with festivals of kingship (Figure 2.14, Bussmann 2006). By 2000 BC, the features of the shrine within the enclosure walls had been transformed, with a stone-clad sanctuary to the local goddess Satet installed between the rocks, facing east across the forecourt to two chapels for the reigning king, also stone clad. Over the second millennium BC, the shrine shifted in scale and monumentality to the rectangular temple structure, entirely of stone, dedicated by Thutmes III to Satet.

In each of these periods, this and any other shrine on the island would have formed one presence within a landscape that included the town and fortress on the island, the river traffic and fishing activity, the links with the adjacent town of Sunet on the mainland, the farming life on islands and mainland, and the sporadic quarrying and building activity around. For around 1800 BC, there is enough archaeological data to set sacred enclosure and less obviously marked space into a single human time and space frame, though the archaeological map is fragmentary, leaving many parts of the town and its specific surrounding landscape unknown. West of the Satet temple, in its early rectangular, partly stone-build form, stood a group of chapels for offerings to local governors going back to Heqaib, in office around 2200 BC, some 500 years earlier (Pilgrim 1996, 17 plan Figure 1). The entrance to the chapel precinct is through a porch at the junction of a broad and a narrow street; the narrower cuts through and connects densely packed houses (cf. Kemp 2006, 199) out to the cemetery to the west. The area to the south was covered later by the temple to Khnum, considered the main god of the First Cataract region after 2000 BC: the temple structure here might have been the largest of the time, though it is also possible that, in 1800 BC, Satet held equal status and equally monumental architecture.

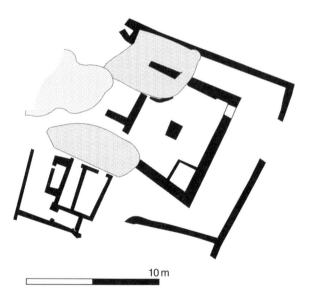

10 m

Figure 2.14   Plan of the temple at the rock hollow on the island of Abu, Early Dynastic level. Drawing © Wolfram Grajetzki.

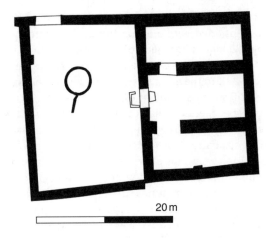

20 m

Figure 2.15 House converted into a three-chamber chapel, with inscription of the officer Sobekemsaf, in Abu town. Drawing © Wolfram Grajetzki, after Pilgrim 1996.

A century later, one house across the street from the Heqaib precinct was rebuilt as a large shrine of its own, with open court before three vaulted halls (Figure 2.15). The entrance to the middle vaulted hall had limestone doorjambs inscribed in hieroglyphs "god's servant Sobekemsaf, repeating life, formed as a child, who modelled himself, whose god made his portion" (left) and "god's servant of Khnum Sobekemsaf, repeating life, says: [I have] gone out as the modeller has gone out, to the chapel of the saviour" (Pilgrim 1996, 150–153). This unusual inscription insists on the motif of *modeling* as a pattern for action, including the action of forming new sacred space; the Egyptian word *qed*, "modeling," is written with the sign of a potter forming a vase of clay, just as the god Khnum is said in other writings to form the body of the king and of mortals. The short passages do not reveal who received offerings in this sacred space: Khnum, another deity, or Sobekemsaf or other mortals. They do, though, confirm the evidence of the triple vaulted hall, already unusual in domestic setting, that the area of more explicitly sacred space could expand over previously less clearly distinctive architecture. Sacred areas could also contract, for within a century the vaults had fallen, and the site made sacred by Sobekemsaf was being quarried for bricks and used for other purposes, with no apparent trace of its short-lived sanctity.

Houses at Abu 1800 BC

The central town streets ending in the precincts of Heqaib, Satet, and probably Khnum were filled with relatively rich houses (Kemp 2006, 199, Figure 70). Here, elegant pillars in papyrus-bundle motifs might have evoked specific divine forces such as Hathor, as well as the idyll of leisurely boating and hunting in papyrus marshes. The walls of the pillared central halls were painted in bright-colored bands (Pilgrim 1996, 123). From this period, there are both large and small houses in the quarter on the other side of the later Khnum temple, to the south. Here stood the house mentioned with the baby burials (see preceding text, Infant burials in houses); by 1800 BC, it had been divided into two separate structures (Pilgrim 1996, 40–43, Figure 7 Houses 23 and 24, and at the next phase p.45, Figure 9 Houses 12 and 22). In the smaller structure, less than 10 × 5 meters, the rear room was found still with its wooden threshold and traces of a single-leaf door; the larger central space, either a hall or an open court, had been a place of work, leaving flint chippings and fragments of wood tools. During the earlier phase in the life of this structure (House 23), a baby less than four months was buried in the entrance room, perhaps after the house had been abandoned; the body had been wrapped in linen, covered with reeds, and then protected by a sandstone block and two polishing stones, perhaps set here as grave markers (Figure 2.16). In the house of the neighbors (House 24), there were too few finds to identify the functions of each room or area within it, but one corner contained two seal impressions from one seal, along with a calcite vase shard and a fragment of a harp, perhaps indicating a certain leisure in the quarter, unless deposited here from use elsewhere (Pilgrim 1996, 43 with n.102).

Some decades later, a larger house again occupied the site, with rooms arranged around a courtyard 6 × 5 meters, with brick granary beside a shallow (20 cm) hollow for standing a round-bottomed jar (Pilgrim 1996, 49, Figure 10, House 10). Each of these architectural changes testifies to the intervention of people with different resources and needs, who would have formed groups of

2 m

Figure 2.16   House 23, excavation of the early to mid-second-millennium BC levels of Abu town. Drawing © Wolfram Grajetzki, after Pilgrim 1996.

different sizes, in ever-changing combinations of ages, genders, and classes. Always multiple, these are the social dimensions of the human space. The covered rooms and open courts of the buildings tended to have varying functions, rather than be fixed in each house as bedroom or reception room, as we might expect. However, secondary architectural features such as granaries, hearths, and water jar installations would establish longer horizons of use in their yards or chambers. In *House 10* of this site, a woman or a man waking in the north room might walk into the court, across the yard to work at the granary, out through a front room into the dead-end alley on the east, turning south to leave the houses beside the temples and head for fields, riverbank, or fishing boats. The sacredness of each step might be a sustained experience or vary according to the season, the time of day or night, and the memory of each space—including, but not restricted to, the memories built into places of burial (in one case on Abu an adult burial, perhaps not so rare within settlements; cf. Pilgrim 1996, 82–83 n.226 for evidence across Egypt 2000–1600 BC). Materially, each person and group would follow a path of varying distinctness or *sacredness*, only visible archaeologically where distinct material form is used or celebrated in ancient writing or depiction. A century or more after the construction of *House 10*, a grander building was laid out over this patch of town, with five column placements in an expanded central court (Pilgrim 1996, 55, Figure 12, House 5). Curiously, none of the usual, more obvious traces of living appeared: no hearth, granary, or animal refuse, as if this building was ceremonial or very seldom used, whether sacred or not.

Excursus: a liturgy on the sacredness of material offerings 1500 BC

By the time the five-columned house at Abu had fallen into ruin, written sources across Egypt record a new rite of offering to the dead, celebrating the divine dimension in every material offering. The words in this liturgy prompt us to consider possible wider ancient awareness of sacredness at every material trace excavated in the houses of the living, as well as materials that evaporate from the archaeological record:

> May Nile Flood give you water,
> May Grain give you bread,
> May Hathor give you beer,
> May the Hesat cow give you milk,
> May you wash your feet on blocks of silver,
> With lips from turquoise,
> May you don pure cloth from the gift of Ptah,
>   (Engelbach 1923, 30, written on two cups from
> Haraga tomb 290, about 1550 BC, UC16128-9)

Here, a divine dimension is found in all the matter of daily living—liquids, food, and cloth. Outside the place of offerings, the same sanctity might have been felt with other material presence, from the mud of floor and field to the domestic and wild animals of towns and countryside.

Were all creatures held sacred at Abu?

On the archaeological evidence carefully recorded at Abu, the streets and rooms of houses at Abu teemed with animal as well as human life, in a way that would abolish our difference between rural and urban living. It remains an open question how the town dwellers regarded the lives of the goats or sheep in their houses, especially in this region. In the hieroglyphic script, the Egyptian word for *dignity* or perhaps *aura* (*shefyt*) was written with the image of a ram. It is not clear precisely how this quality of *dignity* came to be associated with the ram. Within the overall mainly agricultural economy, the pastoral lifestyle of shepherds was always a significant complement to floodplain farming. Whatever the reasoning, the ram was used in formal art from the third to first millennia BC to depict several prominent gods. Most frequent in the surviving sources, from 1500 BC onward, a ram with horns curled to cheek appears as a form of the god Amun, whose cult center was at Waset, later also at major centers in Lower Egypt (for this form of ram head adorning the boat of Amun, see Figure 4.7). More anciently, a ram with horns extended horizontally is used to depict the gods Heryshef, with cult centered on Hutnennesut (Figure 3.10), and Khnum, with cult centers across Upper Egypt at Shenakhen, Shas-hotep, and Abu.

At later times, under Achaemenid domination (525–404 BC), local reverence for sacred qualities in the ram led to conflict between Egyptians and a Jewish community at Abu, over the sacrifice of lambs for the Jewish Passover festival (Joisten-Pruschke 2008). Abu was home at this time to a Jewish community connected with the Achaemenid Iranian garrison stationed at the frontier town. Such communities and conflicts may not have arisen in this form earlier, as the Achaemenid conquest of Egypt placed the country and its people in entirely new conditions; for the first time, the ancient Egyptian view of the world was only one of many, even at the official level. Unprecedented combinations of peoples and approaches may have generated tensions not experienced in earlier times. Moreover, on the ancient Egyptian side, the specific cause of tension stemmed from the reverence for animals by species, a phenomenon not attested before 700 BC. Modern eyes may too quickly misread the objection to animal sacrifice as a desire to protect animals. In fact, meat continued to be included in ancient Egyptian offerings alongside plant-based offerings and hymns. As noted in the preceding section (The separateness of the human in Egypt 3000–525 BC), X-rays of (undated) mummified cat bodies have revealed that many had been killed; evidently, some rites or offerings required the animal body in a form made immortal, not the present living but transient. Yet the later communal conflicts around rituals of sacrifice remind us to question the ways humans related to the presence of animals in the earlier periods too. These relations involve the animals in the wild, often hunted, and those at home—as source of food, protectors, or, in the case of dogs, monkeys, and cats, as luxury pets.

Case Study 3. Sacredness in more urban landscapes: Lahun 1800 BC   A third archaeological fragment set from a *total human geography* can be assembled at the early second-millennium BC site of Lahun, farther north, at the edge of Fayoum. Here, in just ten weeks of AD 1889, a digging team cleared a planned rectilinear town that flourished in 1875–1750 BC. The southwest enclosure wall of the town is close to the Valley Temple of the cult complex, including the pyramid for King Senusret II. The ancient names for these places seem to have been Sekhem-Senusret, "Senusret is Mighty!," for the pyramid complex and Hetep-Senusret, "Senusret is at Peace!," for the town alongside (Horváth 2009). There is no inscriptional evidence for the precise date of the town foundation, but plausibly, it dates to the short reign of Senusret II or just after, between 1900 and 1875 BC. In the immediate vicinity, and across the fields on the outcrop of desert and rock at Haraga, stretch the cemeteries of the period. Little of the original temple reliefs survive, for the pictorial record, but the excavaters harvested papyrus fragments from across the town site, providing an unparalleled written record of more varied activities in life, including scraps of temple ritual, several larger fragments of literary papyri, the earliest mathematical and healing treatises, dozens of personal or official letters, and a great quantity of accountancy fragments. In contrast to the more meticulous excavation of Abu, the relatively rapid clearance of Lahun did not give time for recording much of the detail in finds across the site, and there are only a dozen photographs; nearly all the bricks of the buildings were recycled in the next few decades, but new ground survey and ceramic analysis would help to fill gaps in our knowledge of the site. At present, the combination of finds, 1889 town plan, and the landscape itself can provide some idea of sacredness as experienced and expressed anciently in this more urbanized landscape at the meeting of fields and desert.

The main town is built as a roughly 250 × 250 meter square, or 500 × 500 ancient Egyptian cubits, with an adjacent series of streets forming a veritable second town on the west. A thick, so probably originally high, mudbrick wall separated the main from the west town. Overall population has been estimated between 3,000 and 10,000, depending on unknown factors: the size of households in the larger houses, the number of houses with a second story of living quarters, and the number of houses lost in the eroded area nearest the fields. By far the largest houses are nine palatial mansions, some 60 × 40 meters, located along the north side of the town. Farthest from water supply, this sector would also have been upwind of the rest of society, including the highest area, thanks to the dominant north wind of the Nile Valley. Within the town perimeter walls, the ground slopes dramatically from the north desert edge toward the fields on the south side. A steep escarpment runs west to east near the northwest corner; this was cut back beneath the westernmost and highest of the nine mansions, around a low-lying square, the only more open ground within the town. At the center of one side of this square stood a structure with double-column porch, corridor, and chambers, on a plan of unidentified function—interpreted by some archaeologists as a temple for the town but possibly an administrative point of control or issue of resources. The large house overlooking the square occupies the most favorable position in the town; in a planned town of the same period at Abydos South, the northwest large house is identified on sealings as the *House of the Mayor*, and this seems a plausible function for the Lahun mansion in the same position (Wegner 2010, Figure 2.17).

Over the uneven terrain of the town, the physical access to the outside and the visual horizon of each town quarter would have made for rather different living

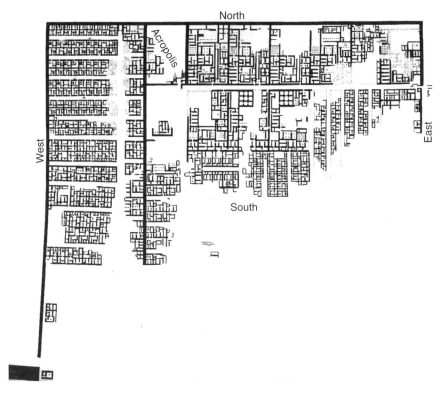

Figure 2.17   The late Middle Kingdom town near modern al-Lahun, as recorded by W. Petrie in 1889. W. Petrie, *Illahun, Kahun, Gurob*, David Nutt, London, 1891, pl.14.

experiences. From the time of its construction, the pyramid over the burial place of Senusret II would have been the visual focus, but in fact, it would have been out of sight for anyone standing at ground level (and perhaps even from the roof level) within the *western town* and west side of the main town. Walking the space today, the pyramid is invisible from the houses on the slope from the westernmost wall; this may have been true, even allowing for higher ancient ground levels. From the northern mansions, the view of the pyramid would have been blocked by the *House of the Mayor* on the escarpment. There might have been only two points from which the whole townscape could have been seen, as well as the pyramid complex: the roof of the Valley Temple south of the main town and the roof of the *House of the Mayor*.

Equipment to protect birth and infancy
Within these physical horizons, we can consider the sight lines and access to sacred spaces for some of the few places where Petrie recorded specific finds in 1889, starting with the *western town*, in the street of houses nearest to the monumental Valley Temple for King Senusret II. The ground immediately south of this street had been too heavily eroded to preserve any traces of building, so we do not know

whether the preserved doors faced other houses or backed onto an open space looking down to the Valley Temple moorings. When the cult flourished, unevenly over the century following the death of Senusret II, this corner of the site could have been one of its busiest points, with arrivals and departures of senior officials on state barges as well as cargo boats laden with material for the economy of the cult. At some point in 1850–1750 BC, a shallow hole was cut in the floor of one room, and someone deposited a remarkable set of ritual items: a pair of beautifully carved ivory hand clappers, made to accompany a chant, along with an extraordinary wooden figurine with a naked female human body, thick-maned lion head, and lion tail, the human arms to the sides, palms inward, and the human feet turned outward, on short pegs for fixing to a base or other object. Lion heads are found for male and female images of those protecting mother and child, notably the male and female forms of Aha/Bes (Figure 2.18a). Another extraordinary find was made in the adjacent room, which might have been in either the same or the next house at the time of the deposits: a starched linen mask painted with the features of a lion, the only mask for the living that has survived from ancient Egypt (Figure 2.18b). Petrie recorded a doorway between the two houses at this point, as if the original plan had been adapted to join one house (7 × 15m) to another (9 × 15 meters), to form one unit of relatively large size within the range of housing at Lahun (smallest 7 × 7 meter, largest the palatial mansions 40 × 60 meters). An adult man or woman living here might have worn the mask and struck the clappers in rituals of birth performed here and/or elsewhere across the town. Someone in the house(s) would inhabit a structure already imbued with the sacredness that is felt in the protection of birth and infancy. It might be more than an accident of survival that these four items were found in the street nearest the Valley Temple: more than half the town inhabitants were named after King Senusret II, perhaps implying widespread personal resonance for the power of his presence and cult. Perhaps, then, the place of the largest quantities of offerings to him might have been the magnet for other senses of the sacred. The street might have been most appropriate for the practitioners of rituals of the human life cycle as well as those on the temple staff rota (for the wide spread of the rota, see Chapter 3, section "Staff in Offering-Spaces".

A central painting in a small house

Few wall paintings were recorded from Lahun, but the 1889 clearance photographs confirm a published line drawing, showing a framed double register of scenes with, below, doorways and plainer rectangular outlines and, above, a man bringing a jar to a seated man, the two figures placed between table laden with vessels, and an indistinct form, perhaps an outline of a canopy or porch building. On his town plan, Petrie pinpointed the location of this painting as the central chamber of one in a series of six- to nine-room houses in the main town. Another painting, depicting columns, he located in the central chamber of a similar house across the street. It is not known whether this part of the houses was a closed room or an open court, with other rooms arranged around the central open space. Nor is it certain that the paintings were added while the building was being used as a living space; possibly, disused house rooms had been turned into offering spaces. Nevertheless, the ambiguity itself shows how

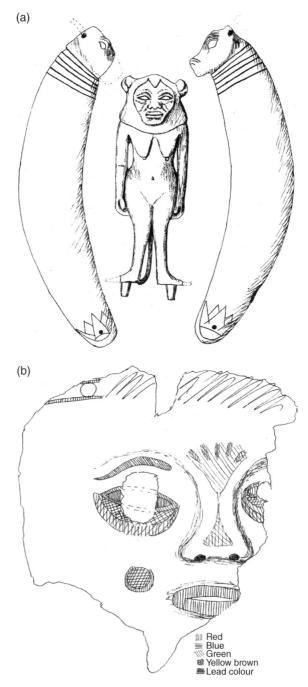

(a)

(b)

Red
Blue
Green
Yellow brown
Lead colour

Figure 2.18 Finds from the Petrie 1889 clearance of Lahun: (a) figurine of a lion-faced naked woman and two clappers found buried with it and (b) painted-plastered cloth leonine mask from the adjoining house. From W. Petrie, *Kahun, Gurob, and Hawara*, Kegan Paul, Trench, Trübner and Co, London, 1890, pl.8.

Figure 2.19   Painting in a house in the late Middle Kingdom town near modern al-Lahun, as recorded by W. Petrie in 1889. From W. Petrie, *Illahun, Kahun, Gurob*, David Nutt, London, 1891, pl.16.

difficult it can be to maintain our division of religious, even funerary, from domestic. The paintings may be an indication of offering practices more frequent than we have imagined, connecting the inhabitants with divine forces—whether deities or ancestors or other. Petrie also received from the clearance teams, though without noting find-place, a series of faience and limestone figures of childbirth protectors: dwarves, lion-faced or lion-masked male and female forms (Aha/Bes), and the standing lion–hippopotamus (Ipy/Reret/Taweret). Some limestone figures supported truncated cones, perhaps lamps or incense burners—Petrie interpreted them as bread altars. We cannot yet locate the figures in a social context, within small, medium, or palatial houses, and though portable, the figures may or may not have been moved around the site. Nevertheless, their presence tends to confirm the evidence of the paintings—that offering practices formed a more widespread part of life than might be assumed from the relative lack of distinctive, figurative finds across the third and early second millennia BC (Figure 2.19 and Figure 2.21).

An enigmatic slab
Another Petrie 1889 photograph of Lahun shows a rectangular limestone slab set in the corner of a room with plastered mudbrick walls. The slab has raised border and short feet to raise it off the ground at the corners and midway along the long side and at its center is a circular hollow. Petrie captioned the image "stone tray for water jar and dishes." The jar emplacement itself implies only that liquid was

Figure 2.20   Stone ablution (?) table at the corner of a house in the late Middle Kingdom town near modern al-Lahun, as it was in 1890, Petrie photograph no.957. © of the Petrie Museum of Egyptian Archaeology, UCL.

present, we cannot in fact be sure whether the jars contained water, milk, or wine, or whether the slab was for special or for regular use. The square pools in other parts of the house might be for washing hands before eating or feet before proceeding into rooms which were kept cleaner. Possibly, the jar on the limestone slab served a similar purpose, and the long table space on either side was for smaller basins for water poured from a central jar. Perhaps, though, the water or other liquid was for drinking, and the long table was for food, offerings for or from guests, or even for forces protecting the house—deities or ancestors. From the period of the houses 1850–1750 BC, there is little other evidence, and we need comparison with other times and places to suggest possible functions. However, the town plan does provide us with a spatial context, and that gives us some idea of the role for the space. Carla Gallorini notes the only stone rectangle marked in the corner of a room on the Petrie plans, at the north end of a double-columned hall, in one of the nine palatial mansions on the site (in Quirke 2011, 782). This takes us to the wealthiest end of living at Lahun 1850–1750 BC, a social context where the word *elite* has some meaning. The mansion floor plans follow a recurring pattern, where functions can be assigned to each space—in contrast to the unpredictable multifunctional use of rooms in the more modest houses on Abu island (see section "Houses at Abu 1800 BC"). Only that one slab is recorded, but a number of other rooms, all in the palatial mansions, had square pools made up of separate limestone slabs at the center of halls with three to ten columns. According to the interpretation of the mansions by Manfred Bietak, the rectangular slab lies within the sphere of the main person in the house, rather than within the subsidiary suites for other family or staff members, or within the economic production or storage quarters of the house (Figure 2.20).

Figure 2.21   Offering stands sculpted as figurines, found in 1889 at the late Middle Kingdom townsite near modern al-Lahun, during the clearance supervised by W. Petrie. From W. Petrie, *Illahun, Kahun, Gurob*, David Nutt, London, 1891, pl.6.

We can, then, use the slab to set in motion a point of meeting between different lives, *elite* and subaltern, within more formal context outside the temple. The slab house is in the quarter farthest from the Valley Temple, but on this side of the site, there is a clear view across the desert to the pyramid of the king a kilometer to the west. The nearest formal place of offerings might be the building in the square below the *House of the Mayor*, but its identity as a temple is not certain. If not, to join rituals of offering or festival at the Valley Temple, someone in this house would need to proceed along the main east–west town street, which has a 55 cm drainage gulley to take some of the winter rain or the liquid refuse, and either down a north–south street to a canal waterfront (area not preserved) or through the only preserved gateway of the town, with brick-paved road down onto the desert to the east of the site.

Serving at the ceremonial inside a mansion

If we woke as domestic servant, we might live, not inside the mansion (though this is possible), but in an adjacent street of the smallest among the preserved houses (7 × 7 meter). There, we would sleep and wake with our own sense of sacred, or not, of the materials within the four rooms (or three rooms and one yard) of our ground floor and in or on the roof space and of the right-angled planned streets from front door to the main east–west town street as wide as our own house and west along to the front door of the mansion. The mansions have an entrance hall made grand by a single column, with a small side room for doorkeeper and supplies. The way into the main part of the house is through either a broad corridor or a narrow corridor, in the first of a series of disorienting side turns, to a second chamber with one column: the great reception hall where a grander visitor might meet the main person in the house is not approached along a single line, like the axis of many formal stone temples (see Chapter Three), but twisting and turning according to a different psychology of the nested, perhaps intended to emphasize the separation of world inside from world outside, so in a sense sacred from the inside. If we are providing our manual labor, we probably take the narrower corridor, past four rooms where possibly we receive orders, clean clothing, or other materials.

From this point on, we stand in the same spaces as the wealthy, but not necessarily same corners or same times: the columned chamber brings us all into the great open garden court, at its northeast corner. Along its southern side, concealed from view when we first enter, an eight-columned portico provides shade for a select few. On this south side of the garden, one door at the east leads to a second suite of rooms, with its own columned halls and pools, while a second door at the west takes us into the transverse hall behind the portico, with three south doors in turn into three different ceremonial spaces of the inner house: the main bedroom, with raised bed bench along the far wall; the main reception hall, with four columns; and the two-columned hall with the limestone slab immediately on our left as we enter. The three rooms are interconnected by doorways, and a door at the rear of the main reception hall leads to the single-columned hall giving access to a final suite of rooms. If food and drink were prepared or stored in that innermost space, we might need to enter here to collect material; it is also possible that external servants had to collect, earlier, anything they needed at rooms closer to the entrance and that only select house staff enjoyed access to the innermost rooms. At the hall with the limestone slab, we might have been needed to lift the heavy jar to pour liquid or to carry heavy trays of food or other equipment. However, these heavier tasks of table setting could have been carried out before ceremonies began, and we might never have been in the room at the time the owner of the house and/ or guests performed those ceremonies. Whoever brought the portable items to the slab, and whenever, the position of the feature within the great house suggests its function: as location for guests to wash and/or receive sustenance, just before entering the main reception hall where they could be received by the owner of the house. No remains of offerings are recorded on the site, and no writings survive to reveal how sacred the participants might have considered the ceremonial in preparing a reception.

Limestone platforms for house ceremonies after 1350 BC

In the late nineteenth and early twentieth century, comparable stone features were discovered in houses at Akhetaten, the short-lived city constructed by King Akhenaten as his residence about 1350 BC (Spence 2007). Shallow slabs have rounded raised edges, with narrow *entrance ramps*, and are found in reception spaces rather than bathrooms where washing installations appear in slightly different form. Evidently, water or another liquid was being poured here in a ceremony with its own space, but the object of the performance is not recorded from depictions or written evidence. In a walled village in the low desert east of the main city at Akhetaten, the painted walls of some rooms include motifs of mother-and-child protectors (Aha/Bes and Ipy/Taweret), as also found in a near-contemporary royal context, the palace complex for King Amenhotep III at Malqata on the low desert west of Waset. More evidence comes from the village built near there, for artists working on the painted corridor tombs of kings in 1300–1100 BC (Deir al-Madina). Here, perhaps reflecting the painting and inscriptional skills of the artists, raised pillared platforms in the front rooms of several houses are decorated with scenes including the nursing of infants and, again, Aha/Bes and Ipy/Taweret figures. The platforms are sometimes large enough to accommodate one or perhaps two persons, with steps for access; they have been interpreted as birthing pavilions, but may have had wider scope, for invoking other protective forces including the reigning king or the past rulers associated with the village, King Amenhotep I and his mother Ahmes Nefertari.

Another focus of offering, or perhaps an aspect of all domestic practice, might be the immediate predecessors as links to a longer line of *ancestors*. Ancestor worship is not considered a major feature of ancient Egyptian practice, including depiction or writing, in comparison with other parts of the world. However, the period 1300–1100 BC also saw the production, across Egypt, of small sculptures in the form of a head and schematic upper body, known in Egyptology as *ancestor busts*. These are not specific to one social group; the finest to survive are perhaps the pair inscribed with the names of Pendjerty and Muteminet, the parents of a high official of Ramses II, Amenmes, perhaps from his Theban tomb chapel, the offering space above his burial place (Habachi 1979). Intriguingly, the inscription for his mother, Muteminet, begins with the words "my mother—Tefnut," as if she embodied the latest in a female line back to the first division of creation, where Atum, "All," produced Tefnut and Shu. His father, Pendjerty, similarly linked him back to Shu. Here, perhaps we find a statement on human identity that each of us bears through our parents a line to Tefnut and a line to Shu. The reverence for immediate parents may then have taken the place, in ancient Egypt, of what appears as a more collective *ancestor worship* in other times and places. Kate Spence has connected the Akhetaten lustration slabs with the literary Teaching of Any, where the good man is reminded to offer to his deceased father and mother. The immediate bonds of parent–child may have framed acts of reverence and invocations for help, involving past generations, even where a collective past *family* or *people* might have been recognized.

CHAPTER 3

Creating Sacred Space and Time: Temple Architecture and Festival

⌐⌐⌐⌐

Formalizing Sacred Space: For Offerings

Ancient sacred monumental architecture survives extraordinarily well at a handful of sites in the Egyptian Nile Valley and Saharan oases. From the period 1500–1100 BC, large temple structures entirely in stone still stand floor to ceiling at Waset/Thebes East (Karnak, Luxor) and West (Madinat Habu, Ramesseum, Qurna) or have been reconstructed (Deir al-Bahari) or rebuilt up to roof level (Abdju kingship temples). From earlier periods, smaller temples are to be found in Fayoum at Qasr Qarun (2500 or 1800 BC) and Madinat Madi (1800 BC), and dismantled sanctuaries of the Middle Kingdom have been reconstructed at Waset (Karnak, 1950 BC). Besides the pyramids at their core, complexes for kingship cult (2600–1800 BC) include well-preserved or reconstructed temple structures at Saqqara, Giza, Medum; museum collections now house the more substantial sections of relief-decorated temple walls from these complexes, from Saqqara and Abusir, and, in part anciently recycled, Lisht. The sum of this remarkable conservation story is curiously limited in range, almost as if we could write a history of religious architecture on just two types, the royal pyramid complex (2600–1800 BC) and the axial procession temple fronted by massive gateways (1500–1100 BC). The archaeological record for less well-preserved structures can reveal a more diverse and intriguing history. The construction of separate sacred space on larger scale falls along a spectrum of informal to formal, where the *built environment* interweaves with spaces cut from the rock and with sands and floodwaters.

Range of different architectural types/engagements with ground

From the late fourth millennium BC, large ceremonial buildings were set up in organic materials, as shown by alignments of substantial postholes at Nekhen, an early kingship center (Kemp 2006). The architectural history of ancient Egypt relies, though, on evidence of stone structures, and new excavations may alter the

Exploring Religion in Ancient Egypt, First Edition. Stephen Quirke.

picture substantially where more mud-brick and organic structures are also recorded. The following examples are not exhaustive, but demonstrate at least the remarkable variety found even for the stone structures:

Type 1 Mounds as platforms: The largest example of this type is arguably the site at the epicenter of ancient Egyptian religious practice, the High Mound for the cult of the sun-god at Iunu (Heliopolis) (Figure 1.5). Early twentieth-century AD excavations found evidence for a rounded stone revetment wall, for a mound supporting the now lost temple or temples of the sun cult. The date of the mound is disputed: the revetment wall includes elements from late third millennium BC, so the structure as found cannot be earlier. Later monuments found within it have been used to date it to the mid-first millennium BC, but the circumstances of their deposition are not clear; they may be from later ditches dug into the mound, perhaps for structures built on top of the mound long after its construction. A fifteenth-century BC manuscript records the decision of King Senusret I (reigned about 1950 BC) to create a new precinct for the sun-god (Lichtheim 1973, 115–118); the first colossal obelisk on the site, the main monument still there, is inscribed for him, supporting the date implied by the manuscript for the temple. A first-millennium BC plaque is inscribed with a plan of the temple, indicating a complex of structures around open courts, their entranceways flanked by massive double towers (Egyptologists use the term *pylons*), as in other temple types of the second and first millennia BC (Ricke 1935). At other sites, the open court is a recurrent feature of sun worship: examples are found at late second-millennium BC temples for kings in Egypt (e.g., Deir al-Bahari) and Egyptian-occupied Nubia (e.g., Abu Simbel). Inscriptions in these sun courts indicate that worship here centered on a sequence of hymns, sung by the king to keep the sun moving through the sky and so the world in orderly motion. For about a century, 2500–2400 BC, pyramid complexes for kings were paired with separate structures, called Sun Temples in Egyptology, but intended to support the cult of the king. In one of these, the Sun Temple for King Niuserra, chambers of approach were decorated in relief with scenes celebrating the full panoply of the creation (Verner 2002, 78–82). At Akhetaten, the city of King Akhenaten, sun worship focussed on the visible solar sphere, in Egyptian *Aten*; the Great Aten Temple contains a series of vast open courts, filled with offering tables for food and drink offerings. In the courts, stepped platforms with balustrade screening walls would raise the king up for the singing of the Aten Hymn (Shaw 1994). The same feature occurs at the other second-millennium open sun courts in temples for kings (Figure 3.1).

Type 2 Rounded mounds enclosing chambers: The *nonformal* type identified by Barry Kemp at several fourth- to third-millennium BC sites, where, in each case, a later rectilinear structure replaced the mound (Kemp 2006, 113–135). At Madu (Medamud), an angular enclosure wall surrounded two central mounds, each with sanded corridor to its center. The main recipient of cult may have been a local deity, or perhaps sometimes the reigning king, as at the Early Dynastic kingship center Nekhen (McNamara 2006) (Figure 3.2).

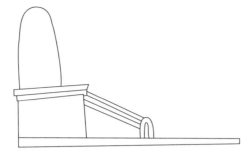

Figure 3.1   Great stela inscribed with hymn to be sung to the Aten, on a raised platform with stepped approach and balustrade, in the court of the Great Aten Temple at Akhetaten, as depicted in the tomb of Meryra, high priest of the Aten at Akhetaten, about 1350 BC. Drawing © Wolfram Grajetzki, after Shaw 1994.

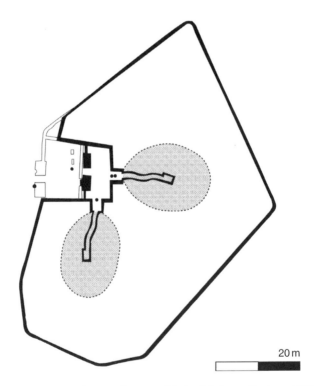

20 m

Figure 3.2   Rounded mounds in enclosure at Madu (Medamud), about 2000 BC, under the later temple of Mont. Drawing © Wolfram Grajetzki.

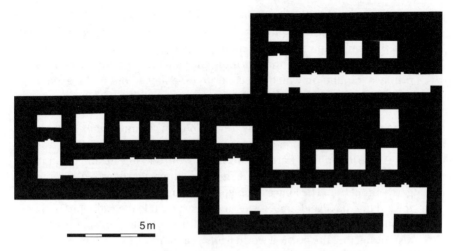

Figure 3.3   Plan of offering chambers within trapezoidal mass cased in limestone blocks, over burial place of a palace official, south cemeteries of Inebhedj, near modern Dahshur, about 2400 BC. J. De Morgan, *Fouilles à Dahchour 1894–1895*, Adolphe Holzhausen, Vienna, 1903, fig. 14.

Type 3 Squared mounds enclosing chambers: The squared mound is a feature over burial places of richer individuals from the third millennium BC onward, and from mid-third millennium, there are offering spaces first at the edge, then leading into the mound (Egyptologists use the Arabic term *mastaba*, "block-bench"); the most elaborate examples have extensive series of chambers, decorated with scenes of offering, and of producing materials for offering, as well as of leisured life. The pyramid with temple at front, burial chambers within, is in a sense a regal transformation of the trend that also generates this type of nonroyal offering place (Figure 3.3).

Type 4 Free-standing rectangular or square structures with principal chamber at rear, façade not always markedly higher, central structure closed to outside:

Single axis to single principal chamber
Multiple axis: dual, triple, unparalleled 7-chamber

The most developed form of architecture with focus on axis from entrance to sanctuary is the *festival procession temple* (Assmann 2001, 27–35). The dominant feature from the outside is the massive double tower at the front of courtyards: the earliest surviving example fronts the pyramid complex for Amenemhat II at Dahshur (about 1900 BC). As noted under type 1 above, this feature may also be found with other temple types, as for structures atop the High Mound at Iunu, and occurs as much in temples for kings and blessed dead (Saqqara temple–tombs post-Amarna, Waset temple–tombs D25–26) as in those for deities. In the developed axial temple, the double tower provided a dramatic point of appearance for the boat-shrine bearing the sacred image as it left the temple on procession at festivals. The spatial logic of the temple as a whole evoked the unfurling of creation: as you move into the temple toward the sanctuary, it becomes darker, the ceiling lower, and the ground higher, transforming the sanctuary ground itself into the primeval mound on which the creator-god emerged out of the expanse of the inert. Outer courts are more open, inner are filled with columns, and the innermost is a solitary dark chamber containing the shrine with the image inhabitable by the divine force. Columns in inner halls have closed buds and those in outer halls open; in the kingship temples in front of the Amun temple at Karnak, the images of the king in inner chambers are wrapped chrysalis-like, and those in outer courts are in ceremonial garments of rule. The long axis creates a channel to radiate a divine force out toward the massive double tower at the entry, while the walls and darkness also help to enclose a force, protecting it from hostile outside worlds but also protecting the outside world from a sacredness that might overwhelm the living (Figure 3.4).

Type 5 Rectilinear, as 4, but without the extended axis, and all or front part surrounded by columns (peripteral): This type survives most often on a smaller scale, in structures of second and first millennia BC. As relatively small sets of hewn blocks, these have often been recycled in both ancient and more modern times. Examples recycled as building material for other temple blocks have been reconstructed more recently, providing an opportunity to appreciate an otherwise lost feature of the landscape. Other examples, such as the Badari temple (Figure 2.11), can be reconstructed at least in plan and then by analogy with the reconstructions or earlier records of other sites (Figure 3.5).

Type 6 With principal chamber cut from rock: Rock-cut chambers have rarely been excavated carefully enough to reveal less substantial features over the approach to them, and so it is not often possible to be certain how they would have appeared anciently; most of the recorded examples are those with depictions carved or painted over interior walls, which received most attention. The best-known examples are primary sources for ancient Egyptian painting, rock-cut tombs of governors, and local ruling class of several periods: 2400–2100 BC at modern Dishasha, Tihna, and Sheikh Said (Middle Egypt); 2000–1875 BC at modern Beni Hasan, Deir al-Bersha, and Meir (Middle Egypt) and at Tjebu/Qau, Waset/Thebes, and Abu (Upper Egypt); 1475–1200 BC at Akhetaten (Middle Egypt) and Waset/Thebes (Upper Egypt); and 700–600 BC again at Waset. The ground in front of the rock-cut feature often included stone structures, such as terraces (as 7) or extensions in structure (as 4), and these have been more fully recorded. Surviving inscribed examples where the rock-cut part dominates tend to be smaller, as at Speos Artemidos near Beni Hasan in Middle Egypt, and at the Gebel el-Silsila sandstone quarries in southern Upper Egypt; the outstanding examples are at Abu Simbel in Nubia, two rock-cut temples for the cult of Ramses II and his wife Nefertari (about 1275 BC) (Figure 3.6).

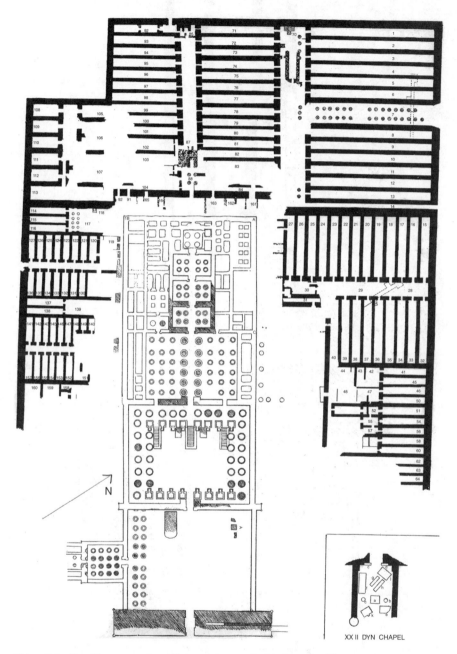

Figure 3.4   Rectilinear temple on linear axis, temple for the cult of King Ramses II, Waset, about 1275 BC. J. Quibell, R. Paget, A. Pirie, *The Ramesseum and The Tomb of Ptah-hetep*, Quaritch, London, 1898, pl. 1.

Figure 3.5   Peripteral temple with columns around the front, temple of Amenhotep III, Abu. From W. Petrie, *Egyptian Architecture*, London 1938, pl. 28.

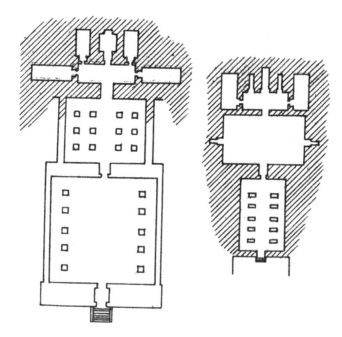

Figure 3.6   Rectilinear rock-cut offering place on linear axis: right, chapel over burial place of Governor Wahka, near Tjebu (Qau), about 1850 BC; left, temple to the cult of Ramses II formerly in Wadi es-Seboua, Lower Nubia, about 1275 BC. From W. Petrie, *Egyptian Architecture*, London 1938, pl. 34.

Figure 3.7   Terraced cliff-front temples to the cult of sovereigns at Waset (covered after AD 300 by a monastery, Deir al-Bahari, now removed): to the left (south) is the temple at the burial place of King Nebhepetra Mentuhotep, in the foreground the temple for Hatshepsut as sovereign. Photograph after unearthing of the sites, E. Naville, *Deir al-Bahri. Part 3*, Egypt Exploration Fund, London 1898.

Type 7 Terraced: Temples built up against an escarpment include one or more platforms connected by central ramps. The best-known example is the reconstructed temple for the cult of Hatshepsut as king, at Deir al-Bahri on the West Bank at Thebes (about 1475 BC); the inspiration for this multiple terrace with pillared tiers seems to have been the adjacent monuments for King Nebhepetra Mentuhotep, reunifier of Egypt (2000 BC), and for his highest officials and predecessors (rock-cut tombs with pillared facades). Large Late Period temples for animal cults at Saqqara stood on terraces that might have required similar but steeper approaches (Jeffreys and Smith 1988, precise form and foundation date uncertain) (Figure 3.7).

Type 8 Within crescent lake: The crescent lake is a natural feature of the Nile floodplain, with high ground within a moatlike outer crescent of water, named *isheru* in Egyptian. The best-known example is at the temple of the goddess Mut at Luxor (Waraksa 2009), and there may be a particular association with the sailing of goddesses. However, the main god at Hutnennesut is called Heryshef "He who is over his lake," and this might refer to a similar feature (Figure 3.8).

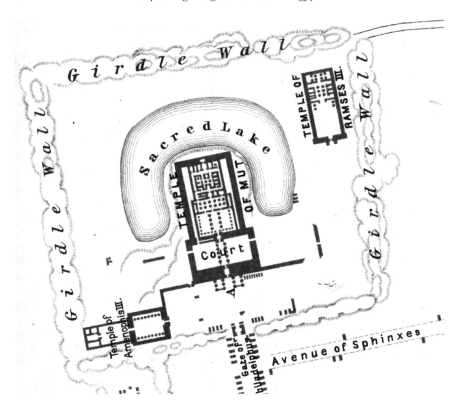

Figure 3.8   Plan of the crescent-shaped lake around temple of the goddess Mut, Luxor. From K. Baedeker, *Egypt and the Sûdân. Handbook for travellers*, Karl Baedeker, Leipzig, 1914.

Recipients of offerings

The pictorial and inscriptional evidence identifies the primary function for all these types as offering places. Prayer and assembly are secondary in the explicit self-image of the ancient Egyptian temple, although they may have been primary in lived experience for many people anciently in their grounds. The evidence also identifies possible recipients of offerings as three categories, each usually with their own separate offering spaces, though they might also receive offerings jointly in one space:

King (Egyptian *nesut*), structures built for the reigning king, rarely for a predecessor.

Gods/goddesses (Egyptian *netjeru/netjeryt*).

Blessed dead (Egyptian *akhu*), structures built for an individual during their lifetime; outside kingship complexes, the inscribed examples are nearly always *his*, but rare exceptions for a woman include the Akhmim tombs of about 2200 BC, the Theban tomb of Senet mother of vizier Intefiqer about 1950 BC (Gardiner and de Garis Davies 1920), and the Saqqara tomb of Maya, nurse of Tutankhamun about 1350 BC (Zivie 2009).

In temples for the first two, the only person who is depicted offering or performing other rituals is the reigning king. In the offering spaces for the blessed dead, the person receives offerings most often from immediate family but may also after 1500 BC appear offering to, or in worship of, a deity or king.

Where the recipient of offering was the embalmed body of king or wealthy nonroyal individual, the focus of offering was in many periods an offering slab in front of a solid stone doorway, known in Egyptology as *door stela* or *false door* (Jánosi 1999). The stone doorway regularly marks the main ground for laying offerings in wealthy nonroyal offering places over the tomb (2500–1800 BC), less commonly in later periods, and in temples built for the cult of the reigning king (2400–2200 BC). Another principal focus, at this and other periods, is the stone image, most often in three dimensions. Although any image might offer a focus for offerings, few surviving images of a deity are likely to have ever served as the principal focus of offerings in a temple. The large stone sculptures that attract attention in museum galleries and art history books tend to be from exceptional ritual settings. Several hundred granodiorite lioness-headed statues of Sekhmet and hundreds more, perhaps the majority of surviving, larger hard-stone images of other deities come from the singular program to ensure the passage of Amenhotep III through his *sed* festivals to enhanced divine status (Bryan 1997). Large stone images of kings also served not as focus of cult at the innermost sanctuary, but, quite the opposite, as guardian forces along the approach to that sanctuary (Figures 3.9). Some of these images are known to have had names and received offerings; these practices demonstrate the divine force felt in the sculpture but seem secondary to their role as active divine guardians of sacred space. The main image in a temple may well have been much smaller, perhaps with precious metal, lapis lazuli, and elephant ivory rather than all in the soft and hard stones of large-scale sculpture: written sources refer to the flesh and bones of deities as being of gold, silver, and lapis lazuli. Any of the rare surviving small-scale images in such precious metals might have been the original images housed in the main sanctuary of a temple, but none is certainly a principal cult image (Figure 3.10). On the written evidence, images were not themselves the object of worship, but provided a material core which could be inhabited by the divine force, to receive offerings, including the word offerings that are hymns, within daily, seasonal, or other rituals (Assmann 2001, 40–47). Similarly, and perhaps the model for the image of king or deity in temples, a nonroyal individual might continue to receive offerings through a statue at any place of offering, either the chapel over the burial place or, from at least 1950 BC onward, at the temple of a king or deity.

Unlike the images of the deities, statues for the eternal offering cult of the individual were more often of soft or hard stone. The main evidence for the consecration of divine images is the composition with the ancient title *Opening of the Mouth and Eyes*. This ritual is primarily for the stone statues of nonroyal individuals, as found from the mid-third millennium BC in chapels over burial places, and perhaps also for stone statues of kings. In the main group of sources, captioned depictions in tomb chapels at Waset (1450–1200 BC), the object of the ritual may be the mummified body, the wrapped and wearing human-form mask, or the

Figure 3.9   Protective statue depicting King Ramses II between two goddesses, from the temple to Min and Isis at Gebtyu (Qift), now Egyptian Museum Cairo CG555. W. Petrie, *Koptos*, Quaritch, London, 1895, pl. 17.

Figure 3.10   Gold statuette of the god Heryshef found at Henennesut temple; cult images are thought to have been similarly small and of precious metal, but this example has a ring at the back as if to wear for protection. W. Petrie, *Ehnasya*, Egypt Exploration Fund, 1905, frontispiece.

human-form inner coffin. The focus of this all-important ritual is overcoming death, and, accordingly, the ritual is outlined in Chapter 7 (see there, Table 2).

Daily offering rituals

The direct evidence for offerings deposited at a site would be physical remains at shrines, but not all offerings were necessarily left with the recipient. An Egyptian phrase *wedjeb khet*, "reversion of offerings," implies removal for consumption by others, whether kings/deities/blessed dead, or other living communities. Temple inscriptions of around 1450 BC record the daily offerings to a statue of Amun-Ra, main deity at Karnak (Barta 1968, offering list Type E), with similar lists for the god Min and, a century later, for the goddess Mut at Luxor. The offerings begin with libation and incense, to purify the space, or intensify its purity, followed by a heading, *offering list of Nun*, the primeval waters, presumably here as source of all life and so of all material to be offered. Three different types of jar with water are presented with natron, another purifying natural material, and, the first food on the table, a large loaf and twenty cakes. Another libation of two different jars of water then introduces the main meal: two different jars of wine; five cuts of meat, including liver, along with the knife to cut them; and a jug of milk with one final wine offering. A ritual note interrupts the flow of material, and the proceedings end with a jug of water and some honey. Although there is no cooking manual, the gist of the ritual evokes a rich formal banquet, as if king/deity/blessed dead take the role of owner in a large estate. On this model, the sacred space is a crucible for a special kind of alchemy, enabling earthly energy to pass to these invisible forces. Any sculpted image in these offering spaces may need to be consecrated, but it seems never to be the object of worship; instead, it provides a material focus to provide orientation for the offerer and perhaps a physical object space where the invisible force could collect the energies being offered in form of food, drink, or incense.

The other inscriptional and pictorial evidence for activity in the innermost part of sacred space confirms that the inhabitant of offering space (king/deity/blessed dead) is treated as the estate owner in a large estate. The principal sources for repeated daily ritual are manuscripts from Karnak temples of Amun and Mut and depictions with hieroglyphic inscriptions in the Karnak Amun temple, on obelisks from the temple, and in the Abdju temple for King Sety I. The main manuscript source (ninth century BC) starts with the words "Beginning of the pronouncements of the god's offerings that are made at the House of Amun-Ra king of the gods, in the course of every day, by the main pure-one who is on his day (of duty)" (for the following series of actions, see Assmann 2001, 47–50). First, the *main pure one* has to light a torch and incense at the approach to the *sacred place* (Egyptian *bu djeser*). He then opens the sanctuary that houses a small shrine containing the little image of Amun-Ra, by breaking a seal on a cord, followed by *the opening of the face* (to light) and *the sight of the god*, where the officiant has to prostrate himself, kissing the ground, before making morning-meal offerings. Crucially, now, comes the *hymn to Amun*. Words are another material to be offered. With another offering of incense, the *main pure one* says the words for *entering the temple* and *entering the sanctuary of the god*, before opening the small shrine itself, prostrating himself, and repeating the words to be recited at *the opening of the face* and *sight of the god*. By this stage, repetition of phrases would be creating chant-like rhythms within the incense and dim torchlight, a powerful psychological combination. A further offering of incense ushers in a whole series of hymns to Amun, culminating in the core rite of "offering What is Right," the primary act of kingship, cementing order in the created world. Incense can then be offered to the *nine deities*, a collective expression for all the named forces accompanying the focal deity in this particular place. The practical task of the morning follows: washing (purifying) the image, clothing it with four sacred cloths of different colors or perhaps more importantly different textures, and anointing the image and applying eye paint, green (copper ore) and black (the lead ore galena, in a preparation like Arabic kohl). To return the image to the small shrine, the main *pure one* strews sand and performs final rites of purification and censing.

Staff in offering spaces

In both popular and scientific imagination, a recurrent orientalist prejudice casts ancient Egypt as a theocracy, a state ruled by priests. In direct contradiction of this, ancient writings provide explicit evidence of a rota system where temple staff served a month at a time (Roth 1991). In the third millennium, staff were divided into five *watches* (Egyptian *sau*); after 2000 BC, the number was reduced to four, each then providing staff for three of the twelve months in the year. On one papyrus from Lahun, names and titles are recorded for all men in each *watch*; each month, one *watch* would have to deliver enough staff for the temple to function—not everyone in the *watch* would have to serve duty every time its month came. In this way, the system could allow flexibly for the busy lives of men generally engaged in other activities, either service for other institutions or managing or manually working on their own fields or other means of procuring food or income. The rota system itself shows that the idea of a priestly caste is foreign to ancient Egypt. Most temple staff were not priests in the sense of individuals trained in a special body of knowledge; at Lahun, the only full-time staff member seems to have been the temple accountant. By the rota of *watches*, far more people would have been included within the circle of *temple staff* at all levels, undermining any separation of *secular* from *religious* spheres that we might expect. There is not even a single word corresponding to the English *priest*: the two titles most often translated *priest* are *wa'b*, literally "pure (for entering a sanctuary)," encountered previously in the daily offering liturgy, and *hem-netjer*, "agent/servant of the god." The word *hem* denoted a force, including a human being, that enabled physical intervention on behalf of another: manual workers were called *hem* of the king in the period 2000–1700 BC, and when Horus fights Seth in a narrative copied in 1250 BC, the aggressive actions are said to be carried out by the *hem* of Horus or *hem* of Seth (summarizing Berlev 1972, 33–41). The term was appropriate for those who had to move material to and from the *netjer*; the same term was used for staff serving the cult of the blessed dead, where the *hem ka*, "servant of the ka-spirit," is the main title in written sources from third to first millennia BC. In centers of cult for kings, the term *wa'b nesut*, "pure one of the king," was most often used. A third term is often found, *it-netjer*, "father of the god," also used for father-in-law of a king in many periods (Blumenthal 1987). No written sources explain how this term came to be used for temple staff or which tasks distinguished the *it-netjer* from the other titleholders; perhaps care for the image was considered analogous to the care of a father for a child.

In the name lists at Lahun and other sources, the temple staff comprises men. Women appear in formal positions within sacred space most often in the role of music provider, as the revivifying force of Hathor, goddess of the sensuous. In the singular, the third-millennium BC sources use the term "god's servant of Hathor," while the second-millennium sources have *chantress*, replaced from 800 BC by *sistrum-player* (Quirke 1999). Since depictions of *chantresses* often show them shaking the sistrum, the metal rhythm marker strongly associated with Hathor, it seems that all three terms denote the providers of music in sacred service at each period (Figure 3.11). The corresponding male term *chanter* is less often found, perhaps because *chantress* and *sistrum-player* are designations for almost all wealthier women, specifically those whose husbands held official positions in temple, palace, or regional administration. In the collective, the Egyptian word *khener* denotes the musicians, particularly women who sang and provided music at rituals and festivals. It is not known how often *khener* groups were called to serve; a Lahun papyrus of 1800 BC shows that the rota system also applied to singers and dancers enlisted for festivals at a temple there (Collier and Quirke 2006, 101–104, UC32191). Staff of larger temples might have included a permanent group of musicians. Around 1800 BC, some women were designated member of the khener, beside their name, their main identity for eternity (Nord 1981). However, the term does not necessarily indicate a full-time indication.

There are also examples of women with the title *god's servant* for goddesses other than Hathor, though these are relatively a small proportion across the surviving written sources. In the third millennium BC, the most prominent is the *god's servant of Neit*, Neit being the main goddess at Sau (Sais) in the western Delta, with a major cult center at Mennefer and later at Esna in southern Upper Egypt. After 1550 BC, in the process of reunification of Egypt under the Theban king Ahmes, a new position is created for his wife Ahmes Nefertari at the Amun temple at Karnak. According to a remarkable inscription immortalizing the legal act, her (inherited?) title *second god's servant of Amun* was transferred to a new position, with supporting agricultural estates, the *god's wife of Amun*. In the following centuries, this is sometimes associated with another leading temple title for women at Karnak, the *worshipper of the god* (often translated *god's adoratrice of Amun*), perhaps specifically lead singer in the chanting of hymns. After 700 BC, the women in this position played a major role in cult and, apparently, in stability and legitimacy of the kingship, as the holder was daughter of the reigning king, and adopted as successor a daughter of the following ruler (Robins 1993). After Assyrian invasions in 671 and 661 BC, the kings of Napata (*Twenty-fifth Dynasty* of Egypt) lost control of Egypt; their god's wife Amenirdis then adopted as successor Nitiqret, daughter of Psamtek ruler of Sau (Sais), then emerging under Assyrian protection as the new king of all

Figure 3.11   A woman in the family of Sennefer, mayor of Waset, shakes sistrum and beads with counterpoise, in the role of the goddess Hathor, bringing life to the sacred space of the family underground burial chamber. Waset, about 1400 BC. © Gianluca Miniaci.

Egypt. Again, an inscription that immortalizes the adoption has survived, record-ing the ceremonial progress from Sau to Waset. The roles of these individuals in political history might be read as exceptions in the surviving record. Yet they keep our attention focussed on the prominence of women throughout sacred space in practice. As much as any other social domain, the gendering of temple ground may be variable, in ways negotiated by a wider population than may appear on the written and pictorial record we select for analysis.

Kingship, temple offerings, and temple staff: in practice

According to the writings and depictions summarized previously, at least one person would enter the sanctuary located at the back of the temple, open the doors of the shrine concealing the image that enabled the deity to be present, and present offerings. Temple depictions regularly show the king alone in this role, but the geographical spread of contemporary temples with these depictions means that a single person could not make offerings at all temples every day. Therefore, the initiation of the king into the lethally pure space of the divine must have been shared, to enable others to substitute for him at each temple where offerings from king to deity were being depicted. The question, how many, remains to be researched for each period. Few of the highest staff held distinctive titles in earlier periods, and the rare examples occur first at the palace and then at the temple centers most closely connected with kingship: the Greatest of Seers at Iunu, Greatest of Directors of Craftsmen at Mennefer, and Greatest of the Five at Khemenu (Grajetzki 2000, 110–111). In later periods, similarly specific titles appear for the highest positions in a series of other regional temples, but, unexpectedly, never at Waset. The temple of the creator as Amun-Ra at Karnak in Waset is the largest of the well-preserved temples and accordingly the place most regularly identified as a center of priestly as opposed to royal power in popular histories of Egypt. Yet here, the most important official held no special or ancient designation, being known simply as First God's Servant of Amun.

In other respects, too, the evidence for relations between kingship and the Amun-Ra temple contradicts general assumptions about *priesthood* in practice. The Karnak temples expanded under the most powerful kings of Egypt, and there is no evidence that the temple staff became a separate political force. After the New Kingdom, the kingship of Egypt was taken up by a military family of west Saharan (*Libyan*) nomadic origins, ruling from a new royal center in the east Delta, Djanet (Tanis); relatives of the Djanet kings took the title First God's Servant of Amun, some adding kingly titles and some moving on to become kings at Djanet. Modern historians often portrayed this change as a *takeover* of the Egyptian state by the Amun priesthood. However, it seems more accurate to see it as almost the reverse: a military takeover using the prestige of the Amun temple to legitimate the unprecedented new separation of powers between northern and southern branches of the new ruling family (Jansen-Winkeln 2006). Despite struggles involving military men at Waset, and despite the evident prestige of the city and its great concentration of temple architecture, the northern kingship seems always to have remained primary.

For occasions when the highest officeholder at the temple was absent or where a temple complex contained numerous shrines to service, additional substitutes would be required. However, for these daily offering tasks, the personnel needed to be physically and ethically clean during temple service, not to have sacred knowledge. None of the regularly attested temple positions previously mentioned—*god's servant*, *god's father*, and *pure one*—can readily be identified as a group of priestly initiates with special knowledge. The ancient Egyptian economy of sacred knowledge does not seem to match the expectations of modern categories and needs to be approached now within its dominant setting, the world of kingship.

Kingship, initiation, and holders of sacred knowledge

Another widespread title, not always so closely linked with the temple, was Bearer of the Festival Book. Rare Middle Kingdom copies of festival book-rolls are written in hieroglyphs, on one example combined with scenes comprising depictions of schematic figures performing rituals. The Bearer of the Festival Book would have had to know how to read hieroglyphic script, as well as the cursive handwriting script in daily use for letters and accountancy. Possibly, then, the Bearer of the Festival Book stands at the center of the history of sacred knowledge. If there were knowledge brokers in ancient Egypt, closer to concepts of clergy in world religions today, the most important would have served not at the regional temples of deities, but at the centers of kingship, perhaps above all at the court of the king. From the Old Kingdom to the Late Period, the royal court included one or more holders of the title Chief Bearer of the Festival Book; the tombs of two of these contained an exceptional range of afterlife literature (Sesenebnef late Middle Kingdom; Padiamenipet, period of Napatan rule to early Twenty-sixth Dynasty). Distribution of sacred writings provides clues for the ways in which sacred knowledge of sacred space might have circulated and how far across the ancient society.

The principal visual and written sources cluster around the ruler, particularly at periods when the tomb of the ruler is decorated. From these, Jan Assmann and Joachim Quack have outlined how the ruler was distinct in having special knowledge of the workings of the solar circuit, in the manner of an initiate into secrets of life (Quack 2002). The key Egyptian word is *bes*, "to initiate"; although it may have sounded similar, this verb is not linked by ancient writings to the slightly differently spelled word *bes*, "fetus/neonate," discussed in Chapter 2. The act of *bes* (initiating) revolves around the person of the *nesut*, "king," between temple of the creator and palace of the king, as if these constitute magnetic poles in the force field of life tensions. In formal terms, within the written and visual record of tomb and temple, there is only one priest in Egypt, the ruler as priest of the sun-god, the creator. Oleg Berlev drew from written and visual sources a picture of ancient Egyptian conceptions of rule as two suns, both rulers, the *netjer 'aa*, "elder god," in the heaven and the *netjer nefer*, "younger god," on earth (Berlev 2000). With this difference in his very being, the ruler remained throughout ancient Egyptian history the primary holder of a sacred knowledge, disseminated across all regions by practical substitution of ruler by the main "readers" of the localized temples. The life of the country was maintained in offering by a double movement of (i) generation of sacred books and (ii) preservation of rituals. Both tasks would be appropriate to a Chief Bearer of the Festival Book and might have been carried out at an institution attached to the palace of the ruler, the House of Life. In Egyptology, the House of Life has come to be seen as a knowledge center equivalent to a European-style university. Such an equation encourages appreciation of its centrality, though at the risk of misreading the specific cultural and social context, and in particular the specific relation to temple *of the creator* and palace *of the king*. In the Ptolemaic Period, every temple may have had its own House of Life, but this is not clearly attested earlier, and the later versions may have been primarily for annual Osiris rituals of rebirth, as part of the Osirification of temple ritual throughout Egypt. The only example of a House of Life attested in architectural remains in the archaeological record is at Akhetaten, where a mudbrick structure with bricks stamped in hieroglyphs "House of Life" stands equidistant from the Aten temple and the official House of the King (Pendlebury 1951, pl. 19). The palace of the ruler may also have been the original home of the principal generator of material production in the sustenance of deities through offerings: the House of Gold, where the sacred images were produced in precious metals. Again, later each temple had its own House of Gold, and the precise history of the spread of the institution remains to be charted. For earlier periods, the constellation *palace—House of Life—House of Gold* perhaps provided a sacred institutional kernel that generated the hegemonic core and its models across the country. All of this landscape seems far from the way in which we have become used to writing about kingship, priesthood, and temples of ancient Egypt.

Formalizing Sacred Time: Festival, Feast, and Foundation

Festival: not necessarily carnival

The English word *festival* implies a certain scale of celebration, public as well as private, with a larger audience as part of the special occasion. Such gatherings are recorded for ancient Egypt, but did not necessarily always occur at every *festival*. There are two Egyptian words for markedly sacred days: *heb* usually translated *festival*, for select days occurring on a cyclical basis, for example, every month, season, or year, and *kha'* literally *appearance*, a special time at which a divine force usually concealed would *appear* outside the usual space, as in divine procession (Redford 1967). The best-preserved monumental temple architecture follows the line of such an appearance of a portable shrine containing the image of the deity, as it was taken from sanctuary to another location. Any longer distance in the Nile Valley or Delta would have required sailing. Accordingly, some festivals are called *khenet*, "sailings," and the main cults had their own festival ships with images evoking the garlanded head of the deity at prow and stern. From 1500 BC onward, depictions indicate that the portable shrine to carry the image of a deity regularly took the form of one of these special boats. The model for the procession and indeed for the concept of *appearance* may have been the journeys of the king; *appearance* could in fact have marked any movement that brought the king into view, even within the palace, and the same word *kha'* was used for the headgear worn on these occasions—as much the plainer headbands or diadems as the more substantial crowns. The distinctive feature of kingship—of both sun-god in the sky and mortal king on earth—was the protective force depicted as cobra rearing with swollen neck, ready to spit fire against any potential enemy. This cobra motif had the name *ia'ret*, "rearing (goddess)," and several different goddesses were said to have played this protective role, the feminine complement to the creator sun-god and to his kingship (Roberts 1995) (Figure 3.12).

Figure 3.12 Limestone stela with depiction of a portable shrine in the form of a sacred boat, being carried by temple staff on procession at a festival. From Gebtyu (Koptos), about 1300 BC. F. Petrie, Koptos, Quaritch, London 1895.

At festivals involving processions, inspired in part by kingship ritual at the palace, larger numbers of people may have participated, or had greater opportunity to participate, in the wider spaces in the broad open courts of a temple or outside its enclosure walls. One of the grandest images of a festival is the series of scenes adorning the great colonnade that extended the temple of Amun at Luxor in front of the courtyard and sanctuary constructed under King Amenhotep III, about 1375 BC (Bell 1997). The scenes, carved under his successors, show the collective celebration accompanying the procession of boats of Amun, Mut, and Khons from the main temple at Karnak along the Nile to Luxor, at the Ipet Festival, in the second month of each year. Here, the public dimension of festival that we expect is foregrounded, while the core rituals and meaning of the festival are not covered; most often, the surviving writings and depictions for festivals give the reverse picture, with details of rituals, but no explicit comment on the scale of participation.

Festivals at the lahun kingship temple (1800 BC)

Indirect information can be gleaned from a fragmented papyrus document from Lahun listing the absence and presence of dancers and singers at festivals for one year around 1800 BC (Collier and Quirke 2006, 101–104). Few monuments with festival lists or scenes survive from 2000 to 1500 BC, making this papyrus one of the most important single surviving sources for festivals in the period. The singers and dancers are grouped, like other temple staff, by membership of four *watches*. On the rota system (see section "Staff in Offering-Spaces"), the watch usually provided new personnel each month, but these staff serve in consecutive months; the existence of the document itself may reflect the need for separate accounts to cover this specialized staff group. Although the list is heavily damaged, it seems that each watch provided two or three dancers and two singers. The singers have Egyptian names, and their ethnicity is not noted, whereas the dancers are either Asiatic (watches 1 and 2) or Medjay, that is, nomads from the eastern deserts of southern Upper Egypt and Nubia (watch 3; watch 4 data lost). In itself, the small number of dancers and singers does not mean there could not have been a large public. Yet when a New Year *festival* has only two singers, we should consider the real possibility that *heb festival* might be a more closed and intimate occasion. The ancient Egyptian term may focus more on mechanisms of accompanying, and ensuring success for, a cycle in its repeating moments, than on the audience numbers we associate with our words for festival and celebration.

The Lahun list records the following festivals throughout the year:

Flood Month 1	Opening of the Year; beginning [...]; jubilation
Flood Month 2	Strewing sand; Cloth of Khakheperra (= King Senusret II)
Flood Month 3	Night offerings of receiving the river; receiving the river; half-moon; raising the sky
Flood Month 4	Sailing of Hathor; *heb* festival of Sokar
Emergence Month 1	Nehebkau; bearing the field
Emergence Month 2	*heb* festival of Sokar; hauling Sokar; full moon; half-moon
Emergence Month 3	Sailing of the land
Emergence Month 4	Full moon; rejuvenation of the year
Summer Month 1	Full moon
Summer Month 2	*heb* festival of the ruler (reading uncertain?)
Summer Month 3	*No entries preserved*
Summer Month 4	*No entries preserved*

Between Flood Month 1 and Emergence Month 2, a *day of butchery for the god* and *day of anointing the gods* were also celebrated. Another fragmentary papyrus from Lahun preserves other festival headings for a name list, but perhaps not for singers and dancers (Luft 1992, 115–117, Berlin 10282). Among festivals in Flood Month 1, it records three known from many other sources, Wag (day 18), Tekh (day 20), and the Great Procession (day 22), and Flood Month 3, day 20 has a festival called "*heden*-plant of Hathor" (*heden* may denote an item made from plants, perhaps a fan or broom; the significance is unknown). The difference between the two documents is typical of the scattered written record across the three millennia, warning us against merging them into a national festival calendar. Each source has its own context and reason for existence, not always as clear as in the Lahun attendance lists. Moreover, many festivals in the lists might have been celebrated only in one locality and for a short period; the *Cloth of Khakheperra* could well have been anchored in renewal of the embalming rituals on an anniversary specific to that one king, Senusret II, buried at Lahun. As long as source context is kept in mind, the written record can still help us chart seasonal patterns and shed light on the dominant concerns raised in the ancient Egyptian festival year. Other written sources give *Cloth* as the name of the second month, when the *Cloth of Khakheperra* was celebrated at Lahun; accordingly, we can revisit the Lahun evidence and interpret the *Cloth* festival as local version of a recurrent ritual performance at other places, perhaps across the whole country.

Clearly, a dominant local concern for the Lahun lists is the cult of King Senusret II. Yet other major days would also have connected the entire country, the Opening of the Year, and perhaps all the lunar festivals may have affected everyone. The festival of the earth god Sokar is also found at other times and places across Egypt; its occurrence in month 4 of Flood links it to the moment in the agricultural cycle when the floodwaters would have almost resided, revealing the silt cover of the fields for the new season of sowing. This crucial moment for growing grain to feed the population attracted a series of rites later called *ka-her-ka* (in Coptic Egyptian Khoiak), "abundance on abundance," or perhaps "*ka*-soul upon *ka*-soul" as a festival for all *ka*-souls (Eaton 2006). The rites culminated in the emergence of a new order on the first day of the second season, called Nehebkau, "yoking the *ka*-souls," when Horus god of kingship took up rule over a new period of life. Finally, the festival names refer to sailings and to goddesses: these are two features common to most later festival sources and demonstrate the central role of the female divine and of the river and its channels in the sacred timescape over the whole floodplain.

Festival lists in monumental inscriptions

The main sources for festivals celebrated throughout the year are as follows (summarizing from Schott 1950): (i) 2500–2200 BC inscriptions in temples at places for kingship cult, echoed in offering chapels over tombs of courtiers—these sources are concentrated in the Mennefer cemeteries (Giza, Abu Ghurab, Abusir, Saqqara) and so may have special connections with the court of the king and the deities of the Mennefer region—and (ii) 1500–1150 BC inscriptions of kings in temples for deities, echoed in offering chapels over tombs of temple staff and officials at Waset (Thebes), again with local coloring. Among the fullest lists are those from the reigns of Thutmes III (1450 BC) for Amun and local deities at Abu, and for Amun in Waset at Ipetsut (Karnak), and of Ramses III (1175 BC) in Waset at the temple to his own cult Khnemetneheh (Madinat Habu).

The most exceptional nonroyal festival calendar, echoing the kingship inscriptions, survives in the offering chapel of a temple staff member called Neferhotep, about 1300 BC (Table 3.1). The main sources for 1500–1150 BC can be summarized as a calendar, keeping the separate monuments in view to avoid the impression that the tabulation itself is ancient. Names for the months survive in other sources,

Table 3.1   The festival calendar in the principal New Kingdom sources

Month	Month name	Day, festival name, source
Flood 1	Djehuty	1 Opening the year (Thutmes III Abu)
		17 Eve of Wag (Neferhotep)
		18–19 Wag (Neferhotep, Ramses III)
		22 Great Procession of Osiris (Ramses III)
Flood 2	Pa-n-ipet	15/18 start-day of the festival of Ipet, lasting 11 to 15 days (TIII Abu, RIII)
Flood 3	Hathor	
Flood 4	Ka-her-ka	1 Hathor (Ramses III)
		18–30 Osiris rites: 22 plowing earth, 25 goddesses, 26 Sokar, 30 raising djed-pillar (Thutmes III Ipetsut, Neferhotep, Ramses III)
Emergence 1	Ta-ʻaabet	1 Nehebkau (TIII Ipetsut, Neferhotep, Ramses III)
		22 Rearing cobra/Heryt (Neferhotep, Ramses III)
		29–30 sailings of Bast/Shesmetet (TIII Ipetsut)
		29 Raising the willow (Ramses III)
Emergence 2	Mekher	1 Anubis (Ramses III)
		30 Raising of Heaven day 2 (Ramses III)
Emergence 3	Pa-n-Amenhotep	30 Entering Heaven day 2 (Ramses III)
Emergence 4	Renenutet	4 Bast (Neferhotep, Ramses III)
Summer 1	Khons	1 Renenutet (Neferhotep, Ramses III)
		11 Procession of Min (Ramses III)
Summer 2	Pa-n-inet	New moon Valley Festival
Summer 3	Ipip	28 Emergence of Sopdet (Thutmes III Abu)
Summer 4	Birth of Raʻ	30 Eve of Opening of the Year (Neferhotep)
"5 days over the year"	1 Birth of Osiris	
	2 Birth of Horus	
	3 Birth of Seth	
	4 Birth of Isis	
	5 Birth of Nebthut	

and are also given here, as they derive from principal festivals, showing how important they could be, in at least formal time frames for life. The eve of a festival day might play a critical part in the rites, and so sometimes a month name relates to a festival on the first day of the following month. Month names also focus on festivals that would center on Waset/Thebes. Amenhotep (Emergence Month 3) refers to the cult of Amenhotep I, known from images, depictions, and ritual manuscripts to have received offerings at Waset centuries after his death, as an enduring localized force of divine kingship. Ipet and *inet* "Valley" (Flood Month 2 and Summer Month 2) are festivals around processions of the main image of Amun at Ipetsut (Karnak). The use of these localized events for month names across the country indicates the national impact of Waset. Major surviving monumental architecture must always be set in proportion to its time, and there is a danger in overestimating the importance of Waset, simply because its temples, of sandstone, have been less heavily quarried than temples at Mennefer, or Delta sites such as Iunu. Nevertheless, it is equally crucial not to underestimate the impact of the city; Ipetsut is still one of the largest temple sites anywhere in the world, it would have been on the same monumental level as Mennefer and Iunu, and in the eleventh to tenth centuries BC it served explicitly as a model for the new royal Residence at Djanet (Tanis) at the northeastern Delta fringes. The month names confirm the extensive role of Waset and its main deity Amun across Egypt from the late second millennium BC onward.

Major new festivals include Ipet and Valley, but several features in the earlier Lahun papyri recur even in this summary of inscriptions. Dominant rites include the Opening of the Year, Wag, and *ka-her-ka* in the Flood season. Goddesses are prominent in their sailings at the start of the sowing season. Perhaps the most important item to note, though, is the place of the Emergence of Sopdet so far from the New Year. For the season, names and many of the major festivals seem firmly linked in the agricultural cycle, anchored in the path of the earth around the sun. Yet, the New Year day in that solar year is the summer rising of Sopdet, the star Sirius, now visible for the first time again ahead of the sun, and heralding the annual rising of the Nile floodwaters. The gap between Opening of the Year and Emergence of Sopdet is a reminder that all these festivals in the official calendar, even when agricultural, were tied not to the solar year, but to the moving year. This poses a basic problem for interpreting even some of the most familiar inscribed objects. In the sixth century BC, faience water flasks are inscribed with invocations of deities to *Open a Good Year*. Presumably, the major deities were being asked to ensure a perfect flood, not too high, not too low, at the late summer rising of the Nile. Yet, at the time these flasks were made, the official calendar of kingship would celebrate New Year, the Opening of the Year, several months apart from the actual Nile flood rise, when divine help might most be needed to guarantee plenty and avoid famine. Was the water in the flask scooped from the Nile at the New Year of the official calendar, under the magnetic force of kingship? Or was the water taken at the moment of the annual flood itself, Hapy (Figure 1.3) during the physical experience of inundation, when Sopdet rose again as the star Sirius in advance of the sun, for the first time since the summer drought began several months earlier? (Figure 3.13).

In general, it is said that there is no absolute dating system in ancient Egypt beyond the reign of the king: as each king came to the throne, the counting of years started again with his Regnal Year 1—there is no AH or BC/AD point to count all time. Yet in practice, there is a longer cycle, set by the official calendar. For efficiency, the year calendar was rounded down to 365 days from the 365 ¼ days that the earth actually takes to circle the sun. A year of twelve thirty-day months, with five end days *over the year*, gave a perfect tool for calculating time. Over a slow cycle of 1460 years, the official *year* in which reigns were counted would slip back against the solar year by one day every four years, ten days every forty years, and a thirty-day month every 120 years, until 1460 years later the two calendars would appear synchronized again for a few years, while the cycle moved relentlessly on backward. In the written record, the regnal year took precedence, as if a divine creation that could still serve as anchor for order, and still generate the desired impact on

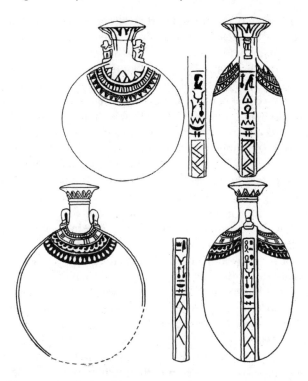

Figure 3.13   Faience water flasks with inscriptions invoking Horus and Thoth (above) and Ptah, Sekhmet, and Amun (below), for the Opening of the Year. From the town site at Natahut (modern Tell el Yahidiya), about 550 BC. After W. Petrie, *Hyksos and Israelite Cities*, British School of Egyptian Archaeology, London, 1906, pl. 21.

flood, sowing, and harvest, even when the regnal year Flood was moving through the harvest months and drought of summer. This observance of festivals out of time is one of the most remarkable features of ancient Egyptian practice. The agricultural rites may have continued domestically as more immediately relevant practices. At the time of the Neferhotep festival calendar, the solar and regnal years would be more closely in harmony—the wandering regnal year cycle rejoined the solar cycle around 1320 BC. At most other periods, for at least two-thirds of this history, the king would have performed, for example, crucial rites against plague through the terminal *five days over the year* not when needed against high summer flood, but during the seasons of flood or sowing. This is an astonishing exercise of power over time.

Offerings at festivals: written evidence

Inscriptions and depictions give the most detailed evidence for festival offerings at least at a formal level. From 2500 to 2200 BC, great lists appear in spaces for offering to kings (Barta 1968). The earliest example of a great list excavated in its original location is inscribed on the south and north walls of the sanctuary in the pyramid temple of King Pepy II (2200 BC), like a mirror projecting into eternity the acts of offering intended to be performed in the space between those walls. In later periods, this long offering list (Barta Type A) is found in nonroyal offering places, and in both royal and nonroyal, it is sometimes accompanied by a second list (Type B). Other combinations of the two lists are found throughout the second and into the first millennium BC, indicating a continually used frame for the performance of offering rituals. One papyrus, written for a man named Sedekh perhaps after 2000 BC, refers to the long offering list as "this festival-book of fixed offerings" (Egyptian *hebyt ten net imenyt*). This implies that the offerings are not the items presented to king/deity/blessed dead every day, but the special accumulations of material to be given on marked days (see following section "Feasting and Offering in the Archaeological Record"). From about 2000 BC, a shorter list in temples for kings (Type C) introduces a range of new entries (8 out of 22 in the earliest example, for King Nebhepetra Mentuhotep). Inscriptions in the temple for King Sety I at Abdju preserve the words that would have been recited with each offering. Under King Amenhotep III, this list appears in nonroyal offering chapels, sometimes lengthening again (Khamhat has some 60 items). There are also special series of offerings (Type D) for the processions of Amun at Karnak (boat-shrine of Amenhotep I) and in the Valley Festival from Karnak to Deir al-Bahari on the West Bank (Amun sanctuary in temple for Hatshepsut). Within this intricate interlocking network of festival offering traditions, we are fortunate to have many of the words to be recited for each item in the great lists at the start of their written tradition, inscribed within pyramids of kings (2400–2100 BC) (*Pyramid Texts*). Many of these compositions for recital are also found on later monuments and items of burial equipment, not by empty repetition or aesthetic archaism, but in the continual renewal of the ritual performances in which they were used (cf. Assmann 1990).

Feasting and offering in the archaeological record

Festivals are prominent in the inscriptional record, and some festivals are also depicted. The Valley Festival reunited not only Amun and Hathor but the people of Waset with their deceased; in chapels over burial places, wall paintings show offerings of great quantities of flowers from the gardens of Amun and accompanying banquets with images of joy and feasting, sometimes to excess. It is rather harder to trace this banqueting in the archaeological record. Vast heaps of first-millennium BC miniature offering vessels mark the destination of processions to the tomb of King Djer (about 3000 BC) at Abdju, identified after 2000 BC as the tomb of the god Osiris, king of the underworld. From the period of Djer himself, large enclosures for the funeral rites may have witnessed massive feasts, on the evidence of beer jars found at the sites. For other sites at other times, the evidence has either not been found or not been recorded. At the offering chapels of Waset, family gatherings might not have left enough traces, although future more careful excavation might reveal more. Among temple sites, only large deposits of pottery vessels at Hutwaret (Tell el-Daba) help capture the moment at which people joined in feasting anciently. There, though, the practice may be imported from the north; the city of Hutwaret is at the northeastern Delta frontier, the deposits date to the period 1650–1550 BC when foreign kings ruled there, and the best published parallels for such deposits in sacred precincts are from west Asia, not Upper Egypt (Müller 2006) (Figure 3.14).

In sum, there is still little evidence on the ground for large-scale participation in festivals, in the form of debris left over after eating and drinking. This may be contrasted with the more substantial deposits of votive offerings, a variety of items offered in sacred places as material prayers or thanks to divine forces. Many items, though always doubtless a minority, were inscribed, identifying the deity and sometimes a general wish such as life or long age. Sacred material of metal was often cached, presumably too sacred to be melted down for recycling. Earlier deposits preserve sets of temple equipment such as copper alloy vases used in offering rituals (e.g., Akhetaten, 1350 BC). After 700 BC, votive offerings of inscribed metal figures of deities became more common, and these dominate the later deposits on sacred sites, into the late first millennium BC. Far the greatest known is the cachette at Ipetsut (Karnak), famous in Egyptology for its large number of stone sculptures of kings, officials, and deities. The deposit also contained literally

Figure 3.14   Deposits of pottery vessels from festival processions to the tomb of King Djer of the First Dynasty, identified in second to first millennium BC as tomb of Osiris. The sacred space is oriented toward the great western desert valley, visible as a gap in the background cliffs. © Ute Effland.

thousands of images of deities in faience and bronze, as well as wood, less well preserved in the waterlogged annually flooded ground (Coulon and Jambon n.d.).

Places dedicated to the goddess Hathor attracted a wide range of inscribed and uninscribed objects connected with fertility: wooden phalli, bright blue-glazed vessels and beads, figurines of naked women (fertility figurines), and textiles woven with beads or, in select examples, painted with images of the dedicator(s), often women, before the goddess (Pinch 1993). Images and inscriptions suggest that many, if not all, express prayers for, or in thanks for, safe birth. The hue and texture of blue-glazed faience of many of these offerings may be part of this focus on well-being in the specific context of birth, perhaps seeking to draw on the generative powers of water, creating and supporting plant life.

Founding a temple

In the archaeological record, the primary evidence for the initial conception of a temple-building project is the foundation deposit, comprised of varying types of material according to period and location (Figure 3.15 and Table 3.2, summarizing Weinstein 2001). The contents of later deposits focus on materials and processes of construction, echoing the depictions on temple walls, where the king receives assistance from the divine embodiment of writing (Egyptian *Seshat*) to mark out the ground with measuring rod and cord, before laying the first brick. Earlier examples contain food and dishes for meals, whether for the initial celebration rituals or as eternal motor of sustenance or both. Certainly, the construction and maintenance of monumental sacred architecture would have required vast resources, and the daily offerings of food and drink at any temple needed great farming estates as the foundation of offering cult. From 2400 BC, the fragmented accounts papyri survive for kingship temples on the desert edge at Abusir. These record an intricate web of interlocking estates, requiring elaborate calculations for the theoretical and practical route taken by the grain, flax, and other produce of the estate fields. The complexity arises from the number of different institutions, and the practice of *wedjeb khet*—literally, turning round the material things to be offered. Every example of sacred architecture implies offerings, which in turn imply a supporting estate.

Table 3.2　Main features of foundation deposits, summarized for six periods

Old Kingdom	Food offerings, pottery or stone vessels, sometimes grindstones
Middle Kingdom	Food offerings, pottery or stone vessels, sometimes grindstones, model tools, inscribed plaques inside mudbricks
Dynasty 18	Pottery vessels, tools, ointment jars, beads, food offerings, model tools, miniature pottery, inscribed plaques (not within mudbricks)
Dynasties 19–20	Standardized mass-produced faience miniature models of offerings and plaques with name of king; longer inscriptions on stone/faience
Dynasties 21–22	Small plaques of copper/bronze, faience, and model pottery vessels
Late Period	Miniature inscribed stone and metal plaques, model mudbricks, pottery, rectangular green faience plaques, resin and ore samples

(a)

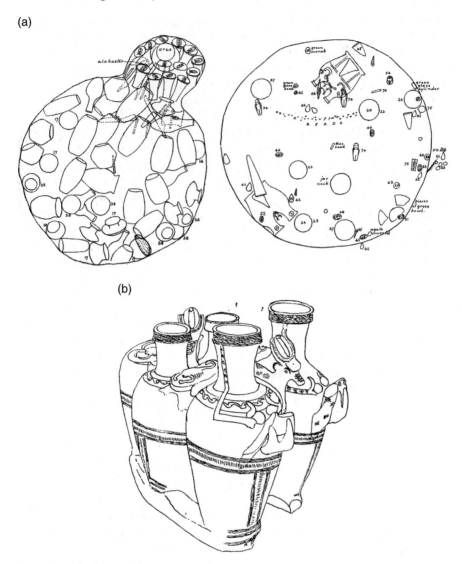

(b)

Figure 3.15   (a) Two of the series of foundation deposits securing the ground of the temple to Min and Isis, constructed by King Thutmes III (about 1450 BC) at Gebtyu (Qift); (b) besides the regular provision of pottery for food and drink, one vessel has an unparalleled form, with central motif of cow and scorpions to the side, indicating variations in foundation rituals; (a) and (b) from W. Petrie, *Koptos*, London 1895.

If anyone wished to construct a new, larger sanctuary or, more decisively, to increase the offerings made at a sacred place, then, within the finite resources of the Nile Valley, there were two choices: either land reclamation or redistribution of produce. The *wedjeb khet* is the pragmatic second response. When Akhenaten created an entire new city for the sun-god creator, Ra in the form of the solar sphere Aten, he would have had to redirect the resource web of the country. Since his reform was reversed after his death, and his city dismantled, he appears in the later Egyptian record as a criminal, or is removed. Yet his crime was to exclude all deities and offering cults other than his own, in his kingship and its expenditure—the act of redistribution of lands in itself was regular kingship practice.

Large-scale diversion of revenue in each reign can be seen in action in a unique record of the offerings during the reign of Ramses III, copied onto a magnificent papyrus book-roll, the longest surviving, at the start of the reign of his successor Ramses IV (Grandet 1994, Papyrus Harris). The document has often been used to show the resources of the king being lost to the temples, but in fact, nearly all the donations by the king are for his own temple, Khnemetneheh (Madinat Habu), and his cult around Egypt and Nubia, not for the temples of gods in themselves. The great temple of Amun at Karnak receives only a tiny proportion of the new staff and offerings assigned to Khnemetneheh. There, a whole new kingship cult comes into existence on a majestic scale that can still be seen at the site in the sandstone architecture, one of the best-preserved temples in Egypt. Exceptionally, for Ramses III, we can see the process of diversion in action, thanks to the inscriptions of his commissioner, the Head Keeper of Documents Penpata, sent in Year 15 of the reign to *swa'b*, "purify," temples of any flaw and *sedjeser*, "hallow," them by reorganizing staff and, by implication, staffing resources including estates. The inscriptions identify the process as *sipty wer*, "the great review" (Spalinger 1991). Ironically, it included a standard clause to *khu meki*, "exempt and protect," the temples under review. From 2650 to 2000 BC, inscribed copies of decrees by kings survive at temples from Gebtyu (Qift) in Upper Egypt to the Mennefer pyramid fields. Evidently, an eternal stone version of an exemption decree was needed against the continual reviews and accompanying redistributions for new royal initiatives. Probably, like a city wall, the exemption decrees in stone did help deflect minor infringements by the perennial stream of royal officials moving up and down the country and perhaps in regional disputes between neighboring estates, including temple estates. However, they probably could not withstand periodic initiatives that involved decree by the king affecting all temples of Upper and Lower Egypt, as in the recorded examples of a "great review" under Merenptah and Ramses III and the equally major transformations under Amenhotep III, Akhenaten, and Tutankhamun. Any new king would require a place of offering for his own cult, as the latest in the series of cult places for the reigning king. Larger structures and greater offerings, as for Ramses II and III, imply more massive reform affecting the whole country. In a broad sense, the architectural history of ancient Egypt is also its economic and social history.

For every major temple construction project, then, a still more massive economic enterprise had first to be installed, diverting resources from other offering places. Probably, for kingship temples, the majority of the resources came from the temples of previous kings: archaeology has shown how each king focused construction work on his own temple, while temples for kings of the previous generations fell steadily farther out of sight. The Abusir papyri effectively chart the same history: the temple equipment is carefully inspected by each incoming month of staff, and sometimes repaired, but maintenance also needs resources. The most dramatic example of decline is at the greatest architectural site of all, the Giza pyramids. Here, the third, smaller pyramid complex for king Menkaura (about 2550 BC) was maintained as a place of offerings for well over a century after the death of the king, but evidently with diminishing external support, for they turned the temple into a production site of its own. Out of the sculpture originally intended a focus of offerings, they cut small stone vases, of a type found in contemporary burials of varying wealth in the area (Kemp 2006, 208–209). Perhaps it was enough, in extreme need, to keep a reduced offering cult for at least one image of the king, sufficient to feed both the image and, after one more reversion, the temple staff. In their daily sustenance, the individuals on rota service at temples would be locked into rhythms of intervention and indifference from the top, on a long-wave history with impact across the country, interwoven with regional and local agendas of overlapping and conflicting interests and resistance.

CHAPTER 4

Chaos and Life: Forces of Creation and Destruction

⌐⌐⌐⌐⌐⌐⌐⌐

Introduction

Chaos and life: identifying and assessing evidence

This chapter turns to the way in which people across Egypt (3000–525 BC) expressed contending forces at play in their lives. Where previous chapters considered individual motifs, here, the focus is on ancient perception and expression of relations and movements between features. Historian Igor Diakonoff argued that language takes precedence: "archaeological data can never let you or me recapture the emotional attitude of these ancient people towards the objects of their culture. We shall not hear what the girl making the pot said to it, what sense its form and ornament made for her" (Diakonoff 1995, 21). Despite the strength of his image, problems arise with a predominantly philological approach to understanding ancient Egypt.

Some ancient writings seem to offer direct accounts of ancient worldviews: *myths* understood as narratives that are set in the world of the divine. Tales of creation and conflict between deities are the stock of *mythology* in European study of religion. Yet for ancient Egypt, such *myths* turn out to be a problem, because so few longer narratives of deities are written down or depicted. As a result, Egyptologists debate whether people in earlier periods produced any such *myth/* extended tale of the divine. Even after 1350 BC, when tales of the gods do survive as connected series of episodes, the contexts for each of these writings reveal culturally specific grounds for each narration. These contexts take us far from direct answers in the ethnographic style to questions such as "how was the world created" or "what characters do the main deities have."

Even without this obstacle, major problems remain for studies starting from written evidence (Chapter 1). Fieldwork-centered archaeologists emphasize

Exploring Religion in Ancient Egypt, First Edition. Stephen Quirke.
© 2015 Stephen Quirke. Published 2015 by John Wiley & Sons, Ltd.

how a focus on writing excludes most people and practices. Similarly, literary analyst Vladimir Propp commented on Egyptian mythology, "For the most part we know only the official religion ... The popular strata could have had other ideas, other, so to speak, story-lines, to those of the official cult, and of these popular conceptions very little is known to us" (Propp 1946, 125, cf. Spalinger 2007). Another objection is broader: both speech and writing involve all the potential for misunderstanding in any human communication. The words of others are precious, especially in other languages, because they can lift us out of our own linguistic and conceptual worlds. However, they do not free us from the need to observe context, interests, or values. This is a self-critical observation: present or past, there are no context-free interlocutors, including ourselves. Finally, against assumptions that we acquire knowledge through explicit words of instruction, anthropologist Maurice Bloch argues that nonlinguistic models predominate in daily life learning (Bloch 1998, 3–21). Each medium of communication creates the condition of knowledge, its *logic*: "If the anthropologist is often attempting to give an account of chunked and non-sentential knowledge in a linguistic medium (writing), and she has no alternative, she must be aware that in so doing she is not reproducing the organisation of knowledge of the people she studies but is transmuting it into an entirely different logical form" (Bloch 1998, 15). I return to his arguments later in this chapter (Learning from schemata).

A quest for *myth* may take words out of context, and methodical philologists or historians would object to this as much as field archaeologists. One example is modern construction of ancient *conceptions of the world* on the basis of recitations for embalming and burial. Egyptologists have used names such as *Book of Shu* or *Book of Ha'py* for certain compositions intended to obtain an afterlife for an individual. Harco Willems has shown how close reading reveals an ancient focus very different from that of a modern reader seeking ancient equivalents to European philosophy. In compositions concerning Shu, "air/light," or Ha'py, "Nile flood," Willems notes how these two names evoke specific intangible and tangible elements of embalming ritual and practice. Passages on Shu express not an ancient endeavor to describe the world, but the need to make air available to the deceased for immortality (Willems 1996, 270–324). The Egyptological *Book of Ha'py* comprises five separate recitations at offerings of fresh water in the course of mummification (Coffin Texts 317–321, see Bickel 1994, 146).

These writings speak indirectly of ancient Egyptian concepts of life and afterlife, but they belong with embalming and burial as techniques for obtaining an eternal life and only became *theological/philosophical treatises* in the hands of Egyptologists. Recognizing the different intention of these ancient writings does not mean assigning them to some more mundane level of thinking, as if below European philosophy. If it helps to overcome the persistent Eurocentric racism that denies Africa any intellectual life, we might call ancient patterns of thinking *philosophy*. Equally, we might be more strongly grounded in those different patterns of thought, if we accepted that

human wisdom need not be called philosophy and that such dominant
European words may sometimes block appreciation.

Myth *as Speech in* Religion

Mythic thinking

Against the logical drives of seventeenth-century European philosophers, the
historian Giambattista Vico asserted the value of poetic, *mythical* expression as
crucial for humanity (Horkheimer 1930). This defense came at the risk of confining
mythical thinking to a lower rung on a succession of historical phases from
supposedly primitive human to supposedly modern European. Myth might be
misread as narratives by people assumed unable to articulate scientific, abstract
or logical, thought. In nineteenth-century Europe, such misreading became
dominant; history was written as a line from inferior to superior, reinforced by
concepts of evolution of species in natural history, developed by Lamarck, Darwin,
and Mendel. Twentieth-century philosopher Ernst Cassirer attempted to dislodge
any automatic inferiority of myth to science, by exploring mythic and other patterns
of thought as parallel rather than in historical succession—alternative *symbolic
forms* to formulate life (Cassirer 1923–1929). There remains the danger of
presuming a split between mind, body, and spirit and projecting from these the
separate modern categories of logical/rational, sensual/anatomical, and poetic/
spiritual. Myth then becomes an echo of poetic, the aesthetic as a fourth dimension
or a lost space between the other three. Terry Eagleton has charted the intricate
history of European thinking on these fissions and fusions from a self around the
concept of aesthetic and so reminds us how specific to Europe the entire set of
categories and their assumptions may be (Eagleton 1990).

Within that Eurocentric history, romantics tended to extol myth, especially
ethnic national myth, not only as antidote to the lethal logic of a desensitized
science, but also as pure expression of the soul of a people. Extreme dangers in
idolizing myth as uncontaminated, indigenous thought of a nation were clear by
the time that Cassirer was rewriting his ideas on mythical thinking. Twentieth-
century Egyptological writers on myth stood within (Brunner), or barely a step
away from (Schott), the lethal excesses of Nazism and nationalisms, where myth is
taken literally as timeless, transferred from human context into some overarching,
eternal dimension (Arvidsson and Wichmann 2006). Archaeological objections to
overreliance on written sources are particularly valuable here, as reminders that
attention to context can also save us from negative consequences. Continuing
political use of national mythologies demonstrates how much is at stake in the
words we choose for describing human thought and action.

For our approach to the people of Egypt (3000–525 BC), debates over the
relative value of *mythic* and *logical* thinking are directly relevant, to help us avoid
thoughtlessly assigning *mythic* expression to more *primitive* levels than

presumed higher levels of scientific thought in later societies. The sheer need to survive makes it unlikely that humans at any time or place could escape calculations of risk and danger (Shennan 1999, 876–877, on *delayed-return* subsistence systems as primary among hunter-gatherer societies). Technical advances in knowledge have probably not altered the propensity of humans either to calculate or to dream. Instead, we might ask more generally how people across Egypt in those twenty-five centuries conceived of danger and purity and how they expressed these perceptions materially in word, image, and act. For this enquiry, a favorite source of answers—longer narrations to explain lives or worlds—is not available: ancient Egypt produced no equivalent to the Greek myths in Hesiod or Norse sagas in Icelandic medieval manuscripts.

The myth debate in Egyptology

In a 1977 article, Jan Assmann exposed many assumptions on myth, observing that *myths* in the sense of *longer tales of deities* are not known from Egyptian writing before 1350 BC. He concluded that, far from being a primeval human expression, in Egypt, *myth* arrived only at that relatively late date, 1800 years after development of the hieroglyphic script. In his interpretation, earlier periods knew only short statements around the relations between deities, expressions which he terms icons or *constellations* of deities (Assmann 1977a). In response, Jürgen Zeidler examined the earliest shorter statements, from *Pyramid Texts*, the religious compositions first inscribed in royal pyramid chambers, 2400–2200 BC (Zeidler 1993). Applying methods used by Propp to analyze tales of wonder or fairy tales, Zeidler concluded that these examples went beyond a *constellation* of direct relations between deities and implied underlying connected narrative.

In another constructive response, Katja Goebs observes the distinction between phenotext, the specific and material form of a composition in the surviving written record, and genotext, underlying compositional pool out of which phenotexts are generated. Pyramid Texts may only allude to a longer *myth of Osiris*, but they could be the tangible phenotexts from that preexisting genotext. As Goebs notes, the location and function of the phenotext might have favored shorter over fuller writings. In contexts such as the burial chamber, inscriptions may excerpt from, rather than recount in full, a genotext, not because no longer myth existed yet, but because these words were to be uttered over offerings, when allusions were enough to evoke a mythic dimension in ritual practice. Goebs calls attention to the immediate setting of surviving words: "the form a myth or mytheme takes is dependent on the function of the context in which it is used" (Goebs 2002, 27).

As with other deep structures, the case for a *genotext beneath phenotexts* remains difficult to decide; ancient Egyptian mythmaking might, but need not have been so. Given the efficiency of short early inscriptions, it remains possible that ancient practice and thought operated as *phenotext only*, as Assmann implied. No underlying genotext necessarily existed even on the analysis by Zeidler, whose connected motifs still amount only to short versions of the Propp fable plots. Propp identified the core theme of tales of wonder as initiation through rites of passage, at life changes such as puberty (Gilet 1998). The use of extended narration for rites of passage may be one among several imports from western Asia into Egyptian court life after mid-fifteenth century BC (others include loan words distinctively written in syllabic orthography and diplomatic royal marriages on a larger scale). The clearest example in Egyptian literature, among the stories used by Propp for his analyses, is the Tale of Two Brothers, the gods Anubis and Bata (Assmann 1977b).

The debate may be an argument over definition, or over qualities of different lengths of narration. The term myth might be applied only to longer passages, constellation/icon for shorter expressions, and a different term such as mytheme for individual motifs as the atoms of mythic expression. Susanne Bickel resolves the problem by extending the concept of mythmaking to broader fields of creative expression, including visual and material alongside verbal (Bickel 1994, following Detienne 1981). This more open approach reduces the importance of the date of the first longer tales of deities. The important point would be not to change the words we use, but to lose automatic equations such as "myth = narrative (of divine)." However, if we continue defining mythic against logical, certain evolutionary assumptions may remain intact, around the core Eurocentric notion that humans developed from nonthinking primitives to fuzzy-thinking myth tellers to a modern age of scientists.

Learning from storytelling: the only option?

Much reaction against the Assmann view seems to stem from a feeling that humans learn primarily from direct verbal instruction, spoken or written, and that, therefore, religion too is taught by narrating myths (as Willems 1996, 8–14). How could people learn about the Osiris myth unless someone recited the tale? Its episodes are connected only outside Egypt, by the Greek writer Plutarch (about AD 46–120) in his *On Isis and Osiris*; this remains the basis for accepting the episodes as one myth (Gwyn Griffiths 1970, comparing with scattered Egyptian sources). From our book learning, we imagine ancient Egyptian children reading or hearing how Osiris ruled as king and was murdered by jealous younger brother Seth and revived by his loyal sister-wife Isis to conceive the child Horus and how Horus was protected by Isis until he could challenge Seth and emerge triumphant as king of the living, with Osiris ruling the dead. An alternative to narrating-to-child seems, to the academic *us*, unthinkable, so powerfully is it set in contemporary education, as in the home or school national histories studied by Marc Ferro in his *How we teach history to children around the world*, translated as *The Use and Abuse of History* (Ferro 1981, 1984). Bedtime stories have been powerful formative elements in middle-class European self-consciousness since the mid-nineteenth century, when the brothers Grimm gathered fairy tales, and Hans Christian Andersen invented his own, for that class on its way to political dominance (Dollerup 1995). That is the cultural historical context for the belief that learning must involve storytelling. The belief may not hold true for ourselves and certainly need not dictate our reactions to people in Egypt (3000–525 BC). Anthropologist Maurice Bloch provides a usefully opposed approach.

Learning from schemata information blocks?

Bloch contests two views comparing culture with language: "culture is thought and transmitted as a text through language," and "culture is ultimately 'language like', consisting of linked linear propositions" (Bloch 1998, 4). Instead, life learning works through mental models, "small networks of typical understandings and practices concerning the world." The models may be acquired first as concepts, not words, in "a continual back and forth movement between aspects of classification which are introduced through language and mental concepts, as the child learns to express these concepts through words" (Bloch 1998, 6). Applying the theory of connectionism from cognitive psychology, Bloch sees learning as the recognition of structures operating as explanatory models for perception/action. Whatever the skill to be acquired, learners need to draw on information automatically; the most efficient means of storage and retrieval is not verbal instruction, but more tightly packed and flexible mental models. Therefore, learning involves "constructing apparatuses for the efficient handling and packing of specific domains of knowledge and practice" (Bloch 1998, 10–11).

The schemata of Bloch recall Assmann on the *constellation* as relations between *netjeru*, "deities." Plato (fifth-century BC Greece) and his follower Plotinus (third-century AD Egypt) wrote that Egyptians learned the world through images, using the Greek word *schemata* for these images (Assmann 1992). The starting point in this symbolic instruction is the concept or mental model behind both image and word. Ancient Egyptian sacred imagery matches the nonlinguistic models which Bloch considers the foundation of all human learning. The particular visual–verbal articulation of each learning object in each time and place then becomes the object for comparative archaeological and anthropological study.

Rather than omitting the evidence of words, Bloch aims to place words in context and to analyze their presence:

> To claim that much of culture is neither linguistic nor "language like" does not imply that language is unimportant. Nevertheless, contrary to what anthropologists tend to assume, we should see linguistic phenomena as a *part* of culture, most of which is non-linguistic. Instead of taking language for granted, we should see its presence as requiring explanation.

Methodical philologists also focus on context and are well placed to pursue the phenomenon of explicit verbal instruction. Bloch relates how, in learning complex skills such as weaving, linked-sentence instructions in words are the exception; most learning is by practice, inculcating models or networks of action and thought in apprentices. It then takes time and effort to translate these efficiently packed networks into the linear sequences of sentences, and the resulting words may be far from the knowledge they convey. Therefore, translation into words, whether instructing or narrating, is a secondary and laborious exercise, presumably only undertaken where some gain offsets the effort. Bloch identifies this gain as transformation of fuzzy prototype concepts into rigorous concepts with checklists of features. Though no longer efficiently embedded in practice, the concept becomes available for another area of action: "such extension may well be linked with the process of innovation" (Bloch 1998, 14–15). In the myth debate, Egyptologists could research what gains might have encouraged translation of small networks or constellations of concepts of the divine, into longer verbal narratives after 1350 BC. In the meantime, Bloch and Assmann warn us that our own storytelling of ancient Egyptian religion may distort into a different form/content, the organization of ideas, knowledge, and practice in operation among past people.

The weight of kingship in ancient Egyptian compositions

Study of ancient Egyptian myths and mythemes may be complicated by their focus on kingship (Diakonoff 1995, 124; Spalinger 2007). Rather than just a distortion, the prominence of kingship can also be read as a story of reception, with the gradual adoption across the society of certain models first developed for kingship. Antonio Gramsci applied from linguistics the concept of Prestige as a decisive factor in attracting people toward particular practices, such as speaking in a certain accent or language (Ives 2004). Prestige might promote models or motifs from the rich and powerful, so establishing hegemony in culture. This adoption of models can also be appreciated from the side of the adopter. Acceptance of an outside idea need not be a sign of weakness or insincerity. Instead, despite all the risks of losing your own earlier way of doing/living/thinking, incorporation of that external motif might still be part of a wider social experience of, and strategy for dealing with, life trauma (Chapter 7). Yet Diakonoff raises the question, whether it is possible for us to see an ancient Egypt outside kingship.

Constellations *Outside Writing*

Evidence beyond words and images?

Writings tend, then, to obscure any parts of ancient Egypt prior to or, more neutrally, outside kingship. In order to overcome this silence, I would start looking for broader categories in material from the archaeology of Egypt (3000–525 BC). Rather than excluding written evidence, I aim, first, at a broader archaeological record and, then, at written communication in context within that record. Yet here, in studies of *myth/mythology*, primacy of the written might be replaced by an equally unbalanced primacy of the visual motif, particularly figurative form. In an image-centered approach, all past visual expression can be reduced to a flat compromise between documentary and materialist histories of thought.

Dangers in relying on visual record can be seen most clearly whenever any motif is avoided or forbidden altogether, because considered too sacred or dangerous. Acts of iconoclasm reveal when previously accepted motifs became forbidden. In ancient Egypt, the most extreme example is from the reign of Akhenaten and the subsequent reaction. Under Akhenaten, new imagery of kingship shed all *netjeru* except the single motif of sun disk with rays, denoting the creator sun-god. Royal sculptors produced no new images of other *netjeru*, and certain motifs were physically erased out of the eternal record in formal script and image. Prime targets were the image and name of the creator as Amun, "hidden"; others were his goddess-wife Mut and the plural word *netjeru*, "gods." Outside monuments of kingship, images of birth deities and some other national deities may have continued in production as amulets or for small shrines, even in the city of the king at Akhetaten. However, these smaller images may date to the restoration of the *netjeru* cults in the decade after Akhenaten, when his city continued to be inhabited (Figure 4.1).

Figure 4.1 Limestone wall blocks sculpted with depiction of singers beside the words of a hymn to King Amenhotep III, in which the words *Amun* and *all gods* have been erased during the reign of his successor Akhenaten and restored in the following reigns. Tomb chapel of the high official Rames, Waset, about 1375 BC. © Schott Archive, University of Trier.

Extreme aversion to images during this short period draws attention to the recurrent but variable avoidance of images across time and space. The name for this avoidance in the Egyptian language is *buwt*, prescribed avoidance of a feature in a place, for example, the pig as *buwt* of followers of Horus, god of order (Frandsen 1986). The assistance of language in defining this phenomenon illustrates the difficulty in removing the ancient writing from assessments of the archaeological record. A focus on the visual at the expense of the written would also be hard to achieve for ancient Egypt, where visual and written are so intertwined, that it does violence to extricate one from the other. In formal depictions, script accompanies images, often playing between the hieroglyphs of the script as small images and the images as large hieroglyphs (Fischer 1986).

For visual motifs, tools of geographical analysis may produce guides to time–space distribution or *reach* of motifs. Future study could include, in one direction, the nonfigurative and, in another, material with writing in context. Survey and excavation provide direct evidence in the form of space–time distributions of practices and object categories. Following a model set by Michael Rowlands for researching connections between ancient Egypt and other African societies, analysts of material distributions could explore shared underlying conceptions of life, in chains of overlapping circles of practice (Rowlands 2003). Assmann encourages this material turn, by a focus on *constellation* as the immediate close relations between features and forces. Longer chains might be found in comparison of the medicinal properties of specific materials between the archaeological and ethnographic record of beads and amulets (see Chapter 6). The archaeological record offers the fragment, where the level of resolution might be precisely that of the *constellation*. We may be able, after all, to hear the girl talking to, and listening to, the pot.

Principles, forces, and materials

Allowing for differences in social class and the impact of rule (*prestige*), the archaeological record may indicate how past people formed material and moved between action and resting. We might look for patterns of gender, age, and class among groups and individuals in such social practices as:

Walking, clothing, and applying cosmetics: How does it feel to wrap a handwoven linen of different textures and to move in tighter or looser, cooler or warmer garments; how does the oil feel on the skin or the amulet or beads on skin or garment or hair—all these variously combine matter at once in contact with individual body and social world.

Wielding and beating: Authority and violence are materialized not only in hieroglyphs for man with staff and man beating with stick but in third- and second-millennium burials of adult men with sticks and staves (Hassan 1976); with a different tone, the fearsome adult may also become a figure of fun (as in the Judgement of Horus and Seth, summarised at the end of this chapter).

Moving to contain/close/tie: bodily contact with sacks, bags, baskets, and vessels of wood/pottery/metal/stone. In ancient Egypt, the pottery vessels most often have a rounded base for laying to rest on ground (contact with earth) or on pottery ring stands or carrying on pad on head and grain and liquid in vessels with wide or constricted mouths/necks. For special contents, the bag or box needs to be sealed with string or rope, secured with mud, in wealthier contexts marked with a seal or signet ring; these actions of containment may deploy the strategy of nesting, as also in architecture and funerary contexts (Roth 1998).

To help us see life forces in these movements and to read the world in a basket or textile, makers in nonindustrial societies offer other views: "Life grows out of the land, woman grows out of the earth, the Beautyway ... Women change the world rear sheep, shear sheep, and weave all the movements into a rug" (unnamed Navajo weaver cited M'Closkey 2002, 214).

Small-scale carving as a widespread source of imagery

Some motifs can be traced across the country and in different levels of society, suggesting a shared relation to life forces. Many images are carved in two and three dimensions on small scale, as amulets protecting the wearer (see Chapter 6). One of the most widespread object types in this history of images is the seal-amulet: first, the cylinder seal and then the stamp-seal, including the scarab-shaped seal. These provide a continuous widely distributed historical index of imagery. There are two constraints on using this as universal atlas of images: forms and motifs may be articulated mainly within richer social circles, and arrangement of motifs may be fostered by the shape of the seal (e.g., symmetrical compositions on disk-shaped seals, processions of figures on cylinder seals).

The cylinder seal is known in western Asia before the first instance known in the Nile Valley (e.g., from Naqada tomb (1863), UC5374), where the earliest examples are imports (Podzorski 1988; Hill 2004). Examples made in Egypt soon follow and are among the main sources for the earliest hieroglyphs, after 3200 BC. During the late third millennium BC, stamp-seal shapes came to replace cylinder seals. Most early stamp-seals are from Upper Egypt, as if the form developed in that region, not at kingship centers (Kemp 2006, 142–143). Yet the concentration of finds may reflect not the epicenter of production, but regional and chronological differences in burial customs. Rare earlier jewelry at royal court cemeteries includes metal headbands with central disks decorated with symmetrical compositions, similar in conception to those found on later Upper Egyptian stamp-seals. Jewelry production at the royal center may be the prestigious model for the later regional imagery (Figure 4.2).

In general, motifs of kingship dominate the entire three millennia in this history. There may be technical factors in the relative centralization of the process. Even where materials for seals are widely available (limestone, steatite) or easy to produce (faience), specific skills in draughting and glazing

(a)   (b)

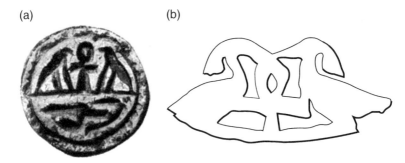

Figure 4.2   (a) Hieroglyph '*ankh*, "life," flanked by facing falcons, on an early type of stamp-seal, perhaps from Upper Egypt (2300 BC). W. Petrie, *Buttons and Design Scarabs*, British School of Archaeology in Egypt, London, 1927, pl.1. (b) Hieroglyph '*ankh*, "life," flanked by facing crested ibis, on an example of residence cemetery jewelry, a gilt copper headband, from the burial of a woman in the cemeteries at modern Giza, tomb G7143B, about 2400 BC. Drawing © Wolfram Grajetzki after C. Aldred, *Jewels of the Pharaohs*, Thames and Hudson, London 1971, Fig. 16.

might have helped confine production to a few centers. As a result, amulet iconography may be generated from the center, as Diakonoff warns of *myth-making* in Egypt in general. Nevertheless, the very distribution of seal-amulets across the country writes a history of the regional reception of kingship, as a social and personal strategy to use prestigious motifs also for individual health (see Chapter 6).

Relations of fertility: movements of seasons, flood, and the return of the distant goddess

One prominent motif is the cow-eared face of a woman, often with broad waving hairstyle, named in earlier inscriptions Bat (perhaps the name of the image type), later as the goddess Hathor (Fischer 1962). The image frequently adorns musical instruments such as wood or bronze rhythm markers known by their Latin name sistra and ivory arm-shaped clappers, as well as the handles of mirrors. The hair-style and the association with rhythmic music and cosmetic equipment identify the theme of the goddess as the sensuous. From the late second millennium BC, numerous votive offerings at shrines throughout the Nile Valley in Egypt and Nubia, and in the desert develop images of Hathor as cow, providing milk and maternal love, or as cat, aggressively protecting against rats (Pinch 1994). Amulets with Hathor motifs are widely distributed, indicating use beyond court circles where they may have first been formed (Figure 4.3).

Other images associated with the goddess appear outside the royal court. By a desert road near Nekhen, ostrich plumes were deposited with a small piece of sandstone inscribed in hieroglyphs *nub-kha'-s*, "the Gold appears," perhaps a per-sonal name Nubkhas (Darnell 1999, 21, 27–29; Meeks 2008, nn.935–938). In other

(a)   (b)

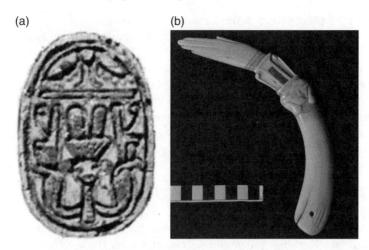

Figure 4.3   (a) Underside of steatite scarab, with a visual motif to bring blessing on the wearer; the motif centers on a scepter-like sistrum with the cow-eared head of a woman, associated with the goddess Hathor and in earlier periods named Bat. Find-place not known, about 1750 BC, now Petrie Museum UC61099. W. Petrie, *Buttons and Design Scarabs*, British School of Archaeology in Egypt, London, 1927; (b) Ivory clapper from a pair, carved with hand terminal and head of a woman with elaborate hair and necklace, associated with the goddess Hathor (Egyptian Museum, Cairo CG 69234-35): photograph © Gianluca Miniaci.

inscriptions, Gold is a name for Hathor; this deposit would connect her with desert roads, specifically to the southern Savannah where ostriches are found. Ostrich plume fans are known from royal circles, but without explicit connection to Hathor, and elsewhere, the double ostrich plume is associated with solar gods rather than the goddess. Nevertheless, the singular plume denotes Ma'at, "what is right," and this find may indicate Nekhen rites celebrating the return of female powers out of the desert, perhaps at the New Year when the Nile Flood rose from the south. In support of this interpretation, John Darnell cites a hymn from an early first-millennium BC ritual for the return of the distant goddess:

> Let us take for her feathers of the backs of ostriches,
> slain for you by the Tjemehu-Libyans with their throwsticks,
> their bindings made of animal-hides.
> Let us make acclamation to you!
> Let the Tjemehu-Libyans dance for you!

Tjemehu is an Egyptian name for peoples living in the Saharan deserts to the west and southwest of Egypt. Different groups may at all times have practiced different or overlapping rites. It is not clear whether ostrich feathers were laid in the ground at Nekhen by people from desert or valley, shepherds or farmers, Egyptians or Nubians. At least one of the people involved knew enough Egyptian hieroglyphs to inscribe the sandstone flake in the deposit.

At most centralized level, the construction of a new kingship city, the same motif of return at the desert edge may be at play. Barry Kemp reads the distribution of outlying shrines and temples at Akhetaten, city of Akhenaten, as a circle fertilizing the central temples of king and creator sun-god (Kemp 1995). These cult places are dedicated to the women around the king: principal wife Nefertiti and daughters Meretaten and Meketaten. All are located in the intermediate space where the desert meets fields, where the goddess would return from afar. The royal city thus maps out a perennial feature of kingship, the cosmic fertility role for the mother, wife, or daughter of the king. Lana Troy has shown how ancient Egyptian queenship operated, not as a royal family in the dynastic European sense, but as a gendered machine for prosperity on the model of sovereign sun Ra/King and feminine complements Hathor/Nut (Troy 1986) (Figure 4.4).

Relations of physical regeneration from immobility: masculine desert, Min and Amun

The desert is site of another fundamental relation recurrent through architectural, visual, and written sources: the mystery of movement emerging out of complete stillness. The earliest freestanding colossal statues in the world, from Gebtyu (modern Qift), include two in form of a standing man, with erect phallus carved as a separate stone. The main ithyphallic deity in later periods is Min, principal *netjer* at the main temples of Gebtyu and, farther north, Khentmin (modern Akhmim). Depictions of Min show a rigidly wrapped body, dramatically breached by erect phallus, left arm extended to support a flail-like scepter of sovereignty, and double falcon-plume crown. Combined, the features convey a stillness about how to impregnate the world with life. Writings associate the Min festival with the harvest season, so directly with fertility. The anchor in static desert aridity remains strong: in visual sources for the festival, a great tent is set up, requiring a broad open area, evoking desert space and nomadic lifestyle.

After 2000 BC, Min imagery becomes associated with the cult of Amun, "Hidden," at the newly dominant southern city Waset/Thebes. Amun expresses on one side the concept of power as invisible authority over unbounded space. Fused with the idea of the sun as creator, Amun-Ra becomes principal deity of Egypt from 1550 BC, when local kings waged war against northern rivals, inaugurating the New Kingdom. In this role, Amun appears as a ruler in human form, with a scepter and double falcon-plume crown of Min. The main cult center at Waset was the temple Ipetsut, "Select of Places" (modern Karnak). Alongside the idea of intangible sovereign power, Amun also continues to express a physical potency, depicted in the same form as Min: wrapped body, phallus, arm extended to flail-like scepter, and double-plume crown. Often named Amun-Kamutef, "Hidden, the Bull of his Mother," this form receives

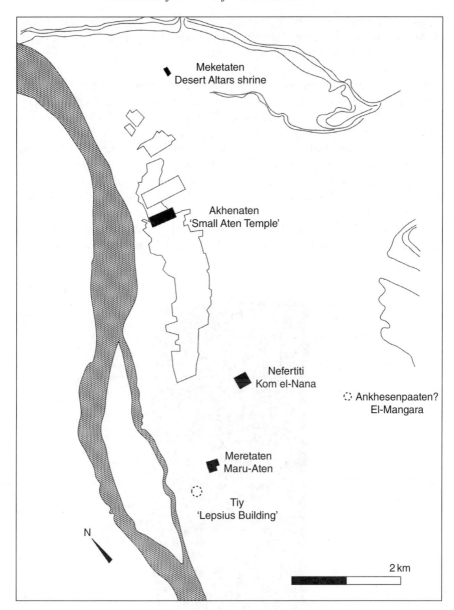

Figure 4.4 Sanctuaries of Akhetaten: the city in the floodplain has central temples to the creator as the sun disk Aten and to King Akhenaten, with major shrines in the low desert around to his mother (Tiy), wife (Nefertiti), and three eldest daughters (Meretaten, Meketaten, Ankhesenpaaten). Drawing © Wolfram Grajetzki.

separate offerings, notably at the temple Ipetreset, "the Southern Private Chamber." Across the river, a temple on the West Bank desert edge (modern Madinat Habu) was dedicated to the primeval form of Amun (Figures 4.5, and 4.6 and Map 4.1).

The fourth corner of this vast landscape of festival was the temple of Hathor (modern Deir al-Bahari), integrating the male potency and female fertility into the monumental architectural map of Waset (Figure 3.7). The kingship monuments project a union of male and female principles that resonated across the social scale, as seen in the votive offerings at these sites. At Karnak, a vast late first-millennium BC cache, the largest ever found in Egypt, included hundreds of stone statues of kings and officials from the temple halls but also thousands of Osiris figures. Excavation of Madinat Habu produced larger numbers of votives, now being published from the archives of the excavations. The offerings to Amun are less well known than those to Hathor, recorded from Deir al-Bahari and other sites (Pinch 1994). Significantly, the Deir al-Bahari deposits include wood models of

Figure 4.5 Depiction of Amun-Ra as sovereign creator, embracing Hatshepsut as sovereign, on her monolithic red granite obelisk at Karnak, 1475 BC. Photograph © Gianluca Miniaci.

Figure 4.6   Depiction of King Senusret I offering to Amun in Min form, reassembled limestone blocks from the White Chapel, Karnak, about 1950 BC. Photograph © Gianluca Miniaci.

phalli; individuals requesting or thanking there included male potency as part of their gift or prayer, either directly to the goddess Hathor or perhaps to the Min aspect of Amun on the festival visits to the temple.

Sailings of the Sun

Formal depictions include imagery of the creator as sun-god traveling over the sky as if by boat on the river. The ever-sailing creator may take the form of a falcon, as in the single most famous early example, incised on a comb (3000 BC), or a disk, or a falcon-headed man wearing a disk. During the reign of Akhenaten, the sailing is rejected in favor of the more static vision of Aten, "disk," with sun rays extending life hieroglyphs to the nose of the king or his wife. Immediately after his reign, the boat image returns. Sailing by boat is the dominant feature of festival processions (Chapter 3), to the point that shrines for transporting sacred images regularly take the shape of a small-scale boat, with carrying poles for a group of men to move it on foot in shorter distances over land. Nile boat travel is the main metaphor for divine movement (Figure 4.7).

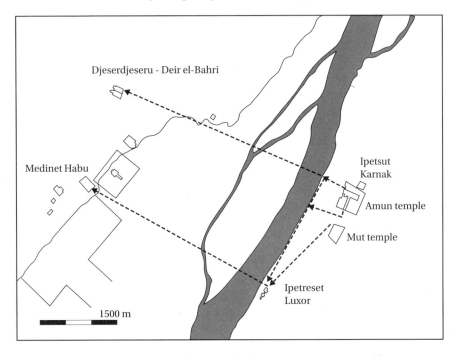

Map 4.1   Plan of festival routes and principal cult centers in Waset. © Wolfram Grajetzki.

Images of a sacred boat in procession are found roughly carved on slabs of the roof over the temple of Khons at Karnak, 1200–1000 BC (Jacquet-Gordon 2003). To judge from names and titles in roof inscriptions, these were drawn by temple guards or timekeepers, watching the processions below. The Egyptian landscape (3000–525 BC) remains otherwise relatively empty of the boat motif, by comparison with rock art in other times and places. Boats are not a dominant feature among the hundreds of inscriptions either on the granite rocks at the First Cataract or in the sandstone quarries at Gebel al-Silsila in southern Upper Egypt (3 out of 551 inscriptions Gasse and Rondot 2007). The Aten image from the reign of Akhenaten shows how a journey might be evoked from a single static instant, such as the high point of midday (Figure 4.8).

Among votive offerings at sanctuaries, too, boats and boat equipment rarely predominate. The main exception is among faience votive deposits at the temple of Satet on Abu (Elephantine Island). After inscribed tiles, the most common type of offering there was a model boat with a hedgehog-head prow, facing back across the boat; over forty examples were found (Dreyer 1986, 76–79). The form is restricted to the late third millennium BC and rare on other sites (one or two only at Abdju and the Delta site Tell Ibrahim Awad, Haarlem, 1997, 168). With pellets in hollow interior, these boat models are small rattles, perhaps appropriate to rites at the first sound of the rising Nile in Egypt. Clay figurines in

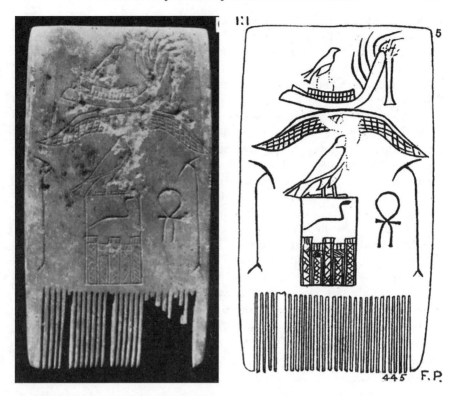

Figure 4.7   Falcon on boat over the name of King Djer, incised on ivory comb, from burial of a palace official, Abdju, 3000 BC, (a) photograph, (b) drawing. W. Petrie, *Tombs of the Courtiers and Oxyrhynchus*, British School of Archaeology in Egypt, London, 1925, pl.12.

Figure 4.8   Roughly incised depiction of the boat of Amun, distinguished by the ram-head terminals, carved on the sandstone roofing slabs of the Khons temple, Karnak. Drawing © Wolfram Grajetzki, after Jacquet-Gordon, *Temple of Khonsu, Volume 3. The Graffiti on the Khonsu Temple Roof at Karnak: A Manifestation of Personal Piety*, University of Chicago Press, Chicago, 2003.

domestic contexts include fewer boats, than animal, human, and plant imagery. In large-scale deposits of bronze figures after 700 BC, the focus is on the deity figure, with boats a rarer secondary feature. Evidently, those votive offerings belong away from the sphere of movement and contained within the stillness of the sacred space, where a supplicant kneels or bows before a divine presence (Figure 4.9).

Boats for kings and boat models for officials are a recurrent feature of burial equipment (Chapter 7) but most often with reference to the life of the deceased, whether king or landowner, or to funeral rites. Only rarely does the form of a model boat explicitly evoke the solar boat and the sky sailing of the sun. Around 1900 BC, some of the wealthiest burials at the royal court cemeteries and around the governors of Middle Egypt contained special solar boats, as if recasting on a divine level the regular fleet for large estates, known from models of 2100–1850 BC (Grajetzki 2003, 49). The short-lived practice, apparently never repeated, is restricted to wealthier burials at the court cemetery of king and regional governors; it remains difficult to track the wider diffusion of the solar imagery across society. After 1300 BC, votive stelae include the motif of the sun Ra in his boat, but these come from centers of production closest to the royal court (Ramesside Deir al Madina). Possibly, the motif may have been avoided as too sacred; on funerary stelae (1500–1300 BC), the motif of cup, water, and ring between two eyes has been interpreted as evoking the circuit (ring) of the sun (eyes) by boat (water sign) over the earth (Westendorf 1966).

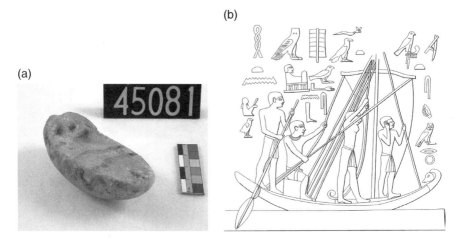

Figure 4.9   (a) Faience hedgehog-boat rattle, provenance unknown, perhaps late Old Kingdom, UC45081. © Petrie Museum of Egyptian Archaeology, UCL. (b) Limestone wall relief with depiction of a river boat with a hedgehog-head prow. From the chapel over the burial place of Seneb, whose dwarf stature is integrated into the task of *raising the sail* of his eternal journey. Cemeteries near modern Giza, about 2500 BC. Drawing © Wolfram Grajetzki.

Figure 4.10   Small-scale votive stela with depiction of a baboon with a crescent, identified in the hieroglyphic caption as *Thoth lord of Khemenu*, limestone, provenance unknown, UC35815. Drawing © Wolfram Grajetzki.

Among other movements in the skies, the evidence for ancient ways of charting and interpreting the circuits of moon and stars belongs mainly within the *elite* sphere (see Section The Nut Image, on the great image of Nut in two Ramesside royal contexts). Crescent moon and star shapes are rare in Egyptian jewelry and amulet forms, in contrast to earlier and later periods. This suggests either a lack of relevance or again an avoidance of a motif, where formal writing and imagery attest freely to star goddess Sopdet (Sirius) and the god Osiris as Sahu (Orion) and to the lunar quality of the gods Thoth, Khons (especially after 1800 BC at Waset), and Osiris (as Osiris-Moon). At centers where written sources show a formal image of local deities as moon gods, there are roughly carved votive images on the same model. Small limestone stelae depict a baboon wearing a crescent moon, in some examples identified in hieroglyphs as *Thoth lord of Khemenu*. Simpler products may indicate a broader social acceptance and use of the form developed in the royal center (Figure 4.10).

Trusting the ferryman? Aggression and defense: fauna of danger and disorder

Disorder and aggression are other forms of movement, which at some places and times were evidently considered to require separate nurturing and to restore or maintain peace. Near Tjebu (modern Qau), the steep cliffs of Gebel Haridi abruptly meet the Nile, before the river turns sharply at the strategic next regional town, Asyut. In Tjebu town cemeteries, massive deposits of fossil hippopotamus bones were placed in disused earlier tombs, intermingled with broken objects made from tusks or materials of similar color or texture and motif, such as limestone hippopotamus figure and calcite cosmetic vase. The artifacts date the deposits (1350–1250 BC). In one find, the excavation director Guy Brunton recorded "two or three tons of bones" (Brunton 1930, 18). The male hippopotamus is the most aggressive Nile animal, no longer found wild in Egypt, but still today feared across other parts of Africa as a bigger killer than crocodile or lion. Given this ferocity, the bone deposits might be collective acts to pacify this force.

On a finely sculpted votive stela from Tjebu, about 1400 BC, local governor Hatiay is depicted in adoration before a hippopotamus in a papyrus marsh, identified in the inscription as "Seth the strong ... lord of Tjebu, overlord of Wadjyt province" (Figure 2.10). In writings and images, Seth regularly stands opposite Horus, as disorder twinned with or balancing order. Other written sources name instead Nemty as local deity of Wadjyt province and Iatfet, adjoining to the north on the east bank. Rare depictions and scattered references confirm his connection with the anarchic Seth; on a stela from Sinai, a deity with a human body and Seth animal head is named Nemty lord of the East. In the literary *Judgement of Horus and Seth* from Deir al-Madina (see the end of the chapter), Nemty has the role of ferryman. According to formal images and written sources, access to a ferryboat was an enduring preoccupation, understandably in the broad Nile Valley of Upper and Middle Egypt: no bridges spanned the river until the construction of barrages in modern times (Tvedt 2003). Within the world of the divine, as a dimension of this landscape, the terrain of Nemty would be the limbo of transit across the river. His disturbing liminal presence would need appeasing in order to maintain the orderly progression of the sun and of life moving forward.

Seth: animal fusion

Imagery of Seth is prominent, though only a small number of votive offerings survived from one principal center of his cult, Nubt/Naqada in Upper Egypt, from 1500 to 1400 BC. Depictions show Seth as an animal of unidentified species, perhaps a formalized rendering of a known species or perhaps intended as a compilation of features that never existed, the ultimate portrayal of anarchic disorder: squared instead of rounded ears, extended curved snout, and tufted tail like an arrow tip. Individually, each feature could find a basis in ancient north-east African fauna, but the combination may intentionally evoke an antiorder (cf. Te Velde 1967). It remains uncertain whether the Seth animal was considered a species living in the desert alongside other animals. In tomb chapels for regional governors (2000–1900 BC), hunting scenes include Seth figures and griffins beside zoologically attested animals. However, these images may not claim to record the desert in the way we might describe fauna in natural science. They belong within a monument for eternity, offering multiple levels of reading, as where a recently published fragment from one chapel adds the leonine-dwarf figure of Aha/Bes, divine protector of childbirth (Figure 4.11).

After 1300 BC, dedications to Seth are found not at Naqada itself, but at Waset and the new royal city of Ramses II Per-Ramses (moved after 1000 BC to Djanet/

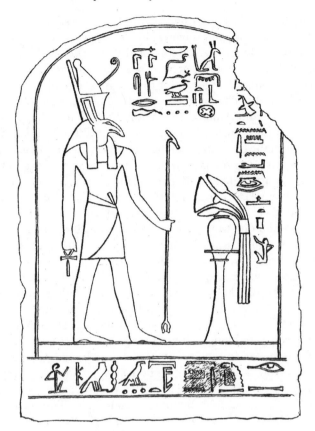

Figure 4.11   Limestone votive stela with depiction of *Seth of Nubet*, inscribed as made by the "pure one of Amun, head of sculptors Nedjem," from Nubet, about 1400 BC. W. Petrie, *Naqada and Ballas*, Quaritch, London, 1896, pl.78.

Tanis, modern San al-Hagar). Like the names of thirteenth–twelfth-century BC Kings Sety and Setnakht, the inscriptions and formal images show how anarchic force could be included in the world of devotion. Any tension in the idea of offering to disorder first emerges violently after 700 BC, when Egyptian temple ritual develops an emphatic focus on Osiris and both name and image of Seth might be erased out of the monumental record for eternity.

Predator as guardian: jackal deities

One prominent relationship in imagery as well as writing is between guardian and guarded. Sacred space received protection from destructive forces—above all, in surviving sources, the jackal prowling at desert edge, where burials were also located and might be vulnerable to scavengers. In funerary context, the most frequent name for the jackal guardian is Inpu, better known in Egyptology in the

Greek form Anubis. In kingship monuments, a jackal on a standard led the procession from the palace; inscriptions name him as Opener of the Ways (in Egyptian Wepwawet). Written sources record Inpu and Wepwawet as the main deities at Asyut, though their temples have not been located on the ground.

In the return to plural imagery after the reign of Akhenaten, animal motifs became a more emphatic focus of attention and production. The image of the individual species is often multiplied for emphasis and perhaps also to assert wider or universal dominion. The principle of multiplication is best known from repetitions of the hearing ear of the deity, as in votive stelae from the Ptah temple at Memphis. At Asyut, in 1922, an Antiquities Service expedition uncovered an extraordinary Ramesside deposit in the great tomb chapel of an earlier governor Djefaha'py (DuQuesne 2009). The main contents comprised some 600 stelae, in fired clay as well as limestone, and some three-dimensional clay images of single and quadruple jackals (DuQuesne 2009, 28: 357 stone stelae, 137 clay stelae, 46 figurines). Some stelae combine deities and species or show different forms. On one, Wepwawet is depicted as a jackal on standard platform with rearing protective cobra, and Amun is shown in different animal forms (DuQuesne 2009, pl.12): the upper register shows as a bull "Amun-Ra bull of his mother"; the middle register has an eel without name, perhaps Amun again; on the lower register, a goose with outstretched wings and erect phallus is named "Amun who comes into being of himself," and behind are two goats. At other sites, Amun is depicted in the form of a goat, and so the double goat here is probably Amun again. The stela deploys both singular and plural approaches to divine forces in the world: strictly separated and singular in the jackal on platform, Wepwawet, and multiple and more open to other identifications (bull as motif also used for Osiris or Ra, eel also for Atum), all as means of visualizing *the Hidden* (Figure 4.12).

The workmanship of the stelae is generally fine, if not the highest quality of kingship sculpture. Even the few depictions of kings offering to deities are not outstanding products. The deposit seems to lie outside the royal court horizon, belonging instead to a world of military officialdom stationed at this strategic bend of the Nile. In sculpture and inscription, these officers and, independently, the women with them expressed their devotions on the model set by kingship in the lost temples of the Asyut floodplain.

Multiple fauna: images and bodies

The multiple animal imagery of the Ramesside period seems to anticipate the development of mass mummification of particular species five centuries later. Despite the gap and differences, it is tempting to draw a line between the two phenomena, as expressions of an underlying sense of connection with the fauna of the valley and desert. There seems a similar tension between features confined to one place and those attested across the country: catacombs of wrapped, often embalmed, cat, dog, falcon, and ibis appear at numerous sites, whereas crocodile, eel, ichneumon, Schilbe fish, and shrewmouse may be more strongly linked to

Figure 4.12 Limestone votive stelae with depictions of supplicants in prayer, the name and image of the god Ptah, and the hearing ears of the god, from the area of the later palace of Merenptah, Mennefer. W. Petrie, *Memphis I*, Quaritch, London, 1909, pl.9.

specific places. The main catacomb species seem to relate to solar kingship: falcon may evoke Horus and Ra directly; the ibis brings the role of Thoth, administrator to the executive sun Ra; the cat evokes leonine qualities of goddesses who are *Eye* of the Sun as his fury; while the dog, as at Asyut, may be a guardian preserver.

Child–god–king

Each dominant constellation provides a template for generating variations around one theme, with localized details, as explored from other societies in structuralist anthropology (Leach 1969). Within the web of kingship features, a prime example is the vulnerable child who emerges to triumph over an enemy. In different periods, the future ruler can take different names, in different places, and merge with other features, all under the triple function child–god–king. At the court of the king, he may be called Horus, while beside Amun and Mut at New Kingdom Thebes, he is Khons. On one small limestone votive stela from a palace city of about 1350 BC, he is depicted facing the hippopotamus–lion protectress at

Figure 4.13   Limestone votive stela with an unnamed child–god–king figure facing hippopotamus–lion protectress of infant and mother at birth. Drawing © Wolfram Grajetzki.

birth, sometimes named Ipy or, later, Taweret; here, the relation to infancy seems to be primary in conception of the small monument (Figure 4.13). Different aspects or episodes of the development to triumphant hero can be foregrounded in invoking, and offering to, this force: Horus the Child may be approached as a divine presence separate from Horus Protector of his Father. After 800 BC, there is a new emphasis on Horus the Child, with increasing use of names on the pattern May (Horus/the king) live! (for the god, Ankh-Hor, Ankh-Horpakhered; for kings, Ankh-Osorkon, Ankh-Sheshonq) as well as special temples for rites and festivals of his birth added to the largest regional and national temples (Mammisi).

Images of order as single and as balance

From the late fourth millennium BC on, kingship imagery moves between balancing motifs and single dominant figure, as two strategies for expressing the triumph of order/good over chaos/evil (Kemp 2006, 92–99). Paired motifs include falcon and composite animal later identified in inscriptions as the god of order Horus and the god of disorder Seth. Single dominant motifs are the falcon, winged sun disk and, more rarely, the lion. Whether paired or single, the imagery of order appears first at the royal court. Balance of motifs continues prominently in late third-millennium BC seal-amulets, with facing or inverted pairs of Seth animals and falcons (Figure 4.2, and examples in Wiese 1996, pl.10–12). Early second-millennium BC pendants of precious metal continue the symmetrical tradition or, at several sites, take instead the form of a single falcon wearing the double crown, as in images of Horus (e.g., Garstang 1902, pl.1). These amulets from different periods testify materially to use of kingship motifs outside kingship circles, as part of broader strategies to defend life and order.

Kingship is disseminated widely as a name and as a royal name ring (cartouche). In the second millennium BC, cosmetic equipment includes cartouche-shaped grindstones for eye paint and perhaps body paint and cartouche-shaped cosmetic boxes. However, the name of the king is the most widely distributed presence of kingship. From 1850 BC, glazed steatite seal-amulets inscribed with the name of the king were produced on a large scale. Similarly, the Residence city of Akhenaten, Akhetaten, was littered with faience rings molded with the names of the king, the women nearest him, and the sun as creator (Quirke and Tajeddin 2010). Faience rings are fragile and break easily, and the psychology of the distribution is ambiguous: did the discarded names fertilize the earth with royal power, or does the ephemeral material indicate a more pragmatic, even less reverent, attitude to kingship across the city? For this question, there is no direct answer in writing.

Speaking and Narrating the Divine

A motif throughout temple ritual: offerings as the eye

The motif of fertility returning after low Nile seems to permeate the entire written record for offerings to deities, kings, and the dead. For ritual performed by or for the king, written sources from 2400 BC onward cast each offering as the return of the healthy eye. Inscriptions and manuscripts of festival and daily temple ritual follow the same model, in periods when they survive (1800 BC onward). Every movement of material for a meal, for sound, for burning incense, and for washing evokes the restoration of wholeness after loss. The pattern may be seen in a purification formula first found for the burial of King Unas, about 2400 BC, and then repeated in different wealthy contexts over the next 2000 years (Pyramid Text 32):

> This is your libation, Osiris.
> This is your libation, O Unas,
> coming -*Libation (and) two pellets of natron*- from your son,
> coming from Horus.
> I have come, I bring you the Eye of Horus,
> so that your heart may be refreshed by it.
> I bring it to you to carry you, under your soles.

The sound of the Egyptian word for each offering becomes material for identifying with the Eye, as seen most clearly in the short assertions accompanying offerings (Pyramid Text 51):

> Unas! Take the Eye of Horus that you may taste (*dep*) it!
> *One depet-loaf*

The English term *wordplay* may obscure the insight of the composers and reciters of these formulae, who are in effect proposing a materialist interpretation of speech several thousand years before Voloshinov wrote his philosophy of language. The sound of a word may be accidental, but it is also specific, with conscious and subconscious links to other words, in a live force field of social practice. In daily conversation and writing, we avoid using words which might give the wrong impression, unless we are actively rebelling against a dominant social practice. In this way, we acknowledge the potential impact of words and sounds: the ancient composers worked more explicitly with this appreciation of the word as a material entity created from physical, bodily moves. Every sound could help to recognize the offering in its divine dimension. For the ancient Egyptian context, Assmann proposed the term *sacramental explanation*, to keep to the sacredness at stake (Assmann 2005, 349–352). These equations of the daily with the divine are the ubiquitous and standard ancient Egyptian use of words, in stark contrast to the elusive narrative *myth*.

Myth *in practice*

Joachim Quack has reassessed the question of longer narrative myth from both the written content and the individual source contexts (Quack 2009). Most examples of longer narrative belong within hymns or rituals in which a deity receives adoration, or where a feature in the world receives explanation in the terms of the divine. The two main functions would then be explanation and praise, perhaps always entwined, with explanation also as a form of praise. For the explanatory compositions, historians of religion have used the term etiology (from Greek *aetios*, "cause," and *logos*, "study") and spoken of charter myths, writings that explain, and so perhaps justify, the existence of a feature in the world. One of the most often cited *myths* from ancient Egypt, the Sky Cow, is full of explanatory passages (see following text).

Quack also notes from the study by James Allen of ancient Egyptian writings on creation that only one of the 16 selected would match the dominant definition of myth as longer narrative composition: the words of the creator in a ritual composition with the title *The Book for Knowing the Becoming of the Sun and for Overthrowing Aapep* (Allen 1988, 28–30, third century BC, so later than the period covered in this volume). Even that declaration is rather distinct from most *mythology* by its use of the first person. In history of religion, a ritual declamation in the first person of divine characteristics and deeds is often called an aretalogy (from Greek *arete*, "virtue," in the sense of good deed or character). The psychological impact of reciting such words may have been overpowering, as the speaker started from such a direct assertion as "I am Isis"—a formula extensively deployed in writings for good health (see Chapter 5). Similar statements recur in writings for eternal life (Chapter 6), where one of the most widely attested compositions identifies the speaker as the creator (Coffin Text 335 = *Book of the Dead* chapter 17, Allen 1988, 31):

> The word comes to be, all is mine (*or* I am the all),
> in my existence alone.
> I am the sun in his first appearances,
> I am the great god who comes to be out of himself.

Total identification with the divine (aretalogy) and seeing the world through the eyes of the divine (etiology) may take us out of myth in our familiar storytelling patterns and into a more surprising and revealing world of imagery and word-craft.

Local, central, or all-Egyptian?

Early Egyptologists constructed myths out of writings from different periods taken together and then concluded that apparently contradictory myths represented the separate traditions of each local area. For example, on creation, there would be (i) a Hermopolitan myth, focussing on primeval forces and the emergence of the primeval mound; (ii) a Heliopolitan myth, on the unfurling of the world through nine deities, from sun-god Ra to Shu and Tefnut, Geb and Nut, and the pairs Osiris–Isis and Seth–Nephthys, on to the kingship of Horus; and (iii) a Memphite myth, around the creative power of Ptah. From her study of the Pyramid and Coffin Texts, Susanne Bickel argues against this idea of early local creation myths. She considers writings after 1500 BC radically different, with earlier writing focussed exclusively on solar creation at Iunu, the later more diverse. Only Atum is attested as creator until the Middle Kingdom; from the New Kingdom, creator epithets are found for Amun, Sobek, Thoth, Ptah, and Ha'py (Bickel 1994, 296). This difference may belong partly to the field of expression, as the New Kingdom is the period when local centers receive monumental architecture (Chapter 3). The new more local creator deities might express in words the claim to solar sovereignty made tangible in the architectural expression which Kemp calls the *Formal* temple. At this same stage, the local deities may more often be associated with the solar creator in the fusions such as Sobek-Ra and Amun-Ra. However, some combinations were not produced: there is no Ptah-Ra, but instead the intricate phrasing in the Shabako inscription from Mennefer (see section "Ptah, Horus and Seth").

Despite such major changes in the expression of divinity, even later sources seem remarkably bound to the centrality of the sun as the primary model of kingship and creation. If a dominant change occurs, it is perhaps less the elevation of the Hidden (Amun), than the increasing focus on the underworld sun-king, Osiris.

How far such change reflects, or draws from, other social classes, remains the question to challenge future archaeology.

Narrative and image as accompaniments

In recent Egyptological studies on myth, a functional approach places the focus on ritual practice as the context for understanding writings (Willems 1996; Goebs 2002). Some monumental writings with no evident place in a performance occupy the space alongside a more clearly liturgical composition, such as a rite to be recited for an offering. From their location beside performative compositions, these writings may be called *accompaniments* (as Assmann 1970). In these juxtapositions, a performative content or practice is reinforced by a separate description or expression in words and/or images. Joachim Quack notes two external parallels that remind us how ritual and liturgy may be interspersed with recitations: from another age, same place, Coptic Martyrdoms are read on feast days of Christian saints; from another place, same age, a creation epic was recited at the Babylonian New Year festival (Quack 2009, 291). These examples from other cultural settings may alert us to other ancient Egyptian patterns of organizing and conveying knowledge and wisdom. Where we may see a myth of creation, there may be a liturgical composition intended to reinforce a highly specific moment such as the burial of a king, or the ceremonies for a new ruler.

The Nut image: world description as accompaniment to burial space

The most monumental ancient depiction of the created world is the image of the sky goddess Nut annotated with hieroglyphic inscriptions, sculpted in relief on the ceiling of the Osiris *embalming-chamber temple* behind the temple for King Sety I at Abdju; another version is painted on a ceiling in the tomb of Ramses IV at Waset (Lieven 2007). The date of composition is uncertain: its astronomical data suggest early nineteenth century BC, 500 years before Sety I. However, its image–word combination could have been compiled in the reign of Sety I from earlier sources, as part of the *repeating of births* or renewal, a generation after Akhenaten ruptured kingship patterns. The rarity of the Nut image and associated inscriptions may simply be caused by their designated location, on ceiling blocks, first part of any monument to disappear (Lieven 2007). In second-century AD Tebtunis, manuscript copies included an explanatory commentary, exceptional among ancient Egyptian religious writings. The same hoard of papyri contained copies of Asyut inscriptions from 2000 BC, and so it is not clear whether the ancient compositions circulated continuously as treasured writings or whether they had been rediscovered at some point, potentially even as late as the Roman Period. The Nut images and inscriptions might have been fundamental to all the learned, a "foundation for the course of the stars" as prescribed in the inscriptions themselves, or a composition restricted to the innermost circle of kingly knowledge, inscribed only exceptionally even for the eternal life of the king himself (Figure 4.14).

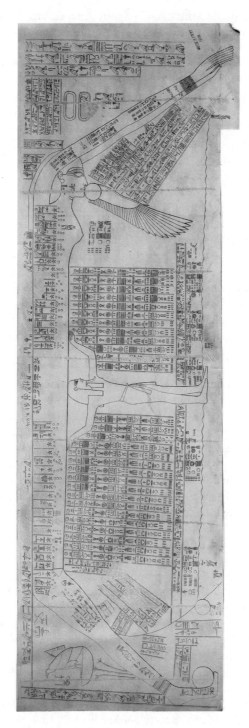

Figure 4.14   Image of Nut on the ceiling of Sety I Osiris tomb, Abdju. Drawing from expedition directed by Henri Frankfort, © Egypt Exploration Society.

In the Sety I monument, the annotated image of Nut is carved at the right end of the western half of the ceiling, followed by four inscriptions: on Shadow Clock, star groups (by decans = ten-day periods), moon, and planets (Lieven 2007, 15). The sky goddess Nut is arched, head to right, feet to left, over a smaller figure of an unidentified god (Shu?), hands supporting her body, standing on a wavy line that runs slightly above the level of her fingertips and toes (Allen 1988, 1–7, pl.1). At the toes of the goddess is a disk, with a smaller disk beside a line to the right, by the start of the wavy line. At her knees is a winged scarab to the inside; here, above the legs and facing out stands a vulture named as the goddess Nekhbet. The crutch of the goddess is labeled *eastern horizon*. Below and touching the mouth of the goddess, labeled *western horizon*, is a disk with one large wing. The image may seem to us a fixed cosmos, but that static word from Greek and our perception of ancient Egyptian formal art fail to convey the dynamism in this expression of created life. In an eternal motion of celestial bodies, the Nut *sky* body is held in tension by Shu *air* as the life bubble of our existing worlds.

The second-century AD papyrus copies and commentaries start from the vertical line at foot end, moving along the annotations below and over the body of Nut, to inscriptions at the winged disk below her mouth, and end at far right. The farthest left line declares, presumably referring to the sun-god: "this god exists on her south-eastern side beyond Punt." As the main source of incense, Punt is generally located at the south-eastern end of the Red Sea, African and/or Arabian side (Harvey 2003; Meeks 2003). On the leg, the position of the sun at her toes is explained: "The power of this god goes out from her lower part, and then moves towards earth, appeared and born! Then he rises, rises on the back, then he parts the legs of his mother Nut, then he moves away to the upper sky!" The winged scarab and lower body inscriptions evoke the red of dawn and union of Ra and Osiris in the zone bordering the horizons of east and west (Egyptian *mesqet*). The series of star groups are inscribed across her body and in the expanse either side of the standing god supporting her. Above her body is written "The upper part of this sky is the total darkness, of unknown limit—south, [north], west, east—fixed in the waters as the inert ones ... its land, south, north, west, east, is unknown to the gods and the transfigured, there is no light there. Any place void of sky, any place void of earth, that is the whole underworld."

In inscriptions at the mouth of Nut, the sun-god enters the underworld "to issue commands to those in the west" (i.e., the dead), followed by the stars until he is born from her again at dawn. To the right of her head are two horizontal ovals, one containing three fattened birds; the second-century AD papyri identify the ovals as "the nests of the Cool Waters." Above is written: "these birds, their faces are of people, their forms birds; they speak to one another in the speech of people; when they arrive, to eat the plants, to fatten up in the Black Land, they touch earth beneath the light of the sky, and take the form of birds." This passage seems to convey the mystery of mass bird migration, as vast flocks fly into the Nile Valley from remote northern regions (for the scale, cf. sightings of 100–150,000 stork and sand martin Goodman and Meininger 1989, 145, 366 150,000). The impenetrable commotion is given human qualities of face and speech, masked by the forms taken as birds once they have alighted on earth. The composition ends with an orientation in darkness, at the upper right corner: "The total darkness, Cool Waters of the gods, the place from which the birds come; this is on her northwestern side from her northeastern side; an opening to the underworld which is on her northern side, her back on the east, her head on the west."

After a passage on the Shadow Clock, the composition continues with accounts of star groups, moon, and planets, in dialogue style, rather than annotated image. Positions and movements in the heavens can be anchored in disputes between divine forces: the earth Geb objects to sky Nut swallowing the stars, as in pig farming the farmer fears that a sow might devour her piglets (te Velde 1967). Throughout the images and words, attentive to time calculation, these sources remain anchored in kingship and its ritual institutions. These concerns may not have been expressed in the same way, or even shared at all, across different life settings and economies. They must be measured in context from palace threshold to farm door and field, where much of the imagery gains its original power (for socially variable articulation of ritual knowledge, especially in relation to time, see Bloch 1998, 131–151).

Ptah, Horus, and Seth: creation at Mennefer, the Shabako inscription

Equally famous in Egyptology is an account of the gods Ptah, Horus, and Seth, inscribed on a block of basalt in the reign of King Shabako (find-place unknown). The heading to this *Shabako Stone*, also known as the Memphite Theology, records that it is a copy from a damaged ancient manuscript. The main content concerns the annual kingship ritual of unification of the two lands, expressed in the terms of actions among gods. The original architectural cult setting and the purpose of the block remain to be established. Crucially, we do not know whether it *accompanied* another composition, a ritual to be performed, or a hymn to be sung. We can only speculate that the contents might have been recited at rites for confirming the kingship on Shabako at Mennefer. One part of the inscription seems to seek a resolution in struggles between Horus and Seth. The other describes the Memphite god Ptah as a creative force in ambiguous terms, exploring his relation to the solar creator Atum (Allen 1988, 43–44 with differing translation):

> It came to be as heart,
> it came to be as tongue,
> in the image of Ptah.
> Great and mighty is Ptah,
> who causes all gods to live,
> and all their *ka*-souls,
> as this heart in which Horus came to be,
> as this tongue in which Thoth came to be
> It came to be that heart and tongue have power over all limbs,
> [...] that he exists as Foremost of the body (of gods),
> as Foremost of every mouth of all gods and all people,
> of all flocks, of all serpents that live,
> in planning, in commanding all that he wishes.

His Nine Gods are before him as the teeth, the lips,
the seed and hands of Atum.

Such condensed, perhaps deliberately ambiguous writing may become clearer from shorter declarations in the writings for the afterlife. One coffin from Inerty (Gebelein), about 2000 BC, preserves a declaration by Ptah, "There is none of them (the gods) that speaks to me, except the [maker] of my name, him alone, for I am Command on his mouth, and Perception that is in his body" (Coffin Text 647, after Bickel 1994, 108). Although a force for creation, Ptah acts as the vital word and sight of a prior creator, as on the basalt block inscribed for Shabako thirteen centuries later.

Creation: centered on the Sun

No readings of these religious compositions can be reduced to the simple or literal, given the special aim of their contexts, as Harco Willems in particular has emphasized. Their social reach is extremely limited in earlier periods, as previously noted. Nevertheless, the compositions first found in the late third millennium (Pyramid Texts) and extended in the early second millennium BC (Coffin Texts) offer a starting point for understanding more specifically the links between named forces and features in the world of kingship, with its hegemonic impact on at least some, perhaps mainly the wealthier, social groups. The principal themes of creation in these sources have been clearly grouped by Bickel, to offer an outline for one part of society 2400–1850 BC (Bickel 1994).

Compositions on creation may be read more effectively as poetic evocations, than as statements from results of scientific research. Variations are to be expected. Some accounts speak of the creator as All (Egyptian Atum) within primeval waters (Egyptian Nun) either masturbating, sometimes then swallowing his seed to give birth to creation, or exhaling, sneezing or spitting out bodily content. One passage advocates one version against another, as words of Shu to refute the idea of his birth from semen (Coffin Text 75):

I am one sneezed of form,
he (Atum) did not give birth to me from his mouth,
he did not conceive me by his fist!
From his nose he sneezed me out,
from the middle of his throat he made me!

Bickel notes that the exclusive emphasis on birth in the element of air may be explained by the context, as this passage comes from a series ensuring the power of Shu, and so the ability to breathe, for the deceased. Modern readers may feel discomfort at these intrusions of body fluids into ethereal questions of eternity. Yet any focus on the physicality of bodily decay stems less from an earthy grounding in realities of life, than from the context of the writings: in the messy business of embalming, the paramount need was to retain the body with all its functions, to eternity.

Place and process of creation

Funerary writings (2400–1850 BC) locate the place of creation, if at all, at Iunu, center of the sun cult. Later compositions take instead male and female versions of the four primeval forces (for four cardinal points addressed in ritual?) as the meaning of the city Khemenu, "Eight," the cult center of Thoth in Middle Egypt. According to the later compositions, Khemenu is a (one?) site of the primeval mound or at least a place with focus on the primeval nothingness out of which dry ground for the sun-god emerged. Since most of the finest coffins with Coffin Texts are from Khemenu, the lack of earlier references is not just a gap in the surviving record. Instead, it seems that writers in earlier periods did not share our need to identify the place for creation in the world. In one of the rare early references, we read (Pyramid Text 600):

> Atum the Becoming One (Egyptian Kheprer)
> You have risen on the Tall Mound
> You have risen from the *benben*-stone in the Domain of the *benben* in Iunu.
> You have spat out Shu, you have sneezed out Tefnet,
> You have extended your arms around them
> in the gesture of *ka* so that your *ka*-spirit may be in them.

The male Shu seems to denote the dry air and light between sun and earth, and the female Tefnet perhaps the complementary force of corrosion, as *tefen* is a word for the corroding of metal. One composition comments on whether there are now three or one, evidently not incorporating Nun the primeval waters in the equation: "Atum made the eldest by his powers, when he gave birth to Shu and Tefnet in Iunu, when was single and came to be three" (Coffin Text 80). In the next phase of creation, Shu and Tefnet engender the earth Geb and sky Nut, who in turn produce Osiris, Isis, Nephthys, and Seth. Some writings look for the principle by which these and other gods came into being and four divine names in particular feature as the creator-sons in these writings: Shu, Ptah, the Nile Flood (Egyptian Ha'py), and the force Heka (creative word: against the translation Magic, see Chapter 1).

In perhaps the most remarkable of these compositions (Coffin Text 1130), the sun-god creator himself declares "I created the gods from my sweat," and "people are from the tears of my eyes." However, no special attention is given to the timing of the creation of humankind, or of gods and goddesses, or even of the order in which humans and deities appeared. They seem to be jointly present from early within the series of unfurlings of the world into its present form.

Overcoming violence after creation: Horus against Seth

Writings for the afterlife cast death as an act of violence against the body. In the context of mummification, rather than the natural violence of age and death, the enemy here is perhaps more specifically the knife cut needed to remove faster-rotting internal organs (see Chapter 7). The cut seemed so heinous that it receives only indirect mention, implicating Seth as the murderer. In one passage, the deceased as Horus speaks of the killer of his father Osiris (e.g., Bickel 1994, 226 no.199). Hymns to Osiris give more information. A great stela from the cult center of Osiris at Abdju describes festivals there, exceptionally celebrated for the king by his treasurer Iykhernefret (1850 BC). At this date, as also attested for the next thousand years, a procession moved from the temple of Osiris at the desert edge over a kilometer to the low desert tomb of King Djer (3000 BC), identified then as the burial place of Osiris. Osiris is felled on the bank of the Nedyt canal, but his enemies are repelled, and his son Horus is declared triumphant. According to other sources, the focus of action immediately after the killing moved to his sister-wife Isis. The longest account is part of a hymn to Osiris on the Abdju stela of the overseer of cattle of Amun Amenmes and his wife Nefertiry (1400 BC, Louvre C286, Lichtheim 1976, 81–85). Within the acclamations of Osiris, one passage describes him as protected by Isis and tells how she sought for his body, implying that it was dispersed, and how she revived his inert body to conceive the child Horus and nursed him to manhood when he could claim the inheritance of Osiris in the judgment hall of Geb, earth god father of Osiris:

> Isis the effective one, protector of her brother,
> she who sought him untiringly, who circled this land in mourning,
> she who would not come to rest until she found him,
> she who makes daylight with her feathers, who causes air with her wings,
> she who performs the dance of joy at the mooring (i.e. burial) of her brother,
> she who raises up the inertness of the weary-hearted,
> who catches his semen, who makes the heir,
> who nurses the child in isolation, his whereabouts unknown,
> who introduces him, once his arm is strong, inside the broad court of Geb,
> the Nine Gods rejoicing "Welcome Son of Osiris, Horus stout-hearted,
> son of Isis, heir of Osiris!" ...
> Horus has been found true of voice (i.e. in his case against Seth),
> and the office of his father is given to him

The end of the world

Twice only, afterlife writings refer to an ending in the present cycle of creation, where they aim beyond even the life of the world and of the gods, to an eternity nestled with the creator. In the great declaration in the Middle Kingdom literature, the sun-god creator declares (coffins from Bersha, 1875 BC, Coffin Text 1130 = Bickel 1994, 229, no.201):

> I have made millions of years between me and that weary-hearted, the son of Geb,
> but I intend (in the future) to dwell with him in one place,
> the mounds will become towns, and the towns mounds,
> domain laying waste to domain.

Six hundred years later, several papyri for the afterlife include a dialogue between Osiris and the creator, here named Atum, the All (*Book of the Dead* chapter 175, Allen 1974). When Osiris asks, "what is a span of life?," Atum replies:

Figure 4.15   Silhouette depicting a figurine of a falcon-headed deity, over which a person should recite the dialogue of Atum and Osiris, in the papyrus for Going Out by Day (*Book of the Dead*), made for the head architect Kha, Waset. Drawing © Wolfram Grajetzki.

> You are to have millions of millions,
> a lifespan of millions.
> when I have had him send out the elders,
> I shall indeed destroy all I made,
> and this land shall turn into Nun,
> as a floodwater, as its original condition.
> I alone am to remain, with Osiris,
> when I have transformed myself into other snakes,
> which men do not know, which gods do not see.

By becoming Osiris, the embalmed dead can escape the end of this world, surviving in the chrysalis of the creator Atum, perhaps for another cycle of creation emerging out of the primeval waters Nun (Figure 4.15).

A longer narrative, 1150 BC: the judgement of Horus and Seth

In the mid-twelfth century BC, a high-placed reader in the community of royal craftsmen at Waset owned what is now one of the finest surviving book rolls from Egypt. The principal composition on the front of the papyrus is entitled *The Judgement of Horus and Seth* by the sun-god Ra/Atum. The opening lines, assuming the equality of the two, present the younger, Horus, as plaintiff to for the office of his father Osiris against his uncle Seth. Over 15 pages of narrative follow, in a seesaw of inconclusive episodes (summary from Lichtheim 1976, 214–223):

> The Gods Favour Horus: Shu and Thoth favor Horus, Isis tells the north wind to tell Osiris, Shu says all gods agree, and Ra is angered by others making a decision.
> Resistance of Ra: Seth requests a duel, and Thoth says he is in the wrong; anger of Ra who favors Seth; Inheret asks "what are we to do?" so Atum summons Banebdjed (elder god at Djedet in the Delta), and he recommends writing to Neit.

Neit Favours Horus: Thoth writes a letter from King Ra-Atum to Neit (primeval *mother of the god* at Sau in the Delta), for a decision after this eighty years of trial, and Neit recommends giving the office of Osiris to his son, doubling the possessions of Seth.

Resistance of Ra: The gods acclaim the decision; Ra calls Horus a bad-smelling child; anger of Inheret and gods; Baba (violent god) tells Ra his shrine is empty; Ra withdraws offended, and the gods are angry with Baba; Hathor exposes herself to Ra to make him laugh and coax him back to his role.

Blocked Judgement: Ra invites statements, Seth says they need his force to smite the enemies of Ra, and the gods agree; Inheret and Thoth say the son should inherit, and Banebdjed says the elder should inherit; the gods and Horus complain; anger of Isis but the gods say they support her; anger of Seth, refusing to continue trial before Isis.

Hearing the Case in Isolation: The gods move to an island but Isis bribes Nemty (ferryman god); disguised, Isis tricks Seth into saying the son should inherit; Seth complains to Ra, and Nemty is punished by having his claws removed; the gods move to the west shore mountain.

Ra-Atum Favours Horus: Ra-Atum tells the gods to end the case, giving Horus the office of Osiris; anger of Seth; Horus is crowned, and Seth swears he will remove the crown from Horus.

Resistance of Seth: Horus and Seth duel as hippopotami; Isis makes harpoon, hits Horus, tells the barb to let go, then hits Seth, but lets go when he cries out; Horus, angry at Isis for sparing Seth, cuts off her head; anger of Ra against Horus.

Loss and Renewal of Eyes of Horus: Seth removes the eyes of Horus, which grow into lotus buds, and he pretends not to have found him, but Hathor finds him and restores his sight with gazelle milk, telling Ra what happened.

False Pause: The gods tell Horus and Seth to stop fighting; Seth seduces Horus, who catches the semen of Seth and tells Isis; Isis cuts off the hand of Horus, throws it into the marshes, and replaces it, then puts the semen of Horus on a lettuce in the garden of Seth; when Seth tells the gods he has done "the work of a male" against Horus, the semen of Seth comes out of the marsh, and the semen of Horus comes out of the head of Seth as a disk, taken by Thoth as a crown; the gods acclaim Horus.

Resistance of Seth: Seth demands a stone boat duel, making a stone boat, while Horus makes a plastered cargo boat; the Seth boat sinks, Seth takes hippopotamus form, and Horus attacks as harpooner, but the gods tell him not to proceed.

Complaint of Horus: Horus goes to Neit to complain of the eighty years of trial.

Correspondence of Ra and Osiris: Thoth tells Ra to write to Osiris; anger of Osiris at the news that Horus has not been given his office and replies reminding Ra that he is the origin of plant life; Ra replies, "If you had not been born, barley and emmer would still exist"; Osiris replies with threat to unleash the disease carriers of the underworld; the gods side with Osiris, and Seth demands a new judgment in the Island in the Midst, "but Horus was declared in the right against him."

Judgement: Atum orders Seth to be brought in chains, which Isis does; he asks Seth why he resists judgment; Seth accepts Horus should be summoned and given the office; Horus is acclaimed as king of Egypt; Ptah asks, what of Seth? Ra says that Seth should be given to him (Ra) as a son, to thunder in the sky; announcement of Horus as king, Ra rejoices and declares celebration; final hymn of celebration by Isis.

The bewildering to-and-fro seems cumulatively comical, apparently intentionally so. The legalistic case pits son against uncle (elder), the first half at court, ending in a first crowning, and the second half in physical duel, ending in the unproductive complaint of Horus and sharp exchange of letters between Ra and Osiris. Finally, more majestically as Atum, the solar creator presides over the chaining of Seth and acclaim at the kingship of Horus.

This long series could offer the myth researcher the longer narrative desired. Yet the episodes seem literarily sewn together, not so much the elusive genotext as a new string of schemata. Alan Gardiner interpreted the rather irreverent tone as a mark of a satirical village tale, but formal religious writing might readily use carnival motifs of fun, shock, and temper. In a striking reinterpretation combining the Tale with other writings on the same papyrus roll, Ursula Verhoeven noted connections with feast days for acclamation of Horus as king, in the formal festival calendars, and concluded that the Tale might have been recited at festivals of kingship (Verhoeven 1996), recalling with Quack the recital of martyrdoms on later Egyptian Christian feast days. Festival acclamation would also return us to the context of hymns, where we find the longer ancient descriptions of the felling of Osiris (stela of Iykhernefret) and the quest of Isis (stela of Amenmes).

Two narratives

Sometimes, anthologists, exasperated by the lack of examples, have included other longer compositions involving deities, of widely varying contexts, and not always narratives from start to finish (James 1971). The prime example of ambiguous function is the composition known today as the Tale of Two Brothers, preserved on a single papyrus, dated 1250 BC, recounting the tribulations of Bata, younger brother of Inpu (Anubis), both gods with cult centers in Middle Egypt (Assmann 1977b). The first part of the tale is set in a farm, on human level, though with superhuman elements (Bata can converse with the cattle he herds); after false accusation by his wife, Inpu tries to kill Bata, who leaves home. The second part moves to exotic locations, Vale of the Cedar (presumably Lebanon) and the royal court, where Bata undergoes a series of transformations. Propp used the story in his analysis of tales of wonder, and it does seem to belong with these rather than serving as an introduction to the two deities, despite points of contact with motifs later attested for Middle Egypt. If the genre serves initiation rites of passage, the composition aptly hovers on the line between literary entertainment and religious experience.

The second composition accounts for the withdrawal of the creator sun-god into the sky, after rebellion by humankind. It is known from five tombs of kings at Waset, 1325–1125 BC. Anthologists tend to extract the first part of the composition, as closer to our expectations of myth as narrative. As this part concerns the punishment of rebels, it is often known in Egyptology as the Destruction of Mankind; the sun-god in fact changes heart, and these lines might also be called the Saving of Humankind. The sun-god sends out his eye as Sekhmet *Fury*, to slaughter the rebels; when he relents, she is tricked into drinking blood-red beer, and reverts to the loving Hathor. Most of the content concerns explanation of features in the present world, with instructions for use, but the overall focus is the withdrawal of the sun-god to the sky, depicted as a heavenly cow supported by the forces of the air. Before assuming that the composition tells us how the ancient Egyptians in general thought that the world assumed its present form, we should consider the physical architectural context for all its surviving copies: the outer gold shrine around the body of Tutankhamun, a special niche off the burial chamber in the tombs of Sety I, Ramses II and III, and a separate niche in the tomb of Ramses VI. In other words, the composition accompanies the body of the king as laid to rest, in one period. The explanations add up to a particular urgent question, the death of the king and, in ancient Egyptian terms, his departure to fuse with the sun-god. In these terms, the part-narrative composition provides not a *myth of creation of the world*, but an accompaniment to the burial of the body of the king (Figure 4.16).

Conclusion: icon, constellation, and tale

From the written evidence, it is unclear whether any underlying myth existed, in the sense of a longer series of connected episodes. Instead, most writings remain, with visual depictions and material practices, within a more tightly drawn focus, the

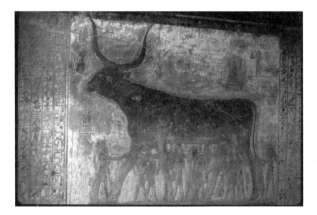

Figure 4.16   Depiction of the heavenly cow, accompanying the narrative which gives explanations for the distance between the creator and people, including the near destruction of humankind. Side chamber in the tomb of King Sety I, Waset, about 1285 BC. Photograph © Gianluca Miniaci.

constellation of Assmann. Over time, this may change, with increasing use of narrative, in longer series. However, there may always be a close connection to specific processes. Rather than the farming cycle, or other seasonal activity, the most prominent ritualized process in our sources is embalming. Funerary literature provides the source for most episodes of deities, and its function may not match our need to know ancient myth; its ethereal features secure air and light for the deceased, and its creation stories of sneezing and spitting may relate to the cleaning of the body as it exudes fluid during embalming processes. Ra and Osiris are indeed the deceased. The better preservation on dry cemetery ground doubtless distorts the picture, although the floodplain sources for later periods seem to confirm that Osiris becomes the dominant model for local religious expression. Perhaps, finally, the Assmann *constellation* is implicit within each divine name/ figure: an ancient Egyptian deity/*netjer* is a relationship internalized already within one name.

For different identifications of daily materials as divine, we may read again the liturgy of offerings for the dead from 1500 BC (Chapter 1). In the temple and offering chapel, the offerings are the Eye of Horus, where there may be connections out to broader material sources with focus on the returning fertile flood and mud after the low Nile. In these equations, there is no need to assume that the words or mythic explanation is later or earlier than the rites. Modern prejudice that ritual is empty may precondition us to expect that the ancient ritualist experienced the same emptiness and that *sacramental explanation* (offering loaf = Eye of Horus) is intended to fill the gap. For ancient Egypt, I see no evidence for a historical progression from a stage where rituals had direct meaning, to a stage where they were being performed but had lost their meaning, to a stage where mythic or divine associations were added to a ritual in order to give them some reason for being performed—an invention of tradition. Instead, with Vico and Cassirer, the evidence can be read synchronously, as two ways of talking about and performing the world: a loaf is offered (tangible this world) and it is the Eye returned to make the world whole (reexpressing the same physical world as interaction between divine forces). The same, as well as different individuals, might see the act in different ways, as an ornithologist and painter and theologian (perhaps all the same person) might see and describe the flight of the heron. Any historical change comes not in a contrast between earlier real and added mythic, but in the impact of the verbal, visual, and material expressions by and on individuals and groups in their varying social historical contexts.

CHAPTER 5

Being Good: Doing, Saying, and Making Good Possible

⌐⌐⌐⌐

Translating Ma'at

On a broad definition, with Gramsci (Chapter 1), we might consider *religion* the interface between a collective understanding of the world and a pattern of social behavior (see Chapter 1). From ways of expressing what or how the world is (Chapter 4), here, we move to how people behaved and gave expression to correct behavior. Social norms are often institutionalized in favor of the powerful, and, historically, groups and individuals support or resist normative power; variance may also, then, be part of our historical study. In the Egyptian language, the word for correct behavior is *ma'at*, "what is right," also translated as truth or justice. Ancient writings oppose *ma'at* to *isfet*, translated "falsehood," "evil," and "what is wrong." In both verbal and visual imageries, ma'at may be a daughter of the creator sun-god Ra and personified as a woman wearing the ostrich plume hieroglyph used to write the word *ma'at*. From 1450 BC onward, tomb and temple wall scenes include depictions of the king presenting to the gods a small image of ma'at in this form (Teeter 1997). Egyptologists have tended to work from this visual expression of ma'at, "what is right," as an icon culturally specific to Egypt and leave the term untranslated. One effect may be a tendency to idealize the past, whereas, as anthropologist Janet Hendricks argues, "few, if any societies, are without some form of domination, whether it is based on age, gender, kinship, or some more institutionalized form of domination" (Hendricks 1988, 217) (Figure 5.1).

Avoiding translation conforms to the idea that the local "what is right" defines every society; any distinctive human group develops a separate identity around notions of correct appearance, behavior, and language. By leaving *ma'at* untranslated, the emphasis falls on the specifically ancient Egyptian, enabling a project of comparative anthropology, to explore differences between languages—between *ma'at*, haqq, right, and Pravda. Yet that comparative project is not emerging. Instead,

Exploring Religion in Ancient Egypt, First Edition. Stephen Quirke.
© 2015 Stephen Quirke. Published 2015 by John Wiley & Sons, Ltd.

Figure 5.1 Depiction of the king offering ma'at, wall-relief in the tomb of King Ramses III, Waset, about 1285 BC. Photograph © Gianluca Miniaci.

Egyptologists seem to assert with *ma'at*, not a universal variation in local expressions of what is right, but some essential quality unique to ancient Egypt. In place of a universal human quest for right, they install without comparison one local answer. However, if every group or *culture* is defined by having its own sense of what is right and wrong, then 'what is right' would be a universal property of human social being. Ma'at should then be translated, "(what is) right," and studied alongside every other social linguistic expression of the concept.

In sum, Egyptological use of ma'at is antihistorical, separating Egypt from all other humans. I prefer to translate *ma'at* as Right, to allow readers to appreciate the ancient Egyptian sources as part of a general human search. The specific expression of Right implicit and explicit in ancient writings can still be used to define the local within that global history. Here, the studies by Jan Assmann have contributed most to defining the particular ancient Egyptian sense of what is Right, including comparison with other ancient writings.

Sources for Ethics

As ever, still insufficiently explored in Egyptology, the question remains whether surviving written sources apply to all, most, or some people in Egypt (3000–525 BC). Feminist writing helps to overturn assumptions in this area, and archaeological theory and methods provide possible broader approaches. How we prioritize sources may depend on whether we are interested in how people treat one another or how they say they should. Writings could be considered the most direct evidence for ethics as statements by (at least some) people in a society on good behavior. For ethics as good or bad behavior in practice, other archaeological material may be the primary sources. The historian of ethics would then look at differences in sizes of houses and quality of clothing, food, and furnishings across the society studied. Condition of bodies and their treatment and arrangement in cemeteries might offer most direct contact with past patterns of social and individual behavior.

In this chapter, I address both approaches to ethics, drawing on three broad sets of sources: (1) the archaeological record across cemeteries and dwellings, as reflection of how people may have treated one another (continuing the discussion of human identity in Chapter 2); (2) direct written evidence on how people treated one another (legal documents); and (3) the indirect written evidence, that is, on how people said people should be treated (autobiographical inscriptions and literary manuscripts with teachings and laments).

Damage as mirror of (In)justice

Violence and peace: bodily evidence

For past generations, preserved bodies offer the most direct evidence for the way people treat one another, though they reveal the results, not the context of action. Recurrent injuries might derive from activity by institution or state, between groups at war, or social custom. As the recorders of human remains were particularly interested in unusual cases, in pathologies, we might expect reasonable prospects for a paleopathology of social life, including such issues as the presence or absence of conflict or domestic violence. Unfortunately, as noted in Chapter 2, too few cemeteries have been excavated and recorded in sufficient detail to write a social history for Egypt at any period down to the twentieth century. Unwrappings or CAT scans of mummified individuals record the presence or absence of a particular condition in single bodies, but only study of larger groups can show whether the condition occurred often or rarely and so begin to show social impact and reaction in those individual lives. Several hundred bodies were selectively recorded and preserved from fourth-millennium BC Upper Egypt (Naqada, 266 at Nag ed-Deir) and Fayoum-Memphis cemeteries of around 3000 BC (Tarkhan) and 600–300 BC (Giza, dating and range highly uncertain). In 1907, ahead of constructing the first Aswan Dam, rescue excavations in the Nubian–Egyptian border zone south of Aswan yielded 6000 burials dated 4000 BC to AD 500 (Jones 1908; summary in Nunn 1996, 177). More recent published reports on larger numbers of individuals also come from the borders of the time–space block "ancient Egypt," where we might expect particularly strong mixture of peoples and social practice: the First Cataract region on its southern border (900, multiperiod, Rösing 1990) and its northeastern fringe, Tell el-Daba' on the east bank of the east Nile Delta branch (257, mid-second millennium BC, Winkler and Wilfing 1991).

Despite valuable detail, these excavations exclude patterns of living across most of the regions of Egypt (3000–525 BC). Marginal time–space scope may be compounded by modern cultural bias. Studies of human remains by specialists outside Egypt may introduce unconsciously external standards; the farther a study from date and place of excavation, the less a researcher may have access to limiting factors in sample preserved and methods used. Research is needed into different patterns of ageing according to ancient climate and diet but also the impact of our own cultures of knowledge production. As yet, published accounts on individual and social violence lie in a vacuum, unable to provide any regional or national picture within the "ancient Egypt" frame.

Continuing excavation with full publication and critical review promises to improve our understanding. Recent excavations at Akhetaten include recovery of over 200 bodies, offering new pictures of life at the city in the fourteenth century BC. Initial reports suggest, as elsewhere, an average lifespan of thirty to forty years, with challenging life conditions, compared by the researchers with Arctic living (Kemp 2010, 2011). Healed wounds on many bodies indicated severe impact of heavy manual labor, in part interpreted, cautiously, as possible result of beating to punish but not disable. Among dietary problems, one-third of adults suffered severe tooth decay. In the current production of archaeological knowledge in Egypt, many interpretations arise out of encounters between past material and a scientific research culture embedded in north European and Euro-American expectations. Like the evidence of ancient writing (particularly the Teaching of Khety, see section "Literary Teachings"), the results could be read productively from different modern environments, including more than one social background.

Architectural and other material equalities and inequalities

A society may declare its own understanding of itself explicitly or implicitly in the way villages and towns are built and grow. New towns express a single moment of planning, as at Middle Kingdom Lahun or New Kingdom Akhetaten. Other settlements grow over time, best documented for Abu (Elephantine), charting social ethics more implicitly. Whatever inhabitants of a society may write, the sizes and arrangement of housing tell the direct story of living conditions and ranges of wealth and health which that society supports. At Lahun and Akhetaten, waterfront buildings are not preserved, removing from our view the densest trading and industrial zones, where the poorest housing might be expected. The Lahun new town, founded in 1900–1850 BC (Figure 4.17), is zoned into three general house sizes on repeating plans and so plausibly from the original town plan (Doyen 2010): (1) a dozen palatial 40×60 m units, (2) separate zones of middle-sized units, and (3) zones of smaller housing units, generally closer to the palatial mansions. Small houses are bigger than smallest houses elsewhere; either these townspeople had larger houses or a lost canal side with wharfs included a fourth category of poorest dwellings. At Akhetaten, the palatial houses may have been planned first, with medium- and small-sized housing following. English 1920s–1930s excavation reports refer to *hovels*, but the smallest houses on the site are again larger than those known at other sites, and so the poorest level may be missing alongside the docks and wharfs outside archaeological view.

In ethical terms, the range of house sizes indicates a society that tolerates major differences in living standards. Preserved palaces of kings (1550–1200 BC) are on an altogether vaster scale, as are the funerary monuments of kings from 3000 to 1070 BC, as if confirming the separate nature of the king, distinct from humankind. If cemeteries reflect social life at least indirectly, funerary archaeology charts material inequality back to the fourth millennium BC. Those tombs relate that, not why, a few are wealthier, nor how individuals enter or leave the wealthy set. The earliest groups of rich tombs with enough written evidence to identify links between the deceased are from the courts of king and regional governors. The two main links are kinship (members of same family buried close or together) and administration or estate management (e.g., officials of regional governor buried with governor, not with family; cf. Seidlmayer 1987, 210–214). These two general patterns in social group formation create a platform for exclusion and inclusion, in preferential treatment of some against others. Groupings formed on other grounds, such as ethnicity, are rarely visible, as in distinctive burials of Nubian desert nomads in Egyptian cemeteries (1900–1700 BC) (*Pan Grave*; for groupings by age, within one social/wealth level, in the funerary record, see Chapter 2).

Material culture confirms patterns of social distinction throughout these millennia. Commissioning and production would start at palaces of kingship, although production sites have rarely been identified archaeologically on the ground; the two main examples are the Akhetaten house ascribed to a head sculptor Thutmes and the walled stone village at Deir al-Madina, base for the project of decorating the tomb of the king. In history of use, it would be wrong to assume that only wealthier Egyptians had exclusive access to highest quality. The finest ancient glassfish vase was found in a small house at Akhetaten. The 1930s excavation report concluded it had probably been stolen—such a prize had no right to live in poverty. Regularly, wealthier classes assume their own monopoly of finery, even, bizarrely, beauty and goodness; the English reporters imposed this view on the Akhetaten inhabitants, without considering in their own society the potential for a working-class woman, for example, to save enough for an object of beauty (cf. on appreciation of modern English literature, Rose 2001). Reassessment of associated finds has raised ethnicity as an explanatory factor: the glassfish may have been in the house of its maker, perhaps Syrian (Shortland 2009). Excavation recorders also assumed theft in the case of a hoard at a well in Akhetaten—a pot containing silver and gold bars and objects. Barry Kemp has compared, instead, a Ramesside letter with instructions on where to find buried bronze and a pot of silver and gold, as if a regular strategy for safeguarding metal (Kemp 2006, 315–317). Small hoards need not automatically be identified as cases of theft; they might more generally document periodic cracks in walls between social groups with different living standards.

Hoards testify to concerns over securing possessions against others in a society. As a negative material record of social ethics, hoards contest ideals of harmony and contentedness. Here, the written legal record provides more explicit material.

Legal cases in archaeological context

Legal documents speak directly about ideals and flaws in social practice, as men and women deliver their protests and appeals, where cases were urgent enough to bring into writing (Lorton 1977; Théodoridès 1971). Mostly, a single document survives from an original mass of paperwork. Moreover, documents tend to give one side of an argument; a judging official would have to assess each plaintiff or accusation. Regardless of the truth in each case, legal writings invoke accepted standards, a powerful guide in reconstructing an ancient shared sphere of ethics, at least in official public view. Disputants may work with implicit rules, or explicitly cite authoritative writings, where kingship is supreme authority. The term *decree of the king* denotes any kingly pronouncement: administrative, judicial, or in letters. A *decree* can include a specific regulation (Egyptian *hep*), which, in turn, might be cited in the way we cite a *law* (Lorton 1977, 60). Examples for regulating estates to support offerings, from 2450 to 2200 BC and 1300 to 1200 BC, provide much of our source material on corporal and capital punishment. Offenders against offering estates may be labeled *rebel* (Egyptian *sebi*), enemy of kingship and Right; in its ruler or ruling class, the formal society defines with this word a boundary across which human can be inhumanly treated (Figure 5.2).

Punishments range in severity to extreme cruelty and apply to officials as often as others. One decree inscribed for perpetuity states that intruders building into a sacred procession path, "craftsman or priest," "shall be branded" (Abdju stela, 1800 BC, Lorton 1977, 18). Later, a decree of Sety I prescribes grimmer sentences: for encroaching on offering-estate fields, cutting off ears and nose and assigning to permanent labor and, for officials failing to prosecute offenders, one hundred lashes, permanent farming labor, and prohibition on burial of the man, his wife, and children (inscription at Nauri, Nubia, 1290 BC, Lorton 1977, 25). In an extraordinary dossier on robberies from royal tombs (1150 BC), witnesses refer to sentences of being mutilated or impaled, and false witness carries the same sentence as committing the crime (Lorton 1977, 34–35). In writings from the village of artists working on the royal tomb (1300–1100 BC), oaths repeat threats of a hundred blows and cutting off ears (Lorton 1977, 38–44). Such repetition might read as a rhetorical motif, as if the most severe possible act by kingship against individual became an accepted device for heightening the urgency of a case, and so the prospect of action. This rhetorical interpretation does not mean that the punishments were never inflicted (Lorton 1977, 45, for one instance), but it reminds us not to take written evidence always at face value. Comparative study of legal rhetoric might provide parallels and methods for assessing the ancient Egyptian writing in practice. Depictions in monuments for eternity need to be read in the same spirit, avoiding both the urge to idealize the society under study and the orientalist impulse to brand the barbarism of the other without measuring against our own (Figure 5.3).

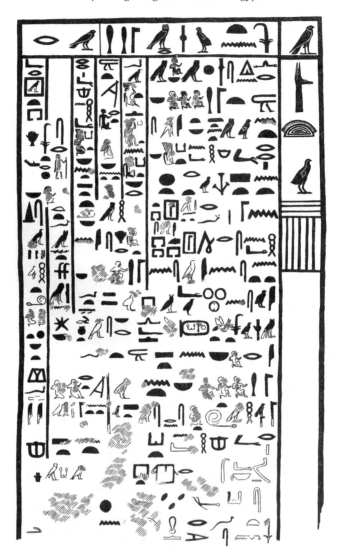

Figure 5.2   Authorizing "what is Right" and prescribing punishment for transgressors: limestone stela inscribed with decree of King Neferirkare, addressed to the overseer of god's servants and to the chief local authority, exempting local temple staff from certain obligations of the central administration and specifying penalties against transgressors. From the main temple precinct at Abdju, about 2400 BC. W. Petrie. 1903, *Abydos II*, Egypt Exploration Fund, London, pl.18.

An earlier decree specifies three drastic consequences for *rebels*: (1) all acquired and inherited property confiscated, (2) not allowed embalming and burial with blessed dead in the cemetery, and (3) not allowed to be among the living (Lorton 1977, 11, decree of a king with Horus name Demedjibtawy, otherwise

(a)

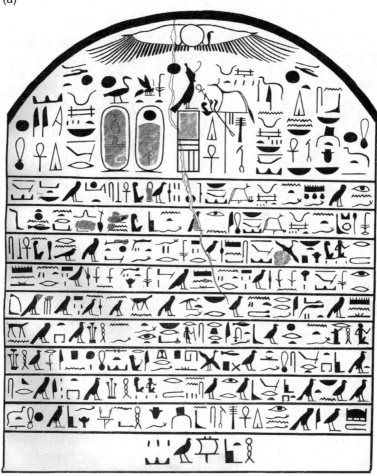

(b)

Figure 5.3 (a) Limestone stela inscribed with decree of a king, whose name has been erased and replaced by that of King Khasekhemra Neferhotep, about 1750 BC. Found at Abdju at edge of town northern cemeteries, on processional route to the tombs of the earliest kings; now in the Egyptian Museum, Cairo. (b) Detail from the decree, where a clause stipulates that any person infringing the sacred space demarcated by the stelae "is to be branded" (the vertical sign at left is the hieroglyph for a torch, used for words involving fire). (a) and (b) Randall-Maciver and A. Mace, *El Amrah and Abydos*, Egypt Exploration Fund, London, 1902.

Figure 5.4 Depiction of King Ramses II poised to smite an enemy from the northeast, in the presence of the creator Atum, presenting him with a curved sword. From Per-Atum (Tell el-Retaba), about 1275 BC. W. Petrie, *Hyksos and Israelite Cities*, British School of Archaeology in Egypt, London, 1907.

unidentified, about 2100 BC). Removal from *the living* might be read literally, as execution, or might denote a symbolic death, ending membership of human society. Among evidence for a symbolic reading, kingship inscriptions apply to war captives a term *seqer-ankh*, "struck-(but)-alive," evoking two inscribed visual motifs of kingship, the *frozen* scene of execution and the curse figurine (Berlev 1989). In the *frozen* execution scene, a king stands poised to smite a defeated enemy (Figure 5.4); the most famous early example is the ceremonial palette for eye/body paint, inscribed for King Narmer, from the great kingship temple deposit at Nekhen around the time of the first recorded unification (3000 BC) (Davis 1992). Although the most finely sculpted examples preserved are monuments of kings, the motif also occurs outside the immediate circle of kingship, as on votive stelae deposited at temples of deities (Figure 5.5). Curse figurines are schematic clay or stone images of bound men, inscribed with recitations against potential enemies of kingship, under direct rule and abroad. In two series, inscriptions are on bowls rather than figurines, but in each case, the objects are broken and deposited in groups at points requiring defense, for example, a cemetery as sacred ground (Figure 5.6). In Nubia, one deposit of about 1850 BC was excavated close to Mirgissa fortress, border town of Egyptian-controlled territory; nearby, a human skull lay on a pottery bowl, beside flint blade, as if one person had been offered up in

Figure 5.5 Depiction of the king poised to smite an enemy, on a votive stela, Ramesside reign of Thutmes IV, about 1400 BC, W. Petrie, *Memphis I,* British School of Archaeology in London, London 1908.

defense of the realm (Vercoutter 1963). Whether the person died in the rite or in fighting beforehand is an unknown and crucial detail for our understanding of ancient Egyptian state ethics. Berlev concluded that *struck alive* denotes the spared captives, while their leader would be killed; there may have been varying responses over time.

Treatment of prisoners may expose and define the ethics of society and state. A remarkable group of legal documents shows kingship reacting to the extreme case of court conspiracy. Various devices, including language, protect the king from being implicated in spilling blood, even, remarkably, of those who would kill him. To remove the accused from humanity, their names are changed, as from "Ra is the one who creates (*mes*) him" to "Ra is the one who

Figure 5.6   Rounded limestone flake inscribed on one side with figure of a bound man, a stream of blood emerging from his forehead. Pyramid field cemeteries, at modern Giza. Drawing © Wolfram Grajetzki.

hates (*mesdjed*) him." Those found guilty of leading the plot are forced to take their own lives, and the king is said to be unaware, so innocent: "All that has been done, it is they who have done it; may all they did fall upon their heads, while I am anointed and protected forever" (Juridical Papyrus of Turin, after Lorton 1977, 30).

Ethical fractures: claims on material possessions and on the labor of others

Surviving legal documents most often record disputes between relatives over inheritance, revolving around two obsessions of propertied classes: material possessions, including land, and rights to labor. Already attested in the earliest copies of documents (mid-third millennium BC), inheritance removes any chance of material equality for all individuals at birth. Continually, the same property relations that bind relatives, and make *family* a central concept, undermine family in the bitterness of litigation. Legal cases show where but not how often harmony breaks down and they are neutral on the question as to whether the property system itself was judged iniquitous; a broader social history of resistance is yet to be written from all the archaeological evidence. Fugitives from labor obligations are a recurrent problem for the authorities at different periods. A register from 1800 BC records a legal review, releasing households held in forced labor for an unknown number of years, after the family head had abandoned his *national service* work obligations; only one case was upheld, a boat captain who lost his name and position because someone escaped on his boat (Hayes 1955; Lorton 1977, 16–17).

The fugitives register papyrus was reused a generation later, to write on the back a separate set of legal documents: two gifts of staff, mainly weavers, listing a total of 95 names, including at least 45 from Syria–Palestine, and the response of an unnamed man, contesting a claim from "my daughter Tihenut" that "my father died, while he had property belonging to me, that my husband had given me; he gave things from it to his wife Senebtysy. Let it be restored to me!" (Hayes 1955). As the man is still alive, either *died* is a statement of rejection or the plain kinship terms father and daughter refer here, as often, to extended relations such as step-father/daughter and grandfather/daughter. Despite its fragmentary condition, the document demonstrates the self-confidence of the propertied woman and her freedom to sue her *father*.

The staff lists on this papyrus reveal how disputes among the wealthy assume rights to labor of others as a norm in social organization. Any such rights clearly remove equality between individuals as forcefully as inheritance of material possessions and land rights. It remains difficult to specify the rights in practice, over different periods. Some Egyptologists speak of slavery and slaves in cases where one person holds or transfers rights to labor of others. However, it is not clear where the rights end, even whether they cover the whole year or just a season, as in a *national service* system of obligations. No legal documents indicate anything as inhuman as ancient Greek or Roman, or more recent European/Euro-American slavery, with torture and killing of the enslaved. Different Egyptian words may denote varying grades of dependency or labor obligation: in documents (1850–1750 BC), *hem*, "power/agency," seems less constrained than *bak*, "worked/worker." In the fugitives register, people in the *hem* category are punished by having to work until released in review; therefore, that category is not equivalent to permanent servitude. Nor does punishment involve being reduced to *bak*, which also, therefore, is not equivalent to *slave*, at least in this period. From the written sources in context, Berlev concluded that rights to labor of *hem* came from the position a person held in state or temple administration, while rights to labor of *bak* came from a personal contract, registered by state officials (Berlev 1972). In one such contract, a man *gives* his brother four foreigners: a woman with Semitic and an Egyptian name, a woman with two Egyptian names, and two children, possibly with Semitic names. The four might be a family of immigrants, with first-generation grandmother renamed, second-generation mother Egyptian named, and her two children recently born inside Egypt. Ethnicity might, like rebellion, form one factor in allowing a society to normalize unequal relations such as the condition of *bak*.

Teachings and their limits

Kingship

Kingship is the political frame for ancient Egyptian ethical writings, most clearly in the remarkable composition which Assmann has called *King as Priest of the Sun*, first inscribed in kingship monuments for Hatshepsut (1475 BC), Amenhotep III (1375 BC), and Ramses III (1175 BC). The words accompany morning rebirth of the sun, when the king raises his arms to "adore Ra in the dawn light." Here (as cited in

Chapter 1), the creator sun-god places the king on earth to make it possible for people to do what is right:

> to judge between people and to satisfy the gods,
> to create what is Right, to annihilate what is Evil

The Egyptian word here rendered *to create* is *sekheper*, "to cause to come into being"; only the king can create the possibility for Right to exist. Once the king has performed his task of *sekheper ma'at*, humans can then *ir/djed ma'at*, "do/say what is right." Before describing his function on earth, the composition defines the distinctive quality of kingship as knowledge, of the speech, forms and hometowns of "the eastern *ba*-souls," depicted as the baboons noisily acclaiming the creator at dawn. Unwritten knowledge separates kingship from humankind and underwrites the function of the king as provider of justice and peace. Kingly knowledge is marked off even from the social stratum of the wealthiest and the highest officials. Judging from surviving copies, the composition was accessible not to the whole circle of highest officials (such as viziers, generals, high priests of Amun), but only those with special access to sacred writing: selective versions for a head keeper of writings at court (Khay, about 1275 BC) and a Third God's Servant of Amun at Karnak (Tjanefer, about 1150 BC) and a more complete version for a chief lector at court (Padiamenipet, about 675 BC). This knowledge seems a function not of all power, nor even of all deities, but of a sacred force uniting creator-god with his form on earth, the king.

Two literary teachings for kings

Two extended literary reflections on kingship practice survive on manuscripts copied after 1500 BC but thought to have been composed earlier. Hieroglyphic inscriptions confirm the idea that a king should teach; the first minister Rekhmira invokes the Teaching of Thutmes III (1450 BC), and officials of Akhenaten (1350 BC) claim to place the teaching of the king in their bodies.

Teaching for King Merykara   Set in the period of disunity (2150–2050 BC), most Egyptologists date this composition under the reunified Middle Kingdom, perhaps after 1900 BC. A king of the north (name lost) addresses a treatise on the practice of kingship to his successor King Merykara, "giving all the rules for a king." The advice operates on three levels (Vernus 2001, 137). The first is about how to rule within and from the court: control of factions and of speech, favor of the *elite* and others close to the king, and care in exacting punishments. The second level concerns relations with the world outside the kingdom, whether nomads on the eastern frontier or the rival southern kingdom of that time. Finally, the king is destined to rule alone in his time, in a chain of unique incarnations of the sun-god across history, and is held accountable for his reign: Merykara is told of the looting of Abdju—"it happened even as something I did, though I learned of it after the deed." The teaching culminates in a hymn to the creator, with a moving description of peaceful intentions (translation by the author, here and for other extended citations in this and following sections):

> Well-tended are people, the herd of the god,
> he has made heaven and earth for their hearts,
> he has driven off the crocodile of the waters.
> He has made the breath of the heart, that their nostrils might live.
> They are his images who came from his body.
> He shines in the sky for their hearts.
> He has made for them plants and herds,
> birds and fish, to nourish them.

Immediately following lines address the conflict in life, in violent terms aimed at legitimating sovereign power:

> He kills his enemies,
> and he has damaged his children
> at their plotting to carry out rebellion.
> He repeats daybreak for their hearts,
> and sails by to see them.
> He has raised a chapel behind them;
> when they weep he can hear.
> He has made for them rulers in the egg,
> commanders to command at the back of the vulnerable.
> He has made words of power for them,
> as weapons to repel the blow of events,
> watchful over them night and day.
> He has killed the disaffected among them,
> as a man strikes his son for the sake of this brother.
> The god is aware of every name.

Teaching of King Amenemhat I   A literary papyrus from about 1250 BC records that the Teaching of King Amenemhat I was written for his son King Senusret I by a man named Khety (Vernus 2001, 161–162, on Deir al-Madina Papyrus Chester Beatty 4); there is no corroboration for this date from their reigns, and it remains possible that it was written later—the earliest surviving copies are from around 1500 BC. Where the Teaching for Merykara seems weary, the tone here is aggressively bitter. Merykara was advised to favor those close to him; the dead King Amenemhat I warns Senusret I, "Trust none as brother, make no friend, foster no intimates—it is worthless," and describes an attack on his life by court conspirators:

> It was after the meal, night had fallen, I took an hour of rest.
> I lay on my bed, for I had grown weary.
> My heart began to follow sleep.
> Suddenly weapons of counsel were turned against me.
> I was like a snake of the desert
> I awoke to my bodyguard.
> I found it was a body blow by a soldier.

> If I had swiftly taken weapons in my hand,
> I would have turned the wretch back in confusion,
> But there is no night champion, no-one who can fight alone.
> There can be no success without a protector.

After lamenting treason, Amenemhat I describes his good deeds, in giving Egypt peace and prosperity, and closes in endorsing his son on the throne.

These two compositions give rules not for human, but for kingly conduct. Nevertheless, they are preserved on manuscripts copied and circulated outside the court and form part of the same reading world as more directly didactic literature. Within the critique of kingly frailty in both works, we learn of how their writers, and at least some of their readers, perceived human life within the relations between creator, ruler, and society.

Literary teachings: father to son

A version of what is right, still restricted to sources from wealthier men, is spelled out in literary teachings and, in more nuanced manner, in the genre of laments over wrong (Vernus 2001 is the most comprehensive collection for the period 2000–525 BC). Some teachings and some laments open with the word *sebayt*, "teaching," like the two kingship teachings in the preceding section, while others are embedded in narrative tales or literary letters. The earliest surviving literary manuscripts date to around 1900 BC, but dates of composition remain disputed. Unlike other writings, many teachings and laments are ascribed to named individuals, but this seems a literary setting rather than historical record, because, in some, the language is later than the date at which the speaker is supposed to have lived. Hordedef and Ptahhotep live under mid-third-millennium BC kings who ruled about 2600–2400 BC, but the language of *their* teachings is centuries later, around 2200–1900 BC (Vernus 2001, 21, 48, 71).

Vernus identifies the readership of this wisdom literature as the "dominated of the dominant class," administrators below the level of the highest court officials (Vernus 2001, 29–33). However, it is not clear that they exclude the wealthiest. In practice, our lack of knowledge over the social profile of ancient Egypt complicates any attempt to assess whether the highest officials stood outside the main administrative circle or whether all middle- to lower-ranking officials are addressed in the teachings. The historical readership may, too, have been wider or narrower than that intended at the time of composition. Broader circles might, over unspecified time spans, gain access to a teaching composed for the royal court or even initially for the king alone (cf. on Teaching of King Amenemhat I, in preceding section).

In rough chronological order, allowing for the continuing uncertainties over dating, the better preserved longer compositions may be summarized for their general ethical guidelines.

Composed in middle kingdom (2000–1800 BC) or earlier

TEACHING OF PTAHHOTEP   An opening passage sets the scene, in which the first minister Ptahhotep asks the king for permission to retire, replaced by his son, and the king accepts provided that Ptahhotep instructs him first, "for no-one is born experienced"; in a remarkable spirit of equality, Ptahhotep first warns his son not to be proud of his knowledge, as "Fine words are more hidden than greenstone, but can be found with the women at the grindstone." There follow 36 maxims of varying length, without any strictly imposed overall framework, and so realistically evoking the more random pattern of advice that a father might give a son. The initial trio of maxims advise different ways for reacting to an opponent in argument, depending on their level of skill or experience. Advice on leadership follows, including "Do not cause fear among people, as the god punishes with like." Rules of etiquette at table, on envoy missions, and at court again depend on the relation to the host. For speaking at court, self-control and clarity are required. Home life is central to the teaching. A house should be founded, and autonomy given to the wife. Good fatherhood means staying close to your son. Friendship receives recurrent attention and requires you "to stay away from the wife" of your host, whether "master, brother, or colleague." If doubts disrupt friendship, "do not make your own enquiries, go direct to him, make the case with him alone, to avoid suffering in his matter." Similarly, "do not repeat slander and do not hear it." Perhaps the greatest evil is greed, with the warning "there is no tomb for the greedy hearted." Conversely, generosity is a blessing with immediate benefit: "Let your face be bright as long as you live ... a man with an empty stomach is a plaintiff." Wealth after lack is a gift from the god, not a reason to lord it over others. The teaching ends with an extended encomium of the obedient son and the blessings of learning. The contents are set within the wealthiest part of society, taking for granted the presence of servants and the opportunity to serve on missions and speak at court.

TEACHING OF A MAN TO HIS SON   Unusually for teachings, the poet chose anonymity for this composition, which opens simply "Beginning of the teaching made by a man for his son." Like the Teaching of Kaires, the first part is a hymn to the king, shorter here, followed by a meditation on destiny: "Can you add a day to a lifespan? Can you subtract from it either?" The birth brick Meskhenet is set by the god, but offers no guarantees, for the god can as easily change course:

> He can transform the ignorant into the wise,
> the hater become the loving,
> he enables the least to be like the great,
> the one in last place to become first,
> the man without property to be a lord of riches
> the miserable to be a lord of jubilation.

In sum, "All this is within a lifetime, beyond the day of Renenet, and Meskhenet can guarantee nothing for it." Change can come from nowhere at any moment from the day of Renenet, "nurture." The same spirit permeates laments of disorder, from the same period (as nos. 5–8 in this section). A second, longer kingship hymn follows, before the main body of the teaching, on similar themes to those in the Teaching of Ptahhotep: correct conduct in official sittings, accuracy in disputes, and avoiding excess speech. However, where Ptahhotep urged taking advice from expert and ignorant alike, here, we read "answer the wise man—avoid the ignorant."

Figure 5.7   The earliest manuscript source for the Teaching of Kaires, with the injunction to care for estate workers as the foundation of well-being. Writing board deposited in a tomb at Waset, early Eighteenth Dynasty, about 1550 BC. H. Carter and Earl of Carnarvon, *Five Years Exploration at Thebes*, Henry Frowde, London, 1912, pl.29, completed by a fragment purchased by Flinders Petrie; now in the Egyptian Museum, Cairo.

TEACHING OF KAIRES (LOYALIST TEACHING)   Without setting, this shorter composition is addressed "to his children" rather than just one son. Opening "worship the king", its kingship hymn ends with the warning: "there is no tomb for one who rebels against His Power." The hymn is also inscribed on an offering-chapel stela for the deputy treasurer Sehetepibra, under King Amenemhat III (1850–1800 BC). The version on manuscripts continues with a second address to the children, warning first against laziness, whereas Ptahhotep had warned more against greed. The next piece of advice is to build up estate staff, with this exceptional appreciation of workers (Figure 5.7):

> It is people who bring what there is into being.
> We live as men who have by their labour.
> If there is a lack of it, poverty takes power.

People here have the same capability as creator-god and king, *sekheper*, "to bring into being." Where labor or workers are missing, there can be no wealth. "No ploughed field comes into being of itself." "A herdsman of evil—his cattle are few." In literary conception, the teaching juxtaposes the cult of kingship with revolutionary recognition of a working class.

TEACHING OF KHETY (SATIRE OF TRADES)   The opening sets the scene: "Beginning of the teaching made by man of Tjaru (?), the Hymn-singer (?) called Khety for his son called Pepy, on the way south to the Residence, to place him in the writing school, among the children of officials, of the foremost of the Residence." Egyptologists have used this one line to conjure up an entire education system on modern lines for ancient Egypt, with promotion by merit, but it remains an isolated instance in the ancient literature. How often anyone from outside could join "the children of officials" remains as unknown as every other stage in the acquisition of writing and reading skills in the ancient society. The scene could as easily be a startling disruption of norms, for literary effect, as an image from regular practice. Encouraging his son to learn how to write, Khety wields stick and carrot: "I have seen violent beatings, so direct your heart to writing ... Read for yourself the end of the Compilation, and you can find this phrase in it saying, *The writer, whatever his place at the Residence, cannot be poor in it.*" The core of the teaching reinforces his message by emphasizing hardships endured by every trade other than that of writing. From coppersmith to fisherman, bleak social portraits gave rise to the Egyptological title for the teaching, Satire of Trades, although every detail is grimly plausible. Where the Teaching of Kaires recognized the value of labor, the Teaching of Khety warns against idealizing labor in this society. If humorous, this is open class war by rich against poor. Yet that modern reading may be too complacent. If realistic, the Teaching would introduce to a dominant class the hardship imposed on the manual professions, with greater awareness than most modern consumers may have in a globalized economy. Judging how to read this teaching is, then, a difficult task. Like the Teaching of Kaires, a new section is marked explicitly, here with the line "Let me tell you in another manner, to teach you so that you may know." The following part turns to themes found in the Teaching of Ptahhotep, on behavior in different social contexts, with some new points of emphasis, as at "Do not tell lies against a mother—that is the extreme for the officials."

LAMENTS OF IPUWER (OPENING LOST, ORIGINALLY ALSO A TALE?) Preserved on one fragmented manuscript from about 1250 BC, this composition includes the words of a man called Ipuwer (name typical of 1850–1450 BC) alongside shorter passages ascribed to the Lord of All—a term used for both king and creator sun-god (Enmarch 2006). Ipuwer bewails the reversal of order, in an overwhelming mass of paired descriptions, as "the woman without her own box is now owner of furniture, the one who looked at her face in the water is now owner of a mirror." From translation, these passages have had great literary impact: in his *Caucasian Chalk Circle*, mid-twentieth-century playwright Bertolt Brecht took a selection of these snapshots of an upside-down world, to celebrate the destruction of an old and evil order (Enmarch 2011). In the ancient manuscript, the laments culminate in a passage headed "Let Lower Egypt weep then!," before turning to demands on the Lord of All, one series with the aggressive refrain to "destroy the enemies of the Residence," another to "remember" a series of cult duties: "Remember the fattened geese, the ganders and ducks, offering god's offerings to the gods ... Remember setting up flagpoles, carving offering-stones." The role of kingship in maintaining offerings recalls the composition "King as Priest of the Sun." A description of violent disorder follows, then an idyllic portrait of good times, before the Lord of All apparently replies, that Egypt can defend itself, and Ipuwer apparently refutes this in terse statements—"ignoring it is what pleases the heart." It is not clear how much is lost from the end of the composition.

TALE OF NEFERTY A narrative introduction sets the work in the court of King Sneferu (about 2650 BC), when the morning hearing has ended, but officials are recalled to advise Sneferu on entertainment for the day. At their recommendation, the great lector Neferty of Bast is summoned, and the king commands him: "Tell me some fine words, choice phrases, to entertain My Power at hearing them." Neferty asks, "what has happened, or what is to happen?" Sneferu opts for "what is to happen, for today is already happened and gone," and sets to write down the precious words. Neferty conjures up a nightmare of destruction, foreign invasion, and loss of sunlight to the point when selfishness merges with civil strife:

> No mourning will be observed today - the heart is turned entirely to itself.
> A man rests on his side—at his back one man kills another.
> I can show you the son as attacker, brother as enemy, man murdering his father.

Similarly to Ipuwer, Neferty says, "I can show you the lower made the upper." However, this composition ends in rejoicing, with appearance of a King Ameny from the Land of the Bow (Nubia and the southernmost province of Upper Egypt). Order is restored, foreign enemies are destroyed, and fortresses are built to guard the eastern border: "Right is returned to its place, Wrong is pushed back out."

TALE OF KHUNINPU (ELOQUENT OASIS MAN) This composition frames nine poems on justice and injustice as petitions within a tale of theft and deception, at a time when northern Egypt was ruled by kings based at, or from, Hutnennesut. "There was a man named Khuninpu," trader in Wadi Natrun, arid territory west of the Nile Delta. Running short of food, he takes his goods to market in Hutnennesut, leaving just enough for his wife to feed the family during his absence. On the way, a servant of the high steward robs him. Khuninpu petitions the high steward so beautifully that he tells the king, who, instead of upholding Right, commands that the trader be kept waiting, to wring more beautiful words from him. The king commands the Wadi Natrun governor to feed the family, without letting Khuninpu know, to keep him fearful for their lives as well as his own. Increasingly desperate, the trader pours out his laments over injustice and his hymns to order, until, at three times three petitions (three being the plural, nine a totality), he declares he will go to petition Inpu, god of the cemetery (in some interpretations a threat of suicide). The tale is brought to an abrupt happy ending: without any legal enquiry, Khuninpu is declared in the right, the servant being sentenced to corporal punishment and confiscation of all his goods in favor of Khuninpu. Such vicious distortion of Right could perhaps only be set in the reign of a king who did not rule all Egypt and perhaps therefore not recognized in full (cf. Merykara in preceding section).

At the end of the ninth petition, Khuninpu thundered or gasped his final cry against those detaining him:

> There is no yesterday for the sluggard,
> There is no friend for one deaf to Right,
> There is no celebration for the grasping.

Jan Assmann expounds this triple declaration as a core definition of *ma'at* Right in ancient Egypt: a sluggard, someone too lazy to act, has no connection to previous action and loses any connection with a human society where good deeds are remembered and repaid; someone deaf to Right has lost powers of communication with their fellow human beings; finally, and fatally, the selfish exclude themselves from the feasting and friendship that are basic to social well-being.

DIALOGUE OF A MAN AND BA   Preserved on one papyrus, from about 1900 to 1850 BC, the Dialogue is among the most remarkable reflections on life in world literature (Figure 5.8). The start is heavily fragmented, but the main content comprises a debate between *the man*, tired of life, and *his ba-soul*, anxious to postpone death. The man ends with a poem on the refrain "To whom can I speak today!," lamenting the strife and isolation in life. Then he compares the end of life paradoxically with the pleasures it should bring:

> Death is in my sight today
> like the scent of myrrh,
> like sitting under the sails on a windy day
> Death is in my sight today
> like the scent of lotus flowers,
> like sitting on the shore of drunkenness
> Death is in my sight today
> like the path of rain,
> like the return of a man from the army to their home

His ba-soul avoids continuing the argument, and asks him to make offerings, accepting his desire for death, "whenever your body may touch the earth, and I may alight after you rest weary, then may we make a dwelling together."

Composed in new kingdom (1550–1070 BC) or later

TEACHING OF ANY   The first line ascribes the teaching to Any, writer (accountant?) of the temple of Nefertari (name of queens of Eighteenth and Nineteenth Dynasties). We learn that it is addressed to his son Khonsuhotep at the end, in an original epilogue of debate, where son despairs of learning, and father insists testily that learning is possible. The advice of Any retraces many themes of earlier teachings, adding charming touches, as in the long command to look after your mother, starting "double the food your mother gave you" with the earthy reminder "as you grew and your excrement disgusted, she was not disgusted." The description of a garden feels like literal refreshment in midflow of the injunctions: "grow yourself a garden,

Figure 5.8   Part of a papyrus roll with the only surviving copy of the dialogue between a man and his ba, followed by a marsh tale. R. Lepsius (ed.), *Denkmäler aus Aegypten und Aethiopien. Nicolaische Buchhandlung*, Berlin 1849–1859, vol.6, pl.112.

plant a gourd row around where you plough, set some trees inside, as the surround of your house, and fill your hands with all manner of flowers, for your eyes to see." Observance of religious duty is more prominent or at least given more detail and phrased more explicitly for a modern reader: "observe the feast of your god," "do not jostle him in order to carry him, do not disturb the oracles."

TEACHING OF AMENEMIPET   The half dozen surviving copies were written down between 1000 and 500 BC, the earliest being a papyrus fragment rather difficult to date within the period 1000–850 BC; the date of composition might be within the range 1200–850 BC. Rather than just stating the title of the teaching father, an overseer of fields Amenemipet, the long opening section gives almost a full description of his official duties, like an autobiographical inscription for eternity, followed by an unusually extended titulary for his son, "the youngest of his children, most junior of his family" Horemmaakheru, ending with the name of his mother, the wife of Amenemipet, a head chantress of Horus Taweret. This long prologue effectively portrays the core of a family, perhaps intentionally evoking Osiris, Isis, and Horus and identifying their home as Ipu, modern Akhmim, to the north of Abdju in Upper

Egypt. There follow 30 chapters, explicitly numbered, the first encouraging the son to hear and learn and the last closing the frame with the exhortation "look, then, over these 30 chapters, they delight, they teach!" The core 28 chapters return to themes in earlier teachings, from Ptahhotep (1, 8, 23, 26) to Any (3, 5), but introduce more recent vocabulary in a changing Egyptian language and a new structure for advice. The Teaching of Ptahhotep would first specify a context, "If you are ...," and then advise positive or negative action, "you should do/avoid X" or sometimes "do not do X." The Teaching of Amenemipet adopts a more rhythmic tone of warning, almost every chapter beginning "Do not ...." Good conduct is discovered in the avoidance of wrongdoing, persistently reinforced by vivid descriptions of good and evil in life. As in the declarations of innocence, for entry into a blessed afterlife (Chapter 6), the evils may be (i) broad-ranging instincts of envy, greed, and selfishness; (ii) specific instances of theft, corruption, or cheating in management of estates and justice; or (iii) the social failings in keeping bad company. In general, the good man is still the silent, self-controlled man, with the emphatic devotion that is now explicit, but could be read just as strongly in the Middle Kingdom teachings with their continual orientation to the god.

From the first modern editions, Egyptology and Biblical studies accepted a direct link between the *thirty chapters* of Amenemipet and another first-millennium BC source, the Hebrew Proverbs of King Solomon, "Have I not written for you 30 sayings, of admonition and knowledge, to show you what is right and true?" (Proverbs 22, 22). Other similar phrasings include the warning not to work always on becoming rich, as riches may fly away to the skies like birds (Chapter 7 and Proverbs 23, 4–5). Diplomatic and trading relations between the court of Solomon and contemporary rulers in neighboring Egypt seem plausible on historical and geographical grounds, even if archaeologically vague. However, each link between the ancient Egyptian and Hebrew wisdom literatures may be more or less direct, potentially involving many other peoples and different zones or sites of contact. The numerous diverse scripts of the first millennium BC should warn us against drawing too few lines on the map of ancient networks. The worlds of Egypt and Palestine might have overlapped with 20–30 written traditions and another 100–200 traditions of peoples without writing; the surviving record leaves us with just a handful even of the written traditions. Accessible literature includes copies from earlier times, as in Iraq, of third-millennium BC Sumer, or, from Syria and Turkey, second-millennium BC Ugarit, and the Hittite kingdom. The history of religion ensures not only that the Hebrew Bible is preserved but also that it occupies a privileged position in research in European languages. Comparative study of any one literature needs to assess not two but all preserved literatures of a period against the general absence of writing across our time maps. Reflections on life may be widely shared, particular to one region, or narrowly local, on a map continually changing as peoples move and meet. Conveyors of wisdom might most easily be less literate nomadic peoples, regularly traveling the farthest—Nubian, Berber, and Arab nomads. How do we assess their impact between literatures? The Teaching of Ptahhotep warned us not to assume where fine words are found.

Autobiographical inscriptions

As Pascal Vernus emphasizes, the same ethical norms permeate autobiographical inscriptions, attested for a longer time span, from mid-third millennium to the Roman Period (Vernus 2001, 22–23). Inscribed in offering chapels and on temple monuments, the ancient Egyptian *autobiography* projects an idealized image of the person, written in the first person (Lichtheim 1988). As there are no direct sources for circumstances of composition and commissioning, many Egyptologists prefer to call these biographies, or to use other terms such as ego-history, to avoid the issue of unknowable authorship. The contents provide either events in a life history, often slanted toward contact with kingship and the divine, or assertions of conformity to ethical social ideals. Early examples emphasize a core series of good deeds, as in an offering-chapel inscription for one first minister, highest official in the administration, Neferseshemra Sheshi (about 2300 BC, Saqqara; cf. Lichtheim 1988, 6):

> I have gone out from my city, I have come down from my district.
> I have done Right in respect of myself, for her lord,
> I have made him content with what he does love.
> I have spoken Right, I have done Right, I have spoken well, I have done well.
> I have seized the good moment; love of me is there among people.
> I judged two companions so that both were content.
> I rescued the weak from the more powerful when I had authority in the case.
> I gave bread to the hungry, clothing to the naked,
> ferrying to the boatless, burial to the man without a son.
> I acted as the ferry for the man without a ferry.
> I respected my father, pleased my mother, and nurtured their children.

In an inscription on an offering-chapel stela from the reign of Senusret I (about 1925 BC), the self-history of Mentuhotep, governor of Armant, mingles assertions of appropriate character and obedience to the king, with record of his own decisive actions as governor, in general adherence to the same principles found in the teachings (Beylage 2003):

> I am steadfast and obedient, one to whom his lord gives his love.
> I am a great one of the privy chamber, attentive,
> free from trembling, not disrespectful towards a powerful man.
> ...
> I am one who rears the child, who buries the old and any pauper.
> I give bread to the hungry and clothing to the naked.
> I am a son of Nepri (grain-god), a husband of Tayt (cloth goddess),
> one for whom Sekhat-Hor (milk goddess) creates cattle,
> a possessor of riches, with all manner of precious stones,
> birthing-brick of Khnum, the maker of people,
> When a low flood occurred during the twenty-fifth year,
> I did not let my district starve, I gave it Upper Egyptian grain and emmer.
> I did not let misery come to pass in it, until high floods came.
> I nourished the children with my donations, I anointed the widows.

There was not a commoner miserable in my time.
I strove to cause that I was beloved, so that my name might be good
and that I might be vindicated in the necropolis.
I taught my children, to speak in contentment, kindness,
not to fight with a youth – no superior who is arrogant is beloved.
I am one well-disposed to him who would tell his troubles,
and to him who would pour out his heart.
I hear his case, I remove his misery,
(for) a man should be placed according to what is right for him.
Furthermore, I am silent when (my) wish is thwarted.
I bowed to everyone, without hiding my face from the starving;
the helping hand is what is beloved, for people are one stock.
I had no conflict with agent or sealer of my estate,
saying, on the contrary: let your heart agree,
do not block a petitioner until he has said what he has come for.
Report is made to me of the condition of commoners,
and of widows and orphans likewise.
I acted for them all, to give breath to one fallen into misery.
The good character of a man is more to him than a thousand arms in action.
The saying of men is heard as that phrase which is on the mouths of the great:
The monument of a man is his goodness;
forgotten is who is evil of character.
If it comes to pass as has been said,
my name will be good and endure in my town,
and my monument will never perish.

Limits to the written evidence

Writings convey mainly the interests of the writer, and in a part-literate society, this introduces a clear social bias. For their own conscience or for public image, the powerful may say they (would like to) protect vulnerable, without necessarily taking action. Conscience, public or private, can also be too easily satisfied by single or limited actions, with no impact on the overall social problem. Indeed, limited action may operate precisely as a strategy to avoid the issue of change. Historically, paternalism does not enforce good governance, but instead highlights the gaps between what people say and what they do; for example, the shift from taxation to voluntary charity brings a collapse in support of public works in the late Roman Empire. The literary and religious writing can be tested against those other areas of written evidence, such as the legal, where past people themselves protested against injustices. All writings, though, remain within relatively narrow social horizons. Therefore, archaeological survey and excavation are needed to provide a broader socioeconomic history, within which to set the claims in ancient writing.

The teachings are particularly useful in exposing limits in writing, because they take the model of father teaching son, an extreme gender bias. One test for our own imagination of the past, and use of past writings, would be to construct a teaching of a mother for her daughter. Gender bias is not the only restriction on visibility of the ancient society. Kinship by blood or marriage, particularly the nuclear family, is not necessarily the primary, certainly not the only, association between individuals in a society: the orphan and the work colleague are both well attested in ancient writings, and neither would neatly fit the family model. Just taking the most common Egyptian family terms—father, mother, sister, brother, husband, and wife—the teachings remain extraordinarily restrictive, even allowing for normative associations of age and gender in literary writing. The six terms allow a range of 14 speech relations, each open to its own learning and teaching:

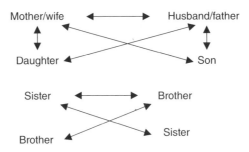

The gaps can only partly be filled from the written record, from ancient letters, where we can find sisters advising one another or sons writing to their mothers (Wente 1990). There are also the legal cases previously considered , where daughter can contest father, adding in effect a negative instruction to the family picture. A father–son model is, evidently, a literary fiction, allowing a past or completed world of experience to inform a present and future, or incomplete, open world of human choice. In those terms, the major omission in the literary model is gender. Too many other social relations may be too easily overlooked, by both the ancient and the modern readers of teachings. Sociologists might ask whether that is not one implicit function of the literary teaching, intended or not.

Echoes in history: eternal Egypt

For the Teaching of Amenemipet, links between Egypt and the Bible were found easy to read out of proportion, given the limited preservation of other literatures among their numerous neighbors. The same warning applies to attempts to find connections over time. First-millennium AD religious teachings in circulation in Egypt draw on varied sources across vast geographic scope, not least from long periods of Nubian, Iranian, Macedonian Greek, and Arab rule. Similarities in spirit or literal content must be treated with great caution, when they span millennia. Yet relatively few places preserve religious writings over these millennia, and the comparative project should include methods for testing connections. North European and American academic and general public may tend to polarize world religions into dogmatic institutions (*bad*) and groups of freer, purer thinkers (*good*). For Egypt, that approach would separate the Coptic Church and Sunni Islam from, respectively, early gnostic and sufi movements. These easy distinctions contradict the content of gnostic and sufi writings, which propose views that have as much potential for dogmatic reading as any other orthodox or unorthodox view. Orthodoxy is a historical development rather than a property of one or other religious content. Modern external preferences for gnostic or sufi may belong within the same Eurocentric reflex as orientalism. This reception complicates comparisons with these writings, on top of the problem of their varied geographical historical sources. Yet the writings remain to be read, both for possible historical echoes and for asking again some of the questions put to more ancient teachings in the same landscape.

Where we found no ancient Egyptian teaching from mother to daughter, one famous gnostic composition gives a Gospel of Mariam, perhaps Mary Magdalene, the woman who gave up prostitution to follow Jesus, in the Christian New Testament (Ehrman and Pleše 2011, 587–599). In the second part, at the request of the disciples of Jesus, Mariam says, "what is hidden from you, I will tell you," and relates the safe passage of the soul past the seven forms of Wrath: darkness, desire, ignorance, envy of death, kingdom of flesh, folly of flesh, and wrathful knowledge. The disciples first refuse to accept her difficult teaching, wondering "did He really speak with a woman secretly from us?," but Levi rebukes them and urges them to go out and teach. Here, elements from Christian evangelism combine with a recurrent theme of gnostic writing, the primacy of spirit over material. For the gnostic emphasis on knowledge and light (Ehrman and Pleše 2011, 306–307), similar motifs might be found in ancient Egyptian writings. Yet the focus of comparison may fall instead on what is absent in the ancient teachings but present in other writings: the teaching woman (see Chapters 4 and 6 for goddesses as instructors and healers).

Equally, comparison with sufi writings might start from the discovery of something previously invisible in writing. The Andalusian writer Ibn Arabi (AD 1165–1240) wrote an account of the life of Dhu al-Nun the Egyptian, a ninth-century mystic at home in the temple of Akhmim, then still standing, said to understand hieroglyphic script (Deladrière 1980); his quest for knowledge looked beyond intellectual knowledge (Arabic *'ilm*) to an intuitive sacred knowledge (Arabic *ma'rifa*). Dhu al-Nun inhabits the same city as the Amenemipet of the first-millennium BC Teaching and where Gnostic writings were also found. An intellectual history of that or another city might be one more productive approach to reading writings from whichever their traditions. If it would be an error to ignore all this later evidence, there remains the danger of constructing an idealized history by lifting similar features out of context. Future reading will require multiple authors in concerted interdisciplinary research programs.

Conclusion: combining the evidence types

Contexts of domination and equality
If modern readers find ancient writings hard to follow, particularly in issues of social organization and justice, part of the problem may stem from evolutionary thinking. Crudely, European history writing may have primed us to expect successive phases of human society, each with its own characteristic manner of treating human beings: a *simple* or *primitive* society, where all are equal; the early civilization or class society, where one set of people can be ruled or exploited by another, with the extreme example of enslaving societies; and then the modern

industrial society, with an aspiration of individual freedom. In such concise terms, some flaws of this scheme are obvious, such as the relocation of enslaving societies from the democracies of Athens, Britain, or the United States to other past tyrannies. However, there may be still more fundamental failures in the vocabulary of primitive and egalitarian. Anthropologists such as James Flanagan have analyzed how misleading the categories may be, because they omit to state what precisely is simple or primitive about the human groups so labeled (Flanagan 1989). Where technology may be simple, other features such as technique, thinking, and indeed language may be extremely intricate. At the same time, the idea of a harmonious egalitarian community in the earliest times fails to account for different treatment of men and women, or adults and children, or differently abled individuals.

In order to understand human groups more clearly, Flanagan proposes that we distinguish between social stratification and hierarchy, with the following definitions:

- Social stratification: one group dominates another such that all members of the group are treated the same way, whatever their age or sex.
- Hierarchy: here, domination is at individual level, one person dominating another.

He also advises against confusing ideal and practice, by separating out:

- Egalitarian ideologies: here, the society or part of it claims to work for equal opportunity, with, for example, the ideal of a fair start in life for all.
- Egalitarian practices: here, the society aims at equal outcome, with methods for removing differences in opportunities.

Historically, so far, as noted from Janet Hendrickx at the beginning of this chapter, there are no egalitarian societies. Yet all societies may offer greater or lesser scope for localized contexts where individuals are treated on equal terms. For more accurate social descriptions, including for ancient Egypt, we can avoid labels such as primitive and civilized altogether and apply labels such as egalitarian to particular aspects of a society rather than to a society as a whole.

CHAPTER 6

Being Well

ᔕᔕᔕᔕ

Health and Well-Being: Starting from Comparative Ethnography

Health and happiness may overlap, but are not identical; a society may include also the serene sufferer and discontented healthy. Definitions of both health and happiness vary under geographical and historical factors such as climate change and population movement, and according to the immediate aspirations of the individual, group, or society. Chapter 5 presented sources for ancient Egyptian senses of Right; for understanding any past strategy for health and well-being, the traces must be approached within the context of particular senses of how individuals and society should work. The modern reader needs to be sensitive to changes over time and disparate opportunities and views according to position within the society. From a study in the 1970s rural Delta, anthropologist Soheir Morsy emphasizes the impact of differences between powerful rich and vulnerable poor, both within the local village level and as part of a larger state:

> The peasants of FatiHa do not live an isolated, independent existence; they are part of a stratified socio-political entity ... Power asymmetry is reflected in villagers' body concepts, their beliefs regarding conception, and their birth practices. (Morsy 1980, 159–160)

Morsy finds gender, class, and age to be useful categories for exploring patterns of variation in the senses of well-being, and of physical and mental health, in this society. For the Delta villagers, she noted how "the body and the mind are regarded as interdependent components of an integrated system ... the proper functioning of the body is not independent of its surroundings, nor is it determined simply by an individual's attempt to maintain his/her body parts in working order" (Morsy [1980], 154). The ethnography of farming villages may help to correct urban foreign misunderstandings in the archaeological study of more distant pasts, particularly

Exploring Religion in Ancient Egypt, First Edition. Stephen Quirke.
© 2015 Stephen Quirke. Published 2015 by John Wiley & Sons, Ltd.

in countries such as Egypt where there is so little archaeology of the countryside (farms, canal systems, villages, rich country houses).

Material health

Rural and urban health

In the countryside, archaeology cannot yet fill in the picture of fauna and flora for each period. The idyll depicted for the afterlife in offering chapels is the result of careful selection, which either conjures threats only in order to overcome them or omits unpleasant features altogether. The presence of biting insects and flies is missing in these chapel scenes, along with common Saharan river enemies such as scorpions and venomous snakes; these have to be sought in the writings for health, in jewelry, or in the iconography of deities. Many chapel scenes show a crocodile lurking near herdsmen and animals as they ford a waterway. Here, the scene of threat becomes a guarantee of life, through a protective gesture against the crocodile, and hieroglyphic inscriptions spelling out terms of protection (Dominicus 1994) (Figure 6.1).

In ancient town life, questions of health become visible in material strategies to promote hygiene. In the nineteenth-century BC new town at Lahun, main streets had central drainage channels, but no other clear system for removing waste. For domestic hygiene at fourteenth-century BC Akhetaten, richer houses had latrines with seat rims of wood or stone (Crocker 1985, 61–62). Bathrooms had no visible sign of special protection in the form of images, as might have been appropriate at purity–dirt boundaries; if daily hygiene was accompanied by ritual words or gestures of protection, these do not materialize in the sites. Both sites include prominent facilities for washing, in part perhaps ensured for ritual cleanliness (Chapter 3).

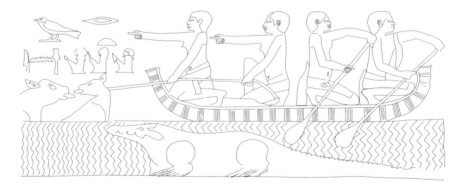

Figure 6.1   Men in a boat make a protective gesture against the crocodile at the ford, as a calf turns back to the cow at the front of their herd. Limestone wall relief in a chapel over the tomb of the high official Ankhmahor, cemeteries of Mennefer, about 2350 BC. Drawing © Wolfram Grajetzki after J. Capart, *Une rue de tombeaux à Saqqarah* 2. Vromant, Brussels, pl.28.

Urbanization creates particular and continual, uphill struggles to sustain health. At Lahun, the schematic excavation report refers to rat holes blocked in every room, and heaps of discarded pottery outside the house of the mayor yielded perhaps the only rattrap so far identified from Egypt (Drummond, Janssen, and Janssen 1990). Rats are often held responsible for spreading disease in human settlements, and from the mid-second millennium, writings refer to a disease called *that of the Asiatics*, sometimes identified as plague (Goedicke 1984). Perhaps not coincidentally, then, by the mid-second millennium BC, the cat was introduced into domestic life. At the divine level, the cat provided an image of triumph over evil in the name of the creator sun-god as *the great tomcat*, depicted knifing the chaos-serpent 'Aapep (Leitz 1994, 99–101). Other domesticated animals might have brought more problems into the town: pigs at Akhetaten, sheep and goats at Abu, and possibly cattle and donkeys would all add to the waste, if not on a modern scale, still enough to threaten human health.

Medicinal matter and the question of shamanism

Sporadically, archaeologists have found assemblages of mixed plant, animal material, and stones, in ways that stand out from the regular pattern of town finds or burial equipment. The interpretation of unparalleled or rare deposits is always hazardous, but one option would be to consider these as materials used in healing practice. One unusual assortment of material was found at a tomb entrance in Waset (Winlock 1942, 206–209, on excavations for the Metropolitan Museum of Art, New York, Asasif Tomb 839). With two baskets, one nested inside the other, and coils of hard plant fiber, there were five pieces of aromatic wood and fragments of copper ore wrapped in cloth, as well as fruits and nuts. The perplexing mixture at least raises the possibility of use in strategies for health and well-being. The items might be burial equipment, cleared out at reuse of the tomb, or they might have been stored beside a tomb because they were being used there, perhaps for the living as much as for the dead. Any modern exclusion of death from life, and rigid line between living and dead, may not apply. This deposit may involve protection with matter to heal individuals in this world and for eternity (see also the following sections and in Chapter 7).

If these items could have been combined for healing rituals or medicinal effect, the next question would be, how many individuals in the society of that time had the skills and access to using them? Modern city dwellers may polarize the possible types of practitioner into two opposite figures: the doctor as a university-trained medic (primary example being the physician) and the folk healer outside modern medicine (in the European literature sometimes as *medicine woman/man*). For the second figure, general and archaeological writers have often used the term *shaman* – a social healer in contact with spirits, in north Asian nomad societies. As the word *shaman* comes from a particular cultural and linguistic background, anthropologists debate how far it can be used for other societies (Hutton 2001). The extreme polarization in general modern concepts of healers may not be useful for understanding the Bronze Age societies of the third to first millennia BC, historically and organizationally distinct from most societies studied in social anthropology and sociology. On the other hand, some of the most productive and insightful new readings of ancient Egyptian evidence have emerged from a conscious shift out of European medical thinking and into the worlds of spirit healers (DuQuesne 1991; Naydler 2004). Rather than applying the category of *shaman* healer directly to past Egyptian sources, I would keep the *shaman* in view as part of the attempt to understand how healers and healing operated within these distanced time–places. Written evidence for specialization in healing is considered in the second part of this chapter (section "Healer Titles and Roles"), but may relate mainly to the royal court and related wealthier social groups. The mixed material finds offer a less confined starting point for considering the healer in society.

Medicinal matter? The burial of an elderly man and woman
Among burials provided with an unusual range of plant and animal material, the most extraordinary collection accompanied an elderly man and woman laid to rest in a southwestern cemetery of Waset, modern Deir al-Madina (Bruyère 1937, 150–157). The man laid in an undecorated coffin. He wore six scarab rings inscribed in hieroglyphs, one of them with the title and name *First God's Servant of Amun Hapuseneb*; this inscription dates the group to no earlier than 1500 BC, because this official is known to have served Hatshepsut. As Hapuseneb had his own burial monument and as the man was buried in a relatively modest, undecorated coffin, the name on the ring does not identify the wearer in this instance or even reveal what relation he might have had to Hapuseneb – a reminder of the limitations to written evidence. A lyre had been placed over the legs of the man, possibly for the reviving force of music into eternity. Alongside, the woman rested in a brightly painted and decorated coffin, inscribed in hieroglyphs, from which we know her name, Madja. The hieroglyphic-inscribed rings and the fine coffin of Madja place these individuals broadly among the middling wealthier in society (Figure 6.2).

Around the two coffins, the excavators found filled baskets and pottery vessels, most closer to Madja; one basket with fine balance set for measuring was beside the coffin of the man. Fruits, bread, and fat are within the range of food supplies known from many other tombs of the period. Yet some items were in tiny packets, not regularly reported for burials of the period, and some materials are treated differently, or rare finds in themselves. A circular basket contained round fruits, one painted blue, with needles and a wood hone; a cattle horn containing fat; and a small ivory-inlaid wood box in which laid little green and pink stones. Three packets were inside a sealed vase, nested inside another sealed vase; one packet contained five smaller packets of grains, the others had miniature clay coffins with winged insects (the excavation diary is not more specific) and one with a double-string necklace of white and blue beads. The small packets and unusual materials have given rise to suggestions that the two individuals, and Madja, in particular, might have been involved in healing (see especially Meskell 1999, 180–181, 193–195).

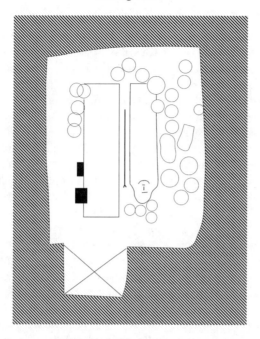

Figure 6.2   The burials of a woman named Madja and an unnamed man. Drawing ©
Wolfram Grajetzki after the online archives of Bernard Bruyère at http://www.ifao.egnet.
net/bases/archives/bruyere/about.

Madja as healing/*knowing* woman?

Two hundred years later, in the same corner of Waset, we read of a *knowing* or wise
woman (Egyptian *rekhet*) from a handful of writings (Toivari-Viitala 2001, 228–231).
In the most poignant, a man called Qenherkhepshef asks a woman Inherwau why
she did not "go to the *rekhet* about the two babies who died in your charge? Enquire
of the *rekhet* about the deaths of the two babies, whether it was their fate, their destiny—and you must enquire about them for me and obtain a picture of my own life
and the life of their mother." Despite the 200-year gap, could Madja be a *rekhet*, specialized in birth trauma and equipped with an array of special items with medicinal
properties? Or is this an imposition from European concepts of white witch, or witchcraft in general, onto the African setting? Anthropologists might provide a range of
possible parallels for healers of both sexes. The gender associations are highly uncertain in the burial of Madja; either one or the other or both the man and Madja might
have been the receiver/user of these baskets and jars of more and less edible items.
Nevertheless, the later references to a wise woman loosely support that interpretation for the find. Contemporary images of a woman with child include some with an
animal horn on her lap, and the fat might be oils for birth or infant health. A set of
miniature bed, stool, and headrest lay on the coffin of the elderly man; again, they
recall images of a woman and child on beds, the dominant form of imagery for safe
maternity at this period. An elderly pair might bring experience of the substances

and unwritten strategies for easing birth against the high risk of death for the infant and mother, the greatest concern of society. Yet Deborah Sweeney recalls the lack of any ancient written evidence for the age of the *rekhet*, inviting caution over assuming that this must necessarily be an elderly woman (Sweeney 2006, 146–147).

Material form: overriding the border of nature/artifice

South of the desert-edge temple at Badari (Chapter 2), in a cluster of half a dozen tombs from about 2300–2150 BC, one simple small pit burial contained an exceptional version of the cosmetic equipment typically included in burials of young women at this period (Brunton 1927, 30, pl.49, burial 3217). A later tomb had cut away more than half the burial, leaving only the items placed at the feet: two copper fasteners from a wooden box, a few beads, blue-glazed cowry-shaped amulet, and *two sliced shells*, recalling later cowrie girdles. There were also three cosmetic vases, one inscribed for the *king's mother Ankhnespepy* (one of the only three royal name inscriptions out of hundreds of stone vases of this age in these cemeteries), and then a more exceptional find: "an elaborate natural shell (*Strombus tricornis?*) was with these, carved with dog's head and monkey, and having a ram's head added in clay and limestone. The spout is of thin bone." Inside the adapted shell was found a seal-amulet in the typical disk form of the period, with symmetrical four-legged motif (Brunton 1927, pl.32.60). The cosmetic set also included a bone spatula and "bone spoon, handle ending in hand with bent fingers" (Figure 6.3).

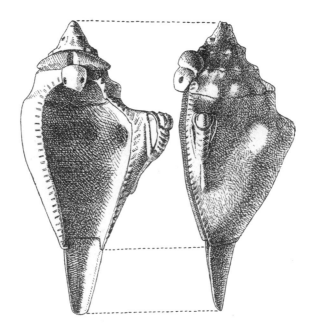

Figure 6.3   Shell with animal depictions and extensions, from Badari burial 3217, about 2200 BC. Brunton, G. 1927. *Qau and Badari I*. British School of Archaeology in Egypt, London., pl.32. © of the Petrie Museum of Egyptian Archaeology, UCL.

The inscribed vase and shell pourer belong broadly to ritual and healing associations of adornment. Inscribed cosmetic vases may only be indirectly connected with the kings and mothers of kings named on them. Perhaps either the vessels or their contents came from kingship rituals, from which they were distributed to select participants and in this way reached regions far from kingship centers. Some vessels of the period, with king name inscriptions, take the form of a monkey mother nestling her young, (Arnold 1999), recalling the monkey carved from the edge of the shell in the Badari burial. It may be misleading to call the animal figures on the shell additions to the natural surface, in our modern division of nature and culture. In formal sculpture for eternity, at the start of the Opening of the Mouth rites, an artist/ritual performer conceives the form in the stone block; here too, perhaps an artist reveals the forms already present within the material. The feature called *dog's head* by Brunton is less easy to identify. The limestone ram face with clay horns curving back might, in this region, evoke Khnum, main deity at Shashotep across the river from Badari, most often depicted with ram head, but perhaps the artist intended no link to any one divine force by name.

Reinterpreting *owners*: patients or healers?

Perhaps, too quickly, we identify the person buried with cosmetic equipment as the receiver of adornment, like the patient in healing treatment, whereas with Madja and the old man perhaps we first think of them as users of the material, the healers active in treatment. With each of these exceptional material deposits, it is worth exploring all three possibilities for the individual closest in view: (1) passive patient, treated or healed, in this life and/or for eternity; (2) active healer, using the materials; and (3) the active patient, using materials and more widely shared skills, to treat her- or himself. Cosmetic equipment raises similar possibilities, as individuals may adorn themselves and others, or be adorned. In any particular society, all, two, or just one might have been the regular social practice; archaeology will not always provide evidence for determining which. As our own social and individual practice may lead us to prefer one without considering the others, contrary options should be considered in assessing finds: Madja as patient and the Badari shell as implement of a (self-)healer.

Meanings in materials and forms

As well as using material and enhancing it with motifs, past makers created forms from material, working the entire surface, on every scale from colossal sculpture to small items worn as jewelry for aesthetic effect and for protection. It may not be clear where the past maker and wearer placed emphasis between aesthetic and protective, though today different terms are used for these as two primary functions: when archaeologists, art historians, or curators consider the protective aspect dominant, the item may be a pendant; when they see more a protective aspect, the terms amulet and talisman are used. When jewelry is found on excavation, archaeologists may distinguish between beads (no precise motif identifiable) and amulets (identifiable motif) and then introduce labels for types and subtypes, to sort larger masses of material for further study. However, any item strung to be worn might have held intense significance for the maker and wearer, whether or not we can now interpret its material and form. In mass production and emulations of motifs, a figurative design may become so schematic that it is no longer clear even at production, further blurring the boundary between these categories. In the archaeology of Egypt, the first attempt at a detailed numerical typology of strung items would combine in one sequence what would later be separated into beads and amulets in one numerical sequence (Engelbach 1923, pl.49–54).

Both ancient writings (see Writings for good health) and twentieth-century ethnography confirm the parallel potential significance of beads as amulets. The Birzeit Museum at Ramallah in Palestine preserves an ethnographic collection of all material means for supporting health, acquired by Dr Tawfik Canaan from rural patients (Ju'beh 2005). In an archaeological museum, many of these items would be called beads rather than amulets, but hand-written labels by Canaan record specific medicinal properties sought by their wearers, such as that two yellow- and white-banded glass barrel shapes were to be worn *against vomiting bile/children up to 4* (Birzeit n.d.). In rural Egypt under British military occupation, the English anthropologist Winifred Blackman also collected items of jewelry, recording age and gender associations and local significance for health (Blackman 1927).

Among ancient finds, recurrent associations of gender or age offer clues to meaning. Leg- and hand-shaped amulets typical for burials of young women (2200–2000 BC) are generally of red carnelian, as if evoking menstrual blood at entry into puberty. However, the same material might carry multiple associations. At a New Kingdom palace by the entrance to Fayoum province, one individual was buried with 16 strings of beads, predominantly blood-red carnelian; one scorpion pendant of carnelian; another of gilt faience; and seal-amulets inscribed with the image of a scorpion (Petrie 1931). The repetition of the scorpion motif might evoke the title *controller of Serqet* (see section Healer Titles and Roles). However, as with the Madja burial, it is not clear whether material with the deceased relates to the role in life or to motifs of eternal protection within the general pattern of burial customs, even, conceivably, a unique strategy thought necessary for someone at the palace who had been struck down by scorpion bite or snakebite.

A papyrus from 1500 BC contains incantations for health of mother and child, in some instances to be spoken over sets of beads of particular materials or strung with specific numbers of knots. Evidently, particular combinations or sequences of material could be as powerful as the individual components, but this is hard to corroborate from excavated examples. Excavations only rarely yield bead strings that are sufficiently well preserved and recorded to confirm their ancient arrangement. In the largest collection, some 2000 strings, fewer than 50, are in original order, despite this being a special interest of the collector and archaeologist Flinders Petrie (Nai 1945). Two examples from the cemeteries at Sidmant indicate the potential for future research into material meanings. From the burial of a young girl, 2100 BC, on a string of green and black faience beads, disk rings alternate with rosettes, punctuated by a cylinder, a *crumb*-coated bead, and a disk on which the *wedjat*, "health," eye is incised. A burial of about 1500 BC had a string of carnelian, blue faience, and ostrich eggshell disk beads, none of which would be classified as an amulet from their form.

A chronology of amulet forms

Most amulets have survived in burials; only more analysis of use-wear and more settlement archaeology can reveal which types were worn in life. The range changes over time with local focus or within a *body grammar* of the full set of material formed, and sometimes inscribed, in each period. Around 3000 BC, figured amulets are rare. In the large cemeteries near Semenuhor (Kafr Turki), only a few richer burials had small figurines, some for wearing as pendants (Petrie 1914, pl.1). Also from the Semenuhor cemeteries, one extraordinary portable form is a small, hollow, beetle-shaped case in calcite, with detachable plug. The excavation director Flinders Petrie identified this as the earliest secure example of reverence for the scarab beetle, but it may be another type; its ancient contents remain unknown. Whichever species served as prototype, the stone case indicates active lines of connection with fauna and geology, comparable in direction with the different deployment of every scale of animal and bird in later periods of Egyptian material production. The burial customs of the mid-third millennium BC did not include the practice of placing jewelry with the deceased, other than ceremonial broad collars made for the burial (Chapter 7), and few town areas of this date have been excavated. As a result, little is known of protective jewelry or amulets for that period, the main pyramid age (Figure 6.4).

The customs change after 2200 BC, and among a wide variety of amulet forms that may continue earlier traditions, some types appear now for the first time in the archaeological record. Flat-based seals for stamping impressions on mud sealings begin to replace the older Mesopotamian cylinder seal, rolling over mud sealings (Wiese 1996). Sealing is a strategy of protection, and seals seem always

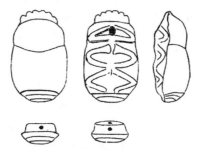

Figure 6.4   Calcite beetle vase, with stopper; the excavation director W. Petrie thought it would have contained a desiccated example of the beetle portrayed. W. Petrie, *Tarkhan I*, 1914, pl.1.

to have been considered imbued with wider protective powers; the term seal-amulet is often used in archaeology to indicate this broad significance, beyond the function of securing contents. Both cylinder seal and stamp-seal continue in use into the second millennium, often on the same strings with beads and amulets. Motifs on the seals, and the forms of the backs, coincide with the pendant amulets, in a unified image world. By 2000 BC, young women of high status in varying contexts, from village to palace, wear buried with girdles of cowry shells, back sliced off to evoke the vulva; examples include actual shells or their form in faience or gold. Fly amulets of glazed steatite are also found, and in the mid-second millennium, larger flies in bone and gold appear; inscriptions after 1500 BC refer to gifts of honor, in military style, perhaps from flies swarming as if on a battlefield (Gestoso Singer 2009). The same form in different materials and scales at different periods seems in this case to vary in meaning.

From the nineteenth century BC, a spectacular series of royal treasures survive from burials of mothers, wives, and daughters of the king, with two sets of jewelry: one placed on or beside the body, made for the tomb, as part of embalming and burial ritual and the other deposited in separate boxes, apparently the items that might have been worn in a ceremony or festival during life (Grajetzki 2014). Items of *life* jewelry include elaborate openwork pectorals with motifs of victorious king; girdles of gold cowries with amethyst ball beads; and, in place of the earlier leg amulets, anklets with gold claws. Outside the court at this time, richer burials include disk rings and sometimes extremely realistic fish amulets of precious metal. From the same period, on depictions of girls and young women, sometimes wearing cowry girdles, the fish amulet is worn at the end of the hair, tied in a single plait. In dancing scenes, the plait terminals are large blue- and black-glazed ball beads, practical counterweights for rotating in dance, but perhaps also with some of the same power to evoke protection, specifically on the water. From the Lahun town or tombs come faience star and dragonfly amulets; these recall the gold five-pronged stars and butterfly pendants from the burial of the king's daughter Khnumet, found at Dahshur. The royal pendants are decorated in granulation, that is, with minute spheres, a technique imported into Egypt at this time from west Asia, and the forms have been associated with Aegean and Anatolian jewelry (Aldred 1971). The Lahun faience examples seem to the local impact of prestigious or sacred motif styles that would have radiated out from kingship centers. The choice of forms might begin with a foreign technique and even a design but also links into earlier Egyptian worlds of significance: the stars are prominent in the literature for the afterlife (Chapter 7), and offering chapel scenes include images of butterflies and dragonflies as part of the rural idyll for eternal good life.

After 1500 BC, the seal-amulets present a twin focus on the name of the king and his father Amun-Ra, fusion of the concepts of hiddenness (Amun of Thebes) and sun-power (Ra). The clearest single series of amulets is the catalogue of forms from Akhetaten, mainly in faience, giving the image world at and immediately after the Akhenaten revolution, about 1350 BC (Petrie 1894). Many amulets and ring bezels give name of the king and sun-god, Aten, in the radical reformulation of kingship as, exclusively, cult of the visible sun. Others create a world of plant and bird forms in praise of the creation, as already found in kingship temple reliefs of 2450 BC. Alongside Egyptian flora and birds appear animals in the style imported from the Aegean and west Asia: dogs racing after deer, or facing goats on their hind legs, nibbling plants. Also, unexpectedly in a city dedicated to Aten, a high proportion of amulets are in the form of protective deities Aha/Bes and Ipy/Taweret; these finds may date after the death of Akhenaten, when the city continued to function under Tutankhamun.

In the early first millennium BC, birth themes continued to dominate production of faience amulets, with Aha/Bes and dwarf motifs. However, new amulet forms refocus on the cults of dangerous goddesses, Bast and Sekhmet, appeased on behalf of the child, and their reverse, Hathor at peace, providing sensuous, including musical, regeneration. Bronze and openwork faience counterpoises for heavy collars evoke Hathor rituals, and the dangerous goddesses are present as faience lioness-headed figurines, found on townsites and in tombs. As in incantations for health (see Writing for good health), the child–patient is modeled on the divine child, simultaneously king and sun-god; though future king, the child is shown as Horus vulnerable in the marshes, needing the protection of the mother Isis.

After 700 BC, there are also amulets evoking the pastoral world along and overlooking the floodplain: goats, ibex, and the branches they feed from are among motifs that had also been prominent in the period of mixed Asian–Egyptian rule east of the Delta, 1700–1550 BC. These forms disappear after reunification of Egypt under rulers from Sais in the west Delta, but it is not clear which images take their place: the period 600–300 BC produced the finest faience figurines for motifs such as dwarf and Ipy/Taweret, but they survive from funerary sets. New finds and analyses of used wear may help clarify whether these circulated outside the specialized environment of temple ritual and burial.

Material defense for safe birth

Among the figurines made not for wearing, but as separate material form, those depicting the young woman are prominent across the three millennia, though still with its own specific history, and always within a changing array of other figures that would affect, if not determine, meaning. In the third millennium BC, the naked female figurine is one of a series of animal and human forms, generally made of faience and found in temple deposits. In the late Middle Kingdom (1850–1700 BC), now mainly preserved in burials, the range continues, though small male figures now tend to be of dwarves and boys (hand to mouth), and the female figurine seems more prominent. In this period, the figurines are often depicted tattooed, and with the arousing and protective jewelry known from depictions and burials, such as the cowry girdles. A wider range of sculptors were involved in production, with different materials: faience, pottery, wood, limestone, and ivory. These vary from schematic painted wood with masses of hair as linen threads with Nile-silt pellets (Morris 2011) to a realistic and expertly sculpted ivory figurine wearing metal earrings – the earliest examples of earrings in Egypt (Bourriau 1988). On many, the genitalia are emphasized, and small versions in mud may reduce the form to a trapezoidal block marked only as reproduction. A spectacular version with leonine mask, evoking childbirth-protector deities, had held copper serpents; in the same tomb find were wood and faience female figurines, faience animals and plants, and papyri for good health (see section "Who Owned Healing Papyri?", with Figure 6.8).

After 1450 BC, clay or stone figurines of the naked female wear jewelry and ornate heavy wig, lying on a bed, often with child alongside. The motif also moves to eye paint containers and dominates a new version of the spoon for ladling or sprinkling, in the wider variety of materials: most often, the bowl of the spoon, sometimes as duck or fish, is held by a naked swimming girl, and sometimes, the handle becomes a new artwork, as in openwork motifs of girl playing music. This form is popular across the eastern Mediterranean (1400–1200 BC), particularly in ivory, and is revived in dark soft stones in first-millennium production, with the distinctive shorter round hairstyles of 750–525 BC.

The lyrical imagery of these works evokes the imagery in love songs preserved on Egyptian papyri 1300–1100 BC. However, in the longer history of the form, safe birth seems the main focus for the figurine, including in palace production of the finest images. Infant and maternal mortality affected every class: the bedroom of the palace of Amenhotep III preserved images of childbirth protectors, and chairs from palace furniture in royal and court burials of 1400–1350 BC include Bes and Ipy/Taweret. Much of the ancient material we classify as art belongs to the battle for safe birth at the highest level (Allen 2005). There is no high/low division in these sources, no religion/superstition divide as some modern writing assumes. Here, the social setting must be considered, from modern parallels that reveal the practicality of caring for mother and child. The art of healing implies wealth; birth protection might always involve the luxury of time, not available to everyone in a farming and pastoral economy. For late twentieth-century Nile Delta villagers, Morsy comments on the social class of birth defense and notes how confinement rituals after birth protection in two directions, for mother and child and for the society around (Morsy 1980, 156):

> In the village of FatiHa, the ideal of confinement of women after birth (practiced only in families whose economic resources permit the temporary release of women from their work obligations) is exercised, not simply as a way of protecting others from their contaminating power, but primarily as protection for women themselves and their newborn infants, all of whom are believed to be particularly susceptible to harm, including death, during the post-partum period

In the ancient Egyptian record, in its different variants, the imagery of fertility and birth protection recurs intermittently throughout the record of votive offerings and burial equipment, including burials of men and women and children and adults, though with a tendency to the female and infant worlds (Figure 6.5).

In one period, 1850–1750 BC, more burials contain more birth equipment, which also appears most varied at this time, with carved hippopotamus tusks and special

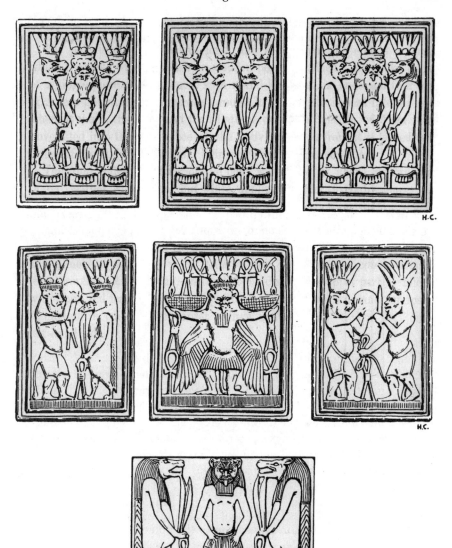

Figure 6.5 Aha/Bes and Ipy/Taweret on a chair inscribed for the king's daughter Satamun, from the burial of Yuya and Tjuyu, parents of queen Tiy, about 1375 BC. Davies, T. 1907. *The Tomb of Iouiya and Touiyou*. Constable, London.

rods decorated with forces of protection, redeployed as additional strategy for securing eternal life (Chapter 7). Finds from second-millennium BC settlement sites indicate that these strategies belong also, or primarily, within at least wealthier town life. The only surviving mask for the living, with lionlike features of childbirth-protector Aha/Bes, was buried in a pit in one of the medium-sized houses at Lahun (1800 BC; see Chapter 2). Recent finds of the same date at Mennefer/Memphis include a fragment of a limestone lamp or incense altar sculpted as a dwarf, in a substantial house where an infant had also been buried (Jeffresy 2012). The modern line between funerary and domestic and living and dead becomes difficult to maintain in this world of protection.

Protection of the body, awake and asleep

After 1550 BC, images of childbirth protectors Aha/Bes and Ipy/Taweret are found on cosmetic equipment, particularly luxurious versions of eye paint containers, eye paint offering medicinal protection as well as adornment (see section "Healer Titles and Roles," for physicians producing eye paint). The imagery is also found on headrests from 1800 BC onward, invoking the same protective powers for the body lying vulnerable in sleep. Other protectors of the vulnerable at home, including adults at sleep, include the female cobra, poised to strike, as clay figurines (Szpakowska 2003b). Serpents might be the enemy as much as defense; from 1350 BC, small wood round-topped plaques are known, incised with images of a young king or falcon overcoming serpents and inscribed with the name Horus or the Egyptian word *shed*, "Savior." After 900 BC, the child-ruler-deity motif is found in the more three-dimensional form of *Horus stelae*, on varying scales, from small portable amulets to larger-scale temple sculptures (Sternberg-el-Hotabi, 1999). On the front, the Horus child stands on two crocodiles, controlling in his hands the hostile forces of the desert – snakes, scorpions, oryx; sides, back and, on small versions, underside are inscribed with incantations against bites (Figure 6.6).

As an aggressive defense of order, the rearing cobra receives early expression in the defense of ruler and divine order (cf. Chapter 2.4). From 2400 BC and later, depictions of rituals set these serpent powers at the forehead, when the king, or later some deities, appears to a wider audience, marking a moment of risk (Roberts

Figure 6.6   Lion-headed and hippopotamus-lion protectors, earliest example on a headrest, inscribed for the accountant of the main recruitment enclosure, Neferhotep, from his burial in Waset, about 1750 BC. Photograph © Gianluca Miniaci.

1995). The protective imagery moves from kingship ritual not only toward the domestic sphere of different social classes but also into temple ritual and furniture in specific locations. After 700 BC, the image of Osiris at Abdju is defended against attack from all cardinal points by four lioness-headed rising cobras with special names. The four *faces* evoke earlier quadruple Hathor-face pillar capitals, a *Complete Hathor*, each side identified as a protective goddess – Bast, Shesmetet, Wadjyt, and Sekhmet (Coulon 2011). Here, in the domain of protection against ills, the imagery returns to the double aspect of Love (Hathor) and Fury (Sekhmet), prominent in the written sources (Chapter 4). For more information on the history of health strategies, with specific naming of the forces arrayed against well-being, the full surviving written record may be addressed next (Figure 6.7).

Health, healers, and healed: written evidence

Healer titles and roles

In written sources, the main titles in the area of healing are physician (Egyptian *sunu*), pure one of Sekhmet (Egyptian *wa'b Sekhmet*), and controller of Serqet (Egyptian *kherep Serqet*). By rationalist prejudice, some histories of medicine excluded the titles referring to goddesses, as too priestly for scientific treatment. However, the ancient writings suggest instead that the difference was in types of ailment treated, rather than any underlying separation of medicine from religion (Känel, 1984). The *sunu*, "physician," seems to specialize in treatment of external wounds, but the term may also be used as a generalized term for healer. In the correspondence of King Ramses IX with the high priest of Amun, Ramsesnakht, about a delivery of galena, the lead ore used for eye paint, the *sunu* presides over this field of protective adornment; "when given to the physicians of the Bureau of Physicians of Pharaoh at the Residence, to be processed, it was found to be such weak galena that it contained nothing useable for the eye-paint of Pharaoh!" (Wente 1990, 37). Men with the other healing titles might also have provided general advice for healing; in one letter (Waset 1250 BC), controller of Serqet Amenmes advises temple accountant Piay on directions for preparing a medicine (Wente 1990, 142).

The hundred and fifty known *sunu*, "physicians," include only one woman, Peseshet, serving in the household of the king's mother about 2250 BC (list in Nunn 1996). However, writing makes visible only some parts of life. Titles define what is considered, in that source, at that time, the primary activity of a person, but they do not seek to describe a social life as the modern job title might. This is clear from instances where physicians hold other titles: on a coffin from Bersha in Middle Egypt, 1900 BC, a man named Gua holds on one side the title physician, on the other estate overseer. Other holders of the common title *estate overseer* might also have served as healers, and other titles may conceal healing practice – including the nonspecific titles of women, such as *lady of the house*. Equally, individuals without titles in written records might have been involved in healing. Our lists of healers are important guides to the social profile in the official record and locate points of social recognition, with all the accompanying prestige, but they must be read in context.

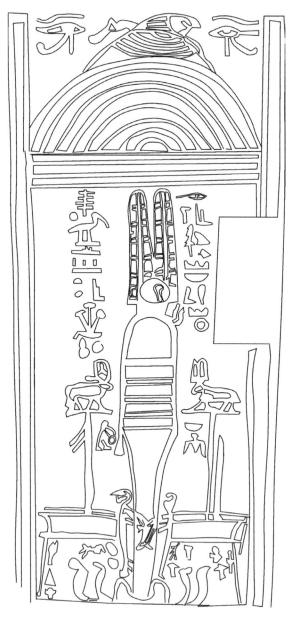

Figure 6.7 Sharp face, flame face, awake face, and alive face: protectors of the image of Osiris at Abdju. On limestone stela from Abdju, now British Museum EA808. Drawing © Wolfram Grajetzki, after Coulon 2011.

Before the name of a man, the term *pure one* most often denotes someone purified for performing rituals and offerings for a named deity at a cult place (Chapter 3). However, men with the title *pure one of Sekhmet* are not associated with temples of the goddess Sekhmet. Instead, the term appears among titles of healers. Sekhmet, the Fury, is associated in writings with the threat of disease and plague at the end of the Egyptian agricultural year, when midsummer heat at the lowest levels of the Nile raised real risks, precisely at the point that food and water were in shortest supply, and anxiety for the height of the next Nile flood at its most intense (Känel 1984). We might expect, then, that the pure one of Sekhmet was involved with what we might call public hygiene, specifically precautions against spread of plague, and checks on any food particularly vulnerable to heat – such as meat in banquets or special offerings (cf. a later manual, first–second century AD, Osing and Rosati 1998).

The controller of Serqet similarly has no known links to any temples of that goddess, and again, no woman is recorded as having the title, whether or not any performed the roles. Serqet, "she who causes/allows to breathe," is depicted in the third millennium as a water scorpion, a small pool insect unrelated to the land scorpion but with a breathing tube that recalls the scorpion's stinging tail. Later depictions show her as a scorpion, particularly as one of the forces enabling the lifeless to regain breath (Chapter 7). A unique late treatise preserves a *collection of remedies in the hands of a controller of Serqet*, which describes each type of snake, the effect of its bite, and instructions for treatment where possible (sixth–fourth centuries BC, Sauneron 1989). In addition to scorpions, the Saharan Nile Valley is home to a far greater variety of snakes, many venomous, like the cobra, and some lethal, like the asp or viper. This geographical context explains the need for a specialist in this area.

Areas of treatment by titled and untitled healers
The three specialist roles of physician, plague expert, and bite expert chart the terrain of healing at formal level, but do not necessarily cover all the types of treatment needed in the ancient Nile. Written records allow us to check the formal picture to at least some extent. From the village of artists working on the project to decorate the tomb of the king at Thebes (1300–1100 BC), documents record reasons for absence for work, including ill health, and offer a means of identifying the most needed treatments (Janssen 1980). One work record cites "sickness" a hundred times but only twice with a specific ailment, "suffering in his eye"; there is also one entry "the scorpion stung him," as known from several other sources from this village. The records of absence thus confirm one specialist area, treatment of snakebites, and draw attention to eye problems, another affliction prominent in the Saharan Nile but one for which there is no specialist title in second-millennium BC sources. One late twentieth-century study notes:

> Even today, Egypt has an inordinate share of blind and otherwise visually impaired citizens—most of them the rural poor and the victims of a chronic and sometimes blinding eye infection called trachoma, which is hyperendemic in rural Egypt. (Millar and Lane 1988, 654)

Other vast areas of challenges to health, above all pregnancy and birth, are also missing from the titles of male healers: for some of these, we turn to the manuscripts which they, and maybe others, were using.

Writings for good health

Surviving manuscripts indicate a recurrent triple strategy for all healers, each with its own Egyptian term: *shesau*, observation-based treatment (diagnosis and prognosis); *pekheret*, medicines, composed of specific ingredients in specific quantities or proportions; and *ru*, incantations, the words to reintegrate the individual back into the society of the healthy. In most manuscripts, one term dominates, so that a papyrus can be identified as predominantly treatments, prescriptions, and incantations already from the headings, before even reading the contents. The division may obscure the likely reality that this triple strategy is deployed by all three categories of healer. Modern prejudice might lead us to disassociate physician from chants and draw comfort from the dominance of *shesau* instructions for treatment of external wounds in the one surviving surgical treatise (Breasted 1930). However, the ancient writings are explicit that chants also accompanied their work; for "a wound in front of his face, shattering the skull shell," requiring particularly risky treatment, the surgical treatise adds a passage of incantation (Allen 2005, 29–80, Papyrus Edwin Smith case 9). In general, modern medical historians excise *magic* from their view of past healing, sometimes allowing for a contaminated interface of *medicomagical*. However, these categories are alien to the unitary or holistic ancient practice of attending to the sick with hands-on treatment, medicaments from the material world around, and the healing power of words.

Who owned healing papyri?
We know the title held by the ancient owner of any other healing papyri in only one case, and it has nothing to do with healing: Accountant of the Project, on the project for cutting and decorating the tomb of the king (Pestman 1982). Perhaps that accountant was a cultured reader, in a society where writings for health might have formed part of the core figure of a knowledgeable person. Although he might have been consulted either for his reading knowledge or for his real experience, the written records for his life at the village do not portray him as a healer. The earliest surviving group of health papyri is from a reused tomb under the Ramesseum: the box of papyri was found in 1896 at the bottom of the tomb shaft, with a range of items, but the body and any coffin had long since gone. The items include figurines associated with birthing rituals, and the combination of imagery and manuscript content has led Egyptologists to identify the original owner of the tomb as a healer (Quack 2006). However, there are three obstacles to this interpretation: (1) the combination of later literary and healing manuscripts recalls the mixed contents of papyri known to belong to the accountant; (2) there may have been more than one person buried in the tomb, and the original association of the objects with the papyri is uncertain; and (3) the presence of birthing objects is typical for burials of the time of these papyri. More serious still, rich burial equipment of the third to first millennia BC tends to

mark not profession, but status and gender: therefore, it would be extraordinary to find a healer buried with healing equipment. Here, the later burial of Madja could be cited as a possible counterexample of healing material with a possible healer; perhaps, then, exceptions were occasionally made with burials of women, supporting the idea that the owner of the papyri was a midwife (Gnirs 2009). However, this remains speculation: there is no body and no secure parallel for special midwife burial equipment, and all other female burials of the period lack such items. In general, the lack of parallel may support a different interpretation for Madja after all, as someone given special healing protection for eternity rather than an owner of medicines.

Among the earliest manuscripts (1800 BC) are two papyri with *shesau* treatments, from the townsite at Lahun. One covers the treatments for women, perhaps specifically once pregnancy is visible but stopping before the birth. Possibly the medic handed over to the midwife at this point. However, on one of the papyri found under the Ramesseum, an incantation series extend beyond birth to (immediate?) postnatal care, as does a later papyrus of incantations for mother and child (Yamazaki 2003). The concerns in these birth papyri include forecasting the sex of the child to be born (on forecasting, see section III). The second Lahun healing manuscript preserves the only second-millennium BC example of veterinary care, perhaps mainly for hygiene of cattle herds used in offerings. A treatise in a Roman Period hieratic papyrus, possibly composed earlier, includes among the tasks of the pure of Sekhmet monitoring outbreaks of contagious diseases and checking cattle meat (Osing and Rosati 1998).

Coping with life crises through the year

A few papyri preserve series of days marked as good or bad, the earliest being a single series of thirty days, as if for each of the twelve months of the year, without its five end days, or perhaps intended for one particular month (from Lahun, 1800 BC, Griffith 1898, pl.25). Two more expansive versions survived from 1300 to 1200 BC, and another from perhaps the seventh century BC. Extending across the year, the entries divide a day into three parts, each of which may be marked good or bad. These more elaborate versions provide reasons from lives of the gods for the good or bad quality of particular days. Equally rare manuscripts survived with incantations to be recited in the dangerous heat of the midsummer days at the end of the ancient Egyptian year. One thirteenth-century BC papyrus preserves a *Book of the last day of the year*, first hailing 12 deities, followed by this invocation (Raven 1997):

> Hail these gods, disease-forces on the arms of Sekhmet,
> going out from the Eye of Ra, envoys throughout the regions,
> inflicters of slaughter, creators of turmoil, racing through the land,
> shooting arrows from their mouths, spying afar!

Following the rest of the incantation, securing the speaker from falling prey to these hostile summer forces, instructions are given for recital: "words to be spoken on a bandage of fine linen, on which these deities are drawn, made into 12 knots." After other incantations for the last five days of the year, the 12 deities are duly drawn as a guide. From the same age, and perhaps source, as the papyrus, five linen bandages are indeed preserved with the images prescribed (Raven 1997).

Intangibles

Recourse to the divine: oracles in writing

Both health incantations and *shesau* treatments aim to affect the course of developments for the good, something many people today may accept in medical prognosis but reject as superstition under any other circumstances. The power of telling the future does not give rise to the role of prophetic seer, found in other cultures. In literary writing, the ability to see the future may be presented as a remarkable virtue but without superhuman associations; in the Tale of a Shipwrecked Courtier, a crew is said able to forecast a storm, but this does not save it from perishing at sea. However, an inscription of 1900 BC does seem to ascribe divine ability to King Amenemhat II for forecasting a miraculous catch of fish (Altenmüller and Moussa 1991). Such marvels (Egyptian *biayt*, "wonder") indicated the intervention of divine powers into earthly events; quarry inscriptions for King Mentuhotep IV (2000 BC) record a flash flood that revealed a desert well and a gazelle giving birth on a block, taken by the quarrying expedition as marking the stone for the sarcophagus of the king, on which the gazelle was then sacrificed in thanks (Vernus 1995).

Procedures for foretelling the future begin to legitimate official action in writings after 1500 BC, when select kingship inscriptions refer to movements of an image of the creator-god being carried in procession, as endorsement of a future king (Hatshepsut, Thutmes III). After 1300 BC, festival processions became more regular opportunities for any person to put a yes-or-no question to a deity, through the image being carried, most often in a boat-shrine on carrying poles (Černý 1962). In these *consultations* (Egyptian *nedjut-re*), a movement of the bearers of the image in one direction or another would give the answer, received as *declaration* (Egyptian *kher-tu*) or *wonder* (*biayt*). The procedure seems to have complemented the regular judicial tribunals, with no structural opposition; high officials of state appear on oracle witness lists. Only later, and perhaps briefly, out at the oases did oracles become decisive even in local land judgments (Gardiner 1933). Nor were oracles automatically accepted; in one dispute between two men, Amenemwia brought an accusation of theft a total of five times before three different forms of Amun, but Patjaumdiamun felt able to reject the verdict against him before finally declaring his guilt (papyrus document, 1250 BC, Blackman 1925).

From 950 to 850 BC, at Waset, over 20 examples are known of oracle pronouncements in favor of the health of a named individual, of high status, including one king's son; these are written on long thin strips of papyrus, to be rolled and worn as amulets, sometimes in cylindrical cases of wood or gold. The following clauses are from the oracle of Mut, Khons, and Amun for a girl or woman named Tashereteniah (Edwards 1960, 51–67) (Figure 6.8):

> We shall make our servant and our children healthy in her flesh and in her bones
> We shall make good every dream she has seen
> We shall make good every dream she will see

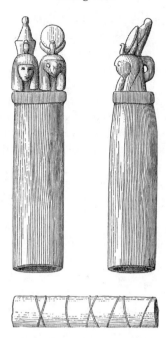

Figure 6.8 Container for a decree of protection issued by an oracle. After the accessions register of the Bibliothèque Nationale, as reproduced by Edwards, I. *Hieratic Papyri in the British Museum. Fourth series.* British Museum, London, 1960, xix.

> We shall rescue her from Khons-enduring-child and Khons-maker-of-condition,
>   the two baboons whose seat is in Pernefer, who rest at right and left of Khons,
>   who issue the books for putting to death and for causing to live.
> We shall rescue her from the fierce lion of Bast ... from the bite of crocodile, snake,
>   scorpion, ... from every evil eye and every evil look,
> ... from all *heka*-power of every *heka*-maker, man or woman,
> ... from the collapse of a wall and the fall of a thunderbolt
> We shall rescue her from any action of a Great (goddess) of   a canal
>   a well
>   a pool
>   a cleft
>   a marsh
> of *khaytu*-disease-demons and of *shemayu*-plague-demons,
> ... from the books of the beginning of the year, books of the end of the year,
>   books of the five days over the end of the year.

Other clauses seek to protect the physical body from head down, starting with hair loss, headache, and problems of the eye, throat, and teeth. Functioning as religious insurance contracts, these documents assemble details on daily matters not always prominent in other sources; the female great powers (Egyptian *weret*) appear localized to specific features in the landscape and might also be attached to the family on side of both mother and father. The world seems a dangerous and fragile structure, against which powers of good must be invoked, at least at this period, at every step.

The god Khons plays a prominent part here, as bringer of divine retribution, a role found in funerary writing a thousand years earlier, before he is attested as *son of Amun* at Waset. He is shown with lunar crescent, the moon changing as fate may change. Lunar deities Khons and Thoth may be depicted in baboon form, perhaps as baboons noisily acclaim sunrise, complementing the sun as the moon does. The moon offers the ambivalent model and influence of celestial bodies for human life; in its rhythms of change, it provides a basis for calculation, a basis for knowledge, and the domain of Thoth, but at the same time, its continual fading threatens the stability of order. One fifteenth-century BC papyrus preserves a series of incantations against corrosive diseases particularly difficult to treat, ascribed to the power of Khons and his emissaries: "swellings, eruptions, gnawings, affliction from a deity, a male or female dead" (Bardinet 2010). The healer invokes the figure of the baboon, recalling the two associated with Khons in the oracle amulet papyri but identified also as *the one from abroad* and from the mountain Laban, interpreted by Bardinet as referring to desert-mountain territory east of the Jordan. An uncontrollable power is seen here as emerging out of foreign lands, threatening sickness and death. Incantations were urgently needed against such forces.

Rarer or less visible traces of divination

In addition to consulting deities on festival procession days, other forms of divination may have been practiced. A unique papyrus of 1250 BC, from the village of artists at Waset (Deir al-Madina), contains evidence for a variety of techniques (Demichelis 2002). The warnings come from the creator sun-god Ra himself, while the person conducting the *good process* (*shemu nefer*) is identified with Thoth, lord of knowledge and script. This person is appropriately identified as *the knower of things* and is to be purified with incense, natron, and an unidentified substance called *dja'a*. One technique involves pebbles, perhaps drawn in lots, as attested for the procession oracles, but there is also divination from liquid in bowls, not otherwise found in Egyptian writings (3000–525 BC). Remarkable schematic images accompany interpretations of patterns formed by moringa oil when dropped in water, with such warnings as "if you see this image on a day of conflict, it is bad for you, do not go beyond words!"

Before 1500 BC, there are no certain written records of consulting divine forces for help in, or information on, the future. However, Sylvie Donnat has proposed to interpret as divination the 15 surviving letters to the dead, the majority from 2200 to 2000 BC, with particular attention to the five written on pottery bowls (Donnat 2002). Pouring water is a ritual act at the core of offering to the dead; at Waset (1300–1100 BC), when artists are absent from work on the tomb of the king to "pour water for the transfigured dead (*akh*)," and first-millennium BC offerers to the dead are called *water pourers*. In scenes of offering for a good afterlife, precisely the same type of wide, fairly shallow bowl appears for use in libations. At Waset (1300–1100 BC), a particular type of stela shows the recipient seated on a formal chair and identified in hieroglyphic inscription as "excellent transfigured one of Ra" (Demaree 1983). Here, communication might happen within the home, as the architecture of houses shows, with closed-platform altars and *false-door* motifs in the village of artists; the Teaching of Any also urges offerings to be made to parents in the home (Weiss 2009). Evidently, the location of contact with the dead might vary. From 1300 to 1100 BC, there are the sculptures known in Egyptology as ancestor busts, small rounded blocks of stone, faience, or wood, with tops carved or formed as a head of a man or woman, more rarely a couple, addressing deceased parents and, through them, the line of ancestors to Shu and Tefnet at the beginning of creation (Chapter 2). The combination of parents and ancestors may be a particularly ancient Egyptian form to more widely attested phenomena of ancestor cults; to call it *ancestor cult* may be to overlook the immediate tie to the biological parents. Within the same frame, the early letters to the dead address the very recently deceased; they appeal for help in daily problems of well-being (domestic conflict) and health (Wente 1990). Comparing the oil-in-water bowls of the papyrus from Deir al-Madina, first-millennium BC divination bowls in west Asia, and recent west African examples, Donnat raises the possibility that the bowls were used to communicate with the dead, perhaps on the very day of the funeral.

Other communication techniques: dreams, nightmares, and the question of games

Communicating with other worlds might extend to the imagery of sleep. The papyri of the accountant in the village of artists (see earlier section "Who Owned Healing Papyri?") include the only known book of dream interpretations. In this manual, interpretations may work by analogy, similar sounds in words, or associations of ideas. Rare second-millennium BC incantations against bad dreams are known, sometimes with instruction for recital over clay figurines of rearing cobras, as known from late second-millennium BC sites (Szpakowska 2003a). The dream might be spontaneous, but there is limited evidence for the practice of incubation or sleeping in a sacred place in order to obtain a dream that might then need to be interpreted. From the family of the book-owning accountant, one man declares on a votive stela to Mut "I have spent the night in your forecourt." Induced dreams may also have been part of the process involving the letters to the dead; Merirtyfy states that he slept in order to see his dead wife (Vernus 1986). According to one intriguing written record from the village of artists, the draftsman Merysekhmet may have spent time in his chapel there, *before his deity*, as part of a healing process after he fell sick; centuries later, as in ancient Greek practice, patients would rest or sleep in sacred precincts to obtain dreams (Fischer-Elfert 2011).

Practices of communicating with divine forces may also leave material traces other than writing. Earlier archaeologists sometimes confidently identified obscure items in burial equipment as toys or material for games. Fourth-millennium BC

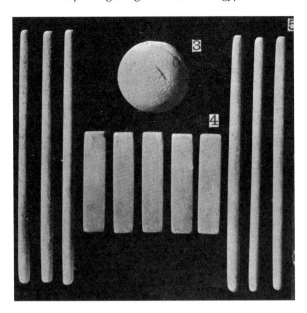

Figure 6.9   Divination equipment, game set, or both? Ivory rods and ball, from a burial in the cemeteries of Semenuhor, (Kafr Turki), about 3000 BC, now Petrie Museum UC15485. F. Petrie, *Tarkhan I and Memphis V*. British School of Archaeology in Egypt, London, pl.12.

balls and square-section rods might be reconstructed as miniature croquet sets, in keeping with the social and cultural background of early twentieth-century excavation directors (Petrie 1896). While they might well have served as pieces for some less European-looking game, they might also be considered instead as divining materials. Around 3000 BC, one burial at Semenuhor/Kafr Turki was provided with two sets of bone rods, one with a square section and one with a circular section (Petrie 1913, pl.12); these could be good materials for a game, as well as for divining. Perhaps it is unrealistic to try disentangling the two spheres of intricate games and divination practices (Flanagan 2009, 67–69). All games of chance automatically invoke destiny and may lead to, or emerge out of, techniques for consulting materially the powers that may reveal or control aspects of life. In an illustration for one of the most widely copied compositions for obtaining eternal life, from 1300 BC onward, the deceased man and woman are at a table playing the board game named in Egyptian *senet* (Piccione 1994). As in Persian, Arab world, and European imagery of chess, games both of skill and chance may simultaneously evoke idylls of leisure and the forces of destiny, where life and afterlife are indivisible (Figure 6.9)

CHAPTER 7

Attaining Eternal Life: Sustenance and Transformation

╒╕╒╕╒╕╒╕

Ancient Egyptian Afterlives: Sources and their Limits

In common with other Egyptological accounts of relations to the dead in Egypt (3000–525 BC), this chapter will struggle, and fail, to escape the straightjacket of a singular unilinear history, emanating largely from written and visual evidence. At the end of the chapter, I return to this problem, reconsidering its causes and the potential for future studies to expand to a wider archaeological base (cf. Grajetzki 2003) and comparative anthropological dimensions (cf. Wengrow 2006). Among the surviving sources, the images, inscriptions, manuscripts, and monumental architecture interweave two dominant themes in concepts of an afterlife: sustenance and transformation (Taylor 2001). In the first, the body is a physical anchor for human life, sustained with material or spoken provisions of food, drink, clothing, and items of status. In the second, the body is transformed into an eternal being, becoming *netjer*-like in immortality. This second goal was secured by techniques of embalming, including rituals for the deceased to share in the identity of Osiris, king of *duat* – the land of those living forever: the practice of mummification with the goal of *Osirification*. The two themes, sustenance and transformation, are complementary strands, each implying the other: a preserved body is already an achievement of human intervention, and, conversely, immortal being implies some need for sustaining energies. Published excavations help to write the history of the interplay and changes of focus between the two. The top-down, palace-centered history of embalming practice and care for the dead echoes the story of writing. As techniques of precision, both *Osirification* and writing seem to creep outward from the center, to achieve hegemonic or normative status across a wider part of society. Even when they achieved their maximum extent, Osirification and writing would still have been accessible only to a minority of the population, in a varying proportion that requires much further research. This chapter charts the chronology of the relationship between the strategies of sustenance and of

Exploring Religion in Ancient Egypt, First Edition. Stephen Quirke.
© 2015 Stephen Quirke. Published 2015 by John Wiley & Sons, Ltd.

transformation, through the architecture of immortality, in different social and geographical locations, and through the words, materials, and images of embalming, funeral, and burial rites. At the heart of these is the relation between living and eternal dead, not only at the moment of burying the dead.

The binary model sustenance + transformation is deduced mainly from inscribed and decorated monumental architecture, best preserved at Waset, Mennefer, and Abdju. All three cities at their height may have set models emulated at other centers across Egypt, and their impact must be read from the archaeological record in each region across the country. The *ancient Egyptians* of our books about the afterlife too may be only richer inhabitants of the larger Valley cities at the times of their greatest wealth. Any unified picture from such select material is unlikely to reflect ancient society, as archaeologist Peter Ucko warned: "in the vast majority of cases known ethnographically, a culture or society is not characterised by one type of burial only" (Ucko 1969, 270). In order to balance the picture, consider any Delta site or any Valley town or village away from those monumental sites, and ask how our standard image of *ancient Egypt* would apply to the inhabitants there, at different periods. Most regions and periods lack localized archaeological investigation and publication on which a series of histories could be written, a precondition for a future overall history. Before reviewing the evidence for the afterlife, reread the map of all Egypt (Chapter 1) to restore some sense of proportion to the modern imagination. As for all topics, we also need to consider dominant modern views on ancient Egyptian afterlife, not least because no area of ancient Egypt has received such heavy modern literary attention and rewriting. Historically, abroad, the ancient *akhet net neheh*, "horizon of eternity," became the primary source of the triple staple of Egyptomania: mummy, pyramid, and hieroglyph. The challenge for archaeology remains to track material evidence for practice on the ground.

Reconsidering Modern Perceptions of Ancient Egyptian Afterlives

A widespread external view accuses *the ancient Egyptians* of being obsessed with death, perhaps under the impact of the largest pyramids and of the intense modern focus on ancient embalming techniques. Egyptological and nationalist responses emphasize how care for an afterlife reflects a deep love of this life and discuss how grand building projects might have unified the country. Against these rather abstract debates, medieval and early modern Arabic and European travelogues can be useful in reconsidering how central such monuments were in life. Most early second-millennium AD visitors to Cairo either never visited the pyramids or encountered them only at the margin of their stay. The same travelers spend varying, but rarely dominant, amounts of time at the equally extraordinary medieval cemeteries. Death is a part, but not a frame, of this Egypt. We might use our imagination to reconstruct, then, not only the original splendors of tomb architecture but first and foremost life in the city, town, and village – not excluding the burials or funerals that take place in all lives. Egyptian archaeology began with urgent tasks of clearing, recording, and maintaining monumental architecture, without ever finding all the resources needed for the scale of either the ancient or the medieval city, or less spectacular graveyards. As a result, we tend to reproduce a picture of this past as monumental tomb and temple (Wendrich 2010, 1–14). In other countries, the reverse general focus may apply; our religious and funerary Egypt contrasts with our economic and urban Iraq or Syria, despite excavation of spectacular tombs and temples there.

The past twenty-five years have brought more publications from settlement excavations in Egypt, allowing new approaches. This shift in fieldwork helps to redress the balance between settlement archaeology and monument preservation. Both branches of fieldwork are needed, but their practitioners have to compete for resources, and as a result, they can become polarized. In the process, the funerary may be lost from the immediate horizon of settlement archaeology, where excavators prioritize knowledge of domestic and working life. Few well-documented excavations publish both a town and its adjacent or internal cemetery, the main examples being at the margins or outside the valley (Abu, Hutwaret, Balat). The resulting *tombless town* corresponds to a blind spot in the society of the excavator: modern consumerism seems the anthropological and historical oddity, in insisting relentlessly on removing death from sight. Life includes burial of the dead by the living.

In sum, the record remains very partial, not only through survival but also through fieldwork strategy, leaving us far from answers to questions, such as: where were most people buried? If most larger cities stood on high ground within the floodplain fields, all but the richest burials might be expected on available high ground nearby. In the few such cemeteries to survive, as at Hutnennesut (Ihnasya), the bodies have rotted away, and the architecture too has decayed in the damp of the river valley. Numerically overshadowing the low desert monumental tomb complexes of Waset and Mennefer, the floodplain *island* cemetery evokes a very different landscape of eternity, where bodies are closer to the Nile (cf. Figure 1.4). The contrast desert valley gives a sharper edge here to the struggles for an afterlife. Even the burials of kings include unexpected choices. Certainly, the most famous kingship cemeteries of third and second millennia are safely in the nearest high desert (Giza pyramid plateau, the Valley of the Kings at Thebes). However, 1900–1800 BC pyramid burial chambers are very deep cut, and after 1000 BC, tombs of kings are in lower-lying temple precincts. Instead of an overfamiliar tale of Osiris, this history of human life may bring a series of surprises.

Burying the Dead: Conceptions of the Tomb

Modern interpretations of ancient Egyptian burial goods seem prone to identifying an ancient individual as a modern census might, by profession. A musical instrument in a burial becomes evidence that the deceased was a musician, a weapon indicates the military (Garstang 1907). Persistently, modern interpreters convert late third-millennium BC sets of miniature metal blades into evidence for ancient medicine – 2000 years earlier than the emergence of special tools for surgery (against this misconception, see already Messiha and Messiha (1964)). Peter Ucko observed instead how "one society will undertake several different forms of burial, and ... these forms will often be correlated with the status of the deceased" (Ucko 1969, 370). In Egypt, most ancient tomb equipment seems to concern social status, in its dimensions of age, class, and gender, with fewer examples of ethnicity and dominant work activity (Seidlmayer 2007). The burial space itself receives a variety of prominent interpretations, outlined in the following section, but all consistent with this frame of social status.

Even in the rare instances where the burial space survived intact under the surface, the ground-level area may not be preserved, or recorded, well enough for us to see whether, and for how long, the living cared for, or communicated with, the dead there. Accordingly, the relations of past peoples to their dead must be assessed from fragments, always asking whether the recorded evidence is a regular or unique pattern from that place and time. A history of burial can give the impression that individuals buried themselves. In practice, even if someone might prepare for their own future burial and afterlife existence, their preparations took shape in the setting of customs across their society and inside the social group to which they belonged within that society. Rather than considering this the story of the individual(s) being buried, we might instead set out to record the practices of those burying their dead. By foregrounding the people burying, alongside the life of the person buried, it may be easier to distinguish the different input of a person thinking of their afterlife and of those involved in burial and offering to the person once dead. Separable histories need to be written for architecture of burial space below ground, for burial-place architecture above ground, for other spaces for offerings to the dead away from the burial place, and for the equipment placed in any of these spaces. The various uniform histories rarely if ever apply to all regions or to all social classes. Different quantities of available evidence can be expected for each history: only richer individuals would have resources for the more substantial architecture and equipment. To this extent, afterlife history can provide a mirror of general social complexity.

Burying, Caring for, and Relating to the Dead: Four Questions

In tracing ancient practice over the centuries, four issues may be used as guides to questioning the published archaeological record:

1. Burial demography: How sociable are the dead expected to be? The living may place in one and the same underground space a single individual, or two or more persons. Burials before 1500 BC tend to be, on these terms, more individual than later burials (Grajetzki 2007). With individual burial spaces, organizers may group burials according to priority in social relations. For example, members of one family or extended kinship group might be placed together, as often assumed, or as around regional governor tombs (2000–1850 BC), officials who worked together may all be buried next to the tomb of their lifetime master (O'Connor 1974; Seidlmayer 2007). At ground level, a large superstructure or enclosure around individual burials may gather together the members of a group, whether kin or colleagues. In the construction of shared space for an afterlife, specific space and timing are

crucial. Therefore, as well as documenting the presence of single/pair/multiple burials, a second key consideration is whether the burials observed took place at a single moment or sequentially over a shorter or longer period of time. Three sets of practices might be kept in mind: (1) burying together people who died at one time (single time of burial, single space), (2) burying people in one tomb but in separate chambers (different times of burial, shared entrance or shaft, but still individual burial spaces). and (3) burying people together in an undivided space over a period of time (sequential burials in single space, opening the burial space for each new burial).

2. Body position: How do the living lay the dead in the ground? Body position offers the best evidence for the geographical spread of embalming techniques. The embalming techniques developed at the royal court in the third millennium BC are reflected in the position of bodies stretched out, lying on their sides, rather than contracted in fetal position, as in fourth-millennium BC burials even of higher status. In the second millennium BC, embalming continues to improve, with less emphasis on padding the body with linen to absorb moisture; perhaps as a result, the body position changes again, as the deceased is lain out flat, face up (Bourriau 2001).

3. Links between the worlds of the dead and of the living: At each burial place, has evidence been found for the uses of the space above ground? This history also requires any well-documented negative evidence, where the surface has been carefully recorded, and found not to yield any evidence of use. Examples of such reporting may be rare in the published record.

4. Material placed with the dead: Why did the living place material with the deceased? Burial equipment varies according to time period and social level, and anthropology warns against assuming the motivation behind each practice (Ucko 1969). Where we might assume that items were the personal property of the deceased, anthropologists can cite examples where mourners gave an item of their own for the burial, making the burial equipment a celebratory posthumous gift. Items might be given not to adorn, celebrate, or protect the deceased, but instead to protect the living from the dead. Modern readers have to approach the evidence on its own terms, asking how we can identify among a range of options: not only gift or property but – more broadly in intent – adornment, healing, protection, regeneration, sustenance, and tradition.

Burying the Dead: Chronological Survey

The preceding general considerations serve as an introduction to the following whistle-blow summary of the dominant practices observable on present evidence of excavated cemeteries. In order to cover the two and a half millennia, the account reduces each period to far too homogeneous a picture and omits the range of variations at any one moment. Without a quick picture of the main visible practices, significant variations cannot easily be identified. Yet the danger remains that unexpected practices are eclipsed by the standard history, even when they may be quantitatively the dominant story. I return to the problem of the normative at the end.

3100–2700 BC Underground provisions store,
overground offering space

At the end of the fourth millennium BC, as Egypt became a unified kingdom apparently for the first time, a large cemetery expanded along desert foothills on the west bank between Fayoum and Mennefer (Petrie 1913; naming the site Tarkhan; summary Grajetzki 2004). Excavators in 1912–1913 recorded 2000 burials from just one century, 3100–3000 BC, implying a relatively urbanized center in the vicinity (=Semenuhor of later sources?), just before development of a new national center at White Walls, the future Mennefer. Deposited materials are well preserved and range across different social levels, so reflecting patterns of burial in at least the urban centers of the time. Overwhelmingly, the living sought to provide all their dead – regardless of age or gender – with individual burial, stocked with a pot for grain and a cylindrical jar for fat, their bread and butter for eternity (Grajetzki 2004). Sometimes (<1 burial in 10), they placed on the deceased an item of jewelry, and occasionally, there were items of weaponry or leisure, very rarely a figurine (Chapter 6). For most burials, the excavators recorded no trace of ground-level chapels or simpler offering installations. However, where tightly packed, no later generation dug into existing burials, as if some marker existed at ground level, and there even seems to be a path through the densest concentration. For some burials, surface structures did survive: single chambers immediately over the burial space, with a small entrance enclosure on any one side (Grajetzki 2008; no preference between north, south, east, and west). Pottery vessels were found stacked alongside, as if for a recurrent ritual of offering to the dead. Three or four tombs stand out as far the richest and grandest, as they had a palatial superstructure with façade of niched brickwork and underground additional stocks of clothing and food (Figure 7.1).

Excavations in the cemeteries of Inebhedj confirm that, at this period, the tomb of the richest was stocked like a warehouse for the deceased (Emery 1961). Above, a solid block of brick – like more recent benches, in Arabic *mastaba* – marked the burial and provided backing for offering chapels now placed along the east side. After 3000 BC, the living begin instead to deposit with the dead not the material food, drink, ointment, and cloth, but rather their eternal presence in the form of empty containers or, increasingly, depictions that would never grow stale or perish. At the central cities and in the regions, great tombs were provided with new means of access for the day of burial, great stairways from outside the *mastaba* block to the chamber beneath, blocked with massive stones after the burial (Reisner 1936). These centuries see transition to a new concept of burial space, where the focus of ornament shifts to the offering space above ground, while the living lay their dead to rest with very little underground equipment. Increasingly, instead of the earlier fetal position, with knees to chin, the richer dead were stretched out and buried on their sides, wrapped in masses of linen, within long narrow coffins. The long coffins and extended position imply either the direct practice or the emulation of the effect of desiccating the body in natron, stretched out for removal of soft inner organs.

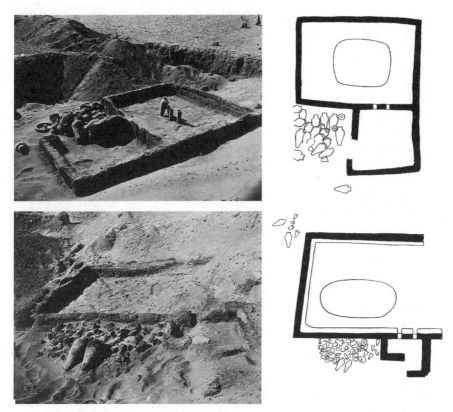

Figure 7.1 Chapels over burials, with stacks of pottery storage jars from the care for the dead, Semenuhor (Kafr Turki), tombs 740 and 1231, about 3000 BC. W. Petrie, *Tarkhan II*, British School of Archaeology in Egypt, London, 1914, pl.14.

2600–2300 BC *Underground blank, overground provisioning/leisure machines for the rich*

During the mid-third millennium BC, while pyramids and their temples were built for kings along the Memphite cemeteries, most burials became so empty, rich and poor, that they are difficult to date without the evidence of the chapels above. Poorer graves of all periods are hard to date, because the body received no datable objects, and archaeologists must rely on other contextual dating criteria such as treatment and position of the body. The same difficulty applies to the wealthy too, during this period. In regions such as the area of Tjebu (Qau) in northern Upper Egypt, in towns and villages, the living chose to bury their dead in the largest pottery vessels available for protection and/or containment. In richer burials, more closely connected with the power centers of kingship, adult men might receive a staff, or set of staves, and a set of miniature tools, and costly linen might pack the coffin around the body. There is also sometimes jewelry, mainly ceremonial items such as broad collars, perhaps made for the tomb. However, in general, the intact burials of the period show how little the living placed with their dead at this time. Instead, over their future burial chamber, the richest at court provided for their own afterlife with lavish chapels, housing an increasing number of offering rooms (Figure 3.3). At first, a smaller offering space opens from the façade of the *mastaba* block; in the cemetery of the Great Pyramid of Khufu (about 2550 BC), the only decorated and inscribed surface here may be a single offering slab of the finest carving and painting (Manuelian 2003). Around the same time, a sculpted portrait head might be deposited at the foot of the shaft to the burial chamber (*reserve heads*). At their most elaborate, 2450–2300 BC, *mastaba* chapel walls teem with scenes of production and leisure in a selective, idealized projection of life into eternity (Harpur 1987). Increasingly over time, governor courts across the regions emulate the royal court ideal tomb type of visual–verbal provisioning and leisure machine, either with *mastaba* block chapels (as at Dandara, Waset) or with chapels cut into the rock (Dishasha, Tihna, Hamamia). With their actively regenerating wall scenes, the chapels are provisioning machines for the sleeping dead, futuristically securing sustenance, and the leisure of music, games, dance, and, though never quite explicitly, physical love (Figures 7.2 and 7.3).

Alongside these two-dimensional projections, eternal life for the wealthy is secured in three dimensions, in the limestone or, more rarely, granite statues of the richest tombs, placed in a chapel or burial space of its own. The status of the

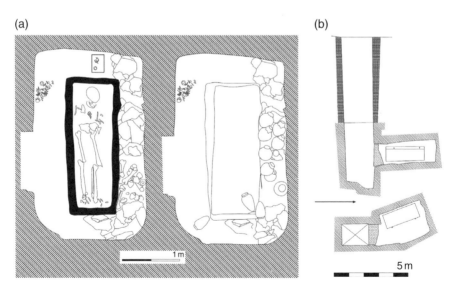

(a)

(b)

Figure 7.2 Burial equipment about 2400 BC, in the cemeteries at modern Giza: (a) underground chamber of tomb 585, Selim Hassan excavations, showing small box of cosmetic equipment to side and predominantly pottery outside and inside the coffin, with second layer (right) with animal bones, food offerings, and/or remains of funeral meal; (b) shaft and burial chamber under mastaba G2220B, George Reisner excavations, found intact and sparsely equipped. Drawings © Wolfram Grajetzki.

Figure 7.3 Motifs selected from provision of offerings for an estate, overseen by the beneficiary, and from fauna and flora of Nile and low desert. Raised relief scene on limestone blocks of wall in chapel over the burial of the high official Ptahhotep, northern cemeteries of Inebhedj (Saqqara). From J. Quibell, R. Paget, A. Pirie, *The Ramesseum and The Tomb of Ptah-hetep*, Quaritch, London, 1898.

three-dimensional image is highlighted by evidence for its own special consecration ritual, named "Opening the Mouth and Eyes" (see Table 7.2). Some burials were reinforced by the provision of more statues, adding to the images of the tomb-owner statuettes of servants at work (Tooley 1995).

2300–1850 BC *Markers of age, gender, and status in the regions: underground and overground provisioning and leisure machines for the richest*

After 2300 BC, above ground, for the wealthy, the decorated surface contracts, though grand offering chapels in regional centers project the life of the tomb owner in words: Weni at Abdju and Harkhuf at Abu eternally recite their expeditions for successive kings (Richards 2002). At the royal court cemeteries, the detailed *mastaba* chapels yield to a new focus on the burial space, now inscribed with images of the essential offerings. Prominent among these are oils and cloth, perhaps reflecting a slightly wider social spread of embalming techniques at least in the Memphite zone. After 2300 BC, increasingly, the long coffin is decorated on the outside with two eyes with falcon marks that identify them as the *wedjat*, "health," eye and enable the deceased, lying with head to north, on his or her side looking east to the rising sun. Statues, now of wood, were placed in the same space with the coffin or in the tomb shaft outside, and wooden models of boats and production scenes begin to be placed with the wealthy, mainly, if not always, men.

Under political division of Egypt (2200–2050 BC), regional ruling groups prospered, with local workshops at all known Upper Egyptian centers, most producing their own images and inscriptions for eternity for the first time (Grajetzki 2003). Reunification around 2050 BC again brought substantial impact in the spread of a widely shared style of burial equipment for the regional ruling courts. Their coffins now have painted friezes of objects, developed from the painted burial chambers, and extensive inscriptions (see Centres of writing or drawing the afterlife for these *Coffin Texts*). Otherwise, workshops continued to produce the same range of burial equipment for the wealthy, ranging from rustic carpentry work (as at Beni Hasan; Garstang 1907) to palace sculpture quality (treasurer Meketra at Waset; Winlock 1955). This new type of burial equipment may have been made specifically for men who were landowners of great estates. Despite their often rustic appearance, perhaps often produced by carpenters rather than trained sculptors, within their time, these models were marks of social distinction. Most individuals received simpler burials, though also often markedly different from other periods; in particular, protective amulets now more regularly accompanied women and children into afterlife existence, apparently at all social levels. Across the regions and the centers of kingship alike, the period witnesses shared burial customs for the less wealthy too: the simplest equipment for adult men, particularly staff, sandals, and headrest for the eternal journey, and jewelry and cosmetic sets particularly for younger women, perhaps as dowry for afterlife wedding or birth (Dubiel 2008) (Figure 7.4).

From this period, kingship focus and regional town intersect in a new pattern at Abdju. Here, around 1950 BC, a new monumental temple to Osiris Foremost of the Westerners was built in the name of king Senusret I (Hirsch 2004). Accompanying this, the temple and adjacent low desert cemetery fields became places for construction of chapels for offerings to high- and middle-ranking officials, from both palace and local governor circles, who were involved in the temple-building kingship project. The chapels fronted a processional route out to the tombs of the First and Second Dynasty kings, a kilometer into the desert, and inscriptions on statues, jambs, and offering stones and tables specify that the named officials and associates – colleagues or family – should receive offerings forever especially at the festivals of Osiris (Simpson 1974; O'Connor 1985). For the next fifteen centuries, local and kingship officials working at, or passing by, Abdju would continue the practice of installing chapels to join, and benefit from, the festivals. The result is a complex archaeological site, with extensive reuse of ground, making it hard to

Figure 7.4 Wooden models as found in the burial chamber of the estate overseer Karenen, cemeteries of Mennefer near modern Saqqara, about 1950 BC. From J. Quibell, *Excavations at Saqqara, 1906–1907*, Institut français d'archéologie orientale, Cairo, 1908, pl.12.

assess which chapels were associated with tomb shafts (as one might expect for the local officials) and which had no associated burials.

In other places, inscribed monuments refer to journeying to Abdju, among other sacred cities, and this has given rise to the modern notion of ancient pilgrimage to Abdju. However, the sources concern rites of the day of burial and were evidently celebrated at any place in Egypt. Instead of literally involving a journey to a sacred place, these rites translate the physical motion of the final stages of embalming and the funeral procession into a sacred geography in which a water offering may become a sailing and the coffin a boat (Willems 1996). The concept of space behind these expressions is far removed from the physical journeys undertaken in other cultures to visit sacred places. Among the thousands of inscriptions at Abdju itself, not one asserts that any ancient individual traveled to Abdju exclusively for a festival, in the manner of pilgrimages in other societies (one only uncertain example in Lichtheim (1988)). Instead, the chapels seem to operate like another all-important Middle Kingdom innovation, the temple statue, inscribed to enable the named individual to participate in festivals (Verbovsek 2004). At least in their inscriptions, the focus of temple statues and

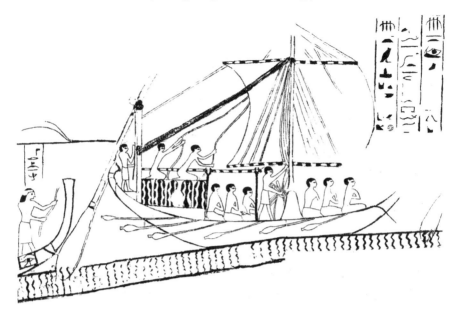

Figure 7.5   Depiction of the sailing to Abdju, painted on the tomb chapel (?) of a man named Sehetepibra, at Waset, about 1750 BC. From J. Quibell, *The Ramesseum*, Quaritch, London, 1898, pl.7.

Abdju chapels is on securing presence at sacred space/time for the sustenance of the deceased. Centuries later, as the focus of burial shifts toward transformation in this normative afterlife history, the need for sustenance may have been met primarily instead in these chapels and sculpture away from the tomb. The social breadth of inclusion or exclusion in each period requires further research, both for the local residents, as variably reflected in the surviving recorded burial equipment, and for the retinue of officials and sometimes kings, where serving staff might be recruited either at Abdju or at the distant residence of king or official (Figure 7.5).

1850–1700 BC Underground solar kingship or birth or leisure, overground provisioning?

The patterns of richest burials become more diverse during the nineteenth century BC, with major change in contents of burials. By 1850 BC, the main features of the previous afterlife world had disappeared: there are few, if any, large governor tombs or coffins with extensive inscriptions and no models of estate production. At royal court cemeteries, the mastaba chapel seems generally to return to the earlier form of solid block, without internal suites of rooms decorated with life scenes; this renewed dominant type might have only limited external inscription, tightly focussed on offering to the transfigured dead (Arnold 2008). Images of fishing and hunting birds, harvest, or musicians do not disappear entirely, including some smaller-scale examples on inscribed elements of chapels at Abdju. However, the general indication is of a radical restructure of machinery for the afterlife.

Surviving tomb equipment points to three separate conceptions of the burial chamber. In the wealthiest burials closest to the Residence, the deceased is transformed into Osiris, with wrapped body lain in anthropoid coffin, equipped with the regalia of his kingship over eternity and supported by the tableware and storage jars for the final meal and eternal sustenance (the best published example is the burial of Senebtysy at the cemeteries of Itjtawy, near modern Lisht; Mace and Winlock 1916). A second, still restricted pattern is the protection of the individual with new types of object, apparently made for use in rituals at birth. Faience, wood, and ivory models of protective and liminal forces were deposited beside or in the coffin (Bourriau 1991). The largest figures are the faience hippopotami, glazed with decorative designs of marsh plant and insect life; the feet are often broken, perhaps ritually, and some were found in the body wrappings at the back. Smaller faience models include other fauna of desert and marsh margins, plant forms such as gourds, small sealed vases, and children or dwarves, sometimes with vases or young animals. One of the largest groups of parallels is from the Baalat/Hathor temple at Jebeil (Byblos) in Lebanon, anchoring the figures in a divine world of female gender (Pinch 2003). With the figurines are sometimes elements from cuboid rods and planed hippopotamus tusks, incised or sculpted with images of birth protectors, especially Aha/Bes and Ipy. A third pattern of burial continues the earlier practices of depositing used domestic items, of cosmetic or leisure, for the adornment and entertainment of wealthy man or woman. To this group belong the burials of women related to kings, preserving remarkable sets of jewelry, some made for burial and some from court ceremonial. In contrast to some other periods, in burials of this time, the domestic equipment includes no furniture other than the headrest. These are all portable materials, as if to accompany the individual on their one last journey and/or the eternal cycle of sailing with the sun (Figure 7.6).

A single burial may combine elements from these varying conceptions of the tomb as Osiris bed, birthing chamber, and cabin. At Waset, an official in labor organization, Neferhotep, was buried resting on his back, looking up, in a new style of anthropoid coffin with feather motif (Arabic *rishi*) and a mace, as if Osiris with his regalia was equipped for eternity (Miniaci and Quirke 2009). However, he was also equipped with a writing tool and two accountancy papyri from managing a visit by the king and the estate of the first minister, and the burial party had also deposited a staff, a gaming set, and a mirror board, as if seeing him off on a standard Nile journey for an official. They also provided a faience hippopotamus figurine and hippopotamus canine section carved with figures, as found in the birthing zone, and a double-scarab seal-amulet inscribed with a protective motif, as well as a headrest inscribed with some of the same images found on the hippopotamus tusk (Figure 6.6).

The body rests here as a vulnerable core, requiring all available strategies for protection and survival. However, already the change in position indicates a new identity: stretched out, as required in fuller embalming, Neferhotep claims the position of ruler of eternity, and this change is found in cemeteries along the Nile Valley (Bourriau 2001). The spread of embalming technique from kingship centers led first to the introduction of the narrow box coffin, body lying on side, and then to its

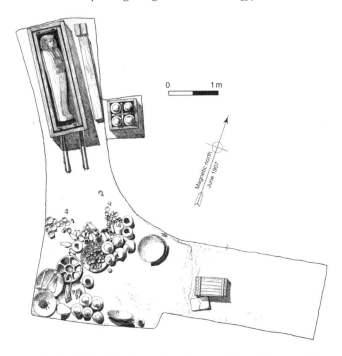

Figure 7.6   Burial of the lady of the house Senebtysy, with regalia and anthropoid coffin including the headcloth of kingship, securing her afterlife through identification as Osiris king of the dead and Horus king of the living. Lisht. A. Mace and H. Winlock, *The Tomb of Senebtisi at Lisht*. Metropolitan Museum of Art, New York, 1916.

replacement with the broad coffin, now often in the form of the human body, with limbs wrapped chrysalis-like and head covered by mask with kingship cloth (*nemes*), protectively encasing the embalmed body, lying flat, facing skyward. The position and its claim to kingship become standard across social classes over the entire following millennium. Accompanying material signs of this divine status include two innovations of the late Middle Kingdom: the shabti, an Egyptian term for a figure invoked to substitute for the individual when called for any heavy manual labor in life after death, and the heart scarab, a scarab-shaped amulet placed over the heart during wrapping after the embalming of the body. For the next fifteen centuries, both object types regularly accompany Osirified individuals into their afterlife.

1600–1350 BC *Underground provisions store and leisure, overground provisioning/leisure*

At some point between 1750 and 1650 BC, gradually or suddenly, the kings at Itjtawy no longer controlled all Egypt, and evidence becomes scarce for richer burials at both the Memphis–Fayoum region and Abdju. Even at Waset, no intact burial group is known, although some must have been found, as complete vaulted box coffins were purchased for some museums in the early twentieth century in Upper

Egypt. Some of these coffins introduce a different range of ritual writings, so far attested at Hu, Abdju, and Waset (Grajetzki 1998). Burials after 1600 BC indicate that coffins maintain the theme of becoming Osiris, while much of the burial equipment picks up on the portable cosmetic and domestic equipment, just beginning to expand from light baggage toward more of a complete household inventory. From 1500 BC, the kings of reunified Egypt were buried at Waset, which became, for the first time since the beginning of the Twelfth Dynasty (1950 BC), the cemetery for the highest officials, receiving unprecedented inflows of wealth. In the richer intact burials, for the century 1450–1350 BC, the idea of packing the tomb like a house store dominates the funerary record (Smith 1992). The wrapped body, with its head cover, lies in a coffin designed to maintain eternal regeneration from the day of embalming, with four protectively inscribed bricks of mud, each with its separate figure, as may have demarcated the embalming space during the weeks between death and burial. Regularly, a papyrus book-roll with the deceased projects around the body the rituals and amulets needed for bodily survival and transformation into a *netjer* (see Centres of writing or drawing the afterlife, *Book of the Dead*). Around, the body is most often accompanied by others, and this smaller or larger community of dead is supplied with the stockpile of food, drink, clothing, cosmetic equipment, and leisure equipment for the rich household (Figure 7.7).

From this point in this normative history of burial, the dead are less often placed into the ground alone. Initially, the more usual combination may still be restricted to a couple, but now, the underground chamber rather than just the wider cemetery becomes a communal unit, creating different social relations in the ground. As with earlier governor tomb chapels, the male head of household may seem visual first point of reference in richer and more monumental examples, but the dominant underlying conception seems to be of gender complementarity. In chapels or in the illustrated papyri for the afterlife, a man is often shown first, and a woman follows in accompaniment. This complementary gendering of the burial space needs more careful reading and decoding, in the manner proposed by Ann Roth for earlier monuments (Roth 2006). Further research is also needed into the relation between the primary figures, whether singular or paired, and all the other persons present in the images and inscriptions of offering chapels and perhaps bodily in the burial chambers beneath them. After 1350 BC, the numbers of burials within one chamber can rise far higher, but already in this period, there are some striking examples. Around 1400 BC, in the Middle Kingdom town at Lahun, apparently depopulated by then, one house cellar was expanded to receive the burial of over 40 men, women, and children of unknown relation to one another, perhaps within a generation. The exact number of bodies is uncertain, as the damp of the ground reduced the contents of the coffins and boxes to dust. Two boxes were used for the burials of children, and the only anthropoid coffin contained a single individual. For the 11 box coffins, the excavator reported that each "contained several bodies, some holding five or six, piled one on the other" (Petrie 1891, 21). The coffins bear no names, but the burial included some gold jewelry and fine amulets, as well as an imported Minoan vase, as well as Cypriot and Levantine pottery, and a chair (front legs removed to prevent reuse). The overall effect is not of a particularly poor

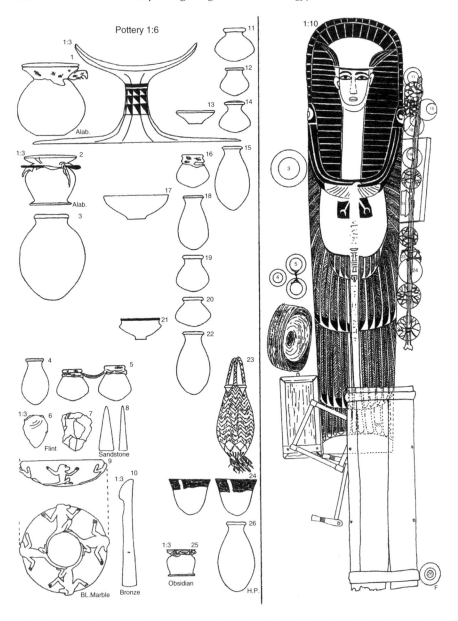

Figure 7.7   Burial of a wealthy woman in a gilt wood anthropoid coffin and two children in wood boxes, pottery, and baskets around the coffins. W. Petrie, *Qurneh*, British School of Archaeology in Egypt, London 1909.

burial, and therefore, there may be other factors behind the use of a coffin for more than one burial. Presumably, the people conducting the funeral felt it was crucial to protect the body by housing it within a secure eternal container. No other period seems to betray quite the same panic at exposure (Figure 7.8).

Figure 7.8   Female–male complementarity as a visual ordering principle: a man raises his hands in adoration, accompanied by his wife in the role of *chantress*, shaking sistrum, in the tomb chapel of the estate overseer Rey and his wife chantress of Amun Nebettawy, Waset (Theban Tomb 255). Photograph © Gianluca Miniaci.

We do not know how the living maintained offerings to, or any links to, their dead buried in the Lahun cellar. There are no record of any preparation of offering ground at the surface and no formal visible trace such as a stela or offering table from a chapel there. Perhaps, they were invoked at home (see Chapter 6). By contrast, in the city where the kings of this period were buried, at Waset, the superstructure above the burial spaces of the richest became an architectural spectacle, integrating into major festivals the tombs of the officials of kingship, including of the Amun temple, after 1450 BC. Like the mastabas and rock-cut governor tomb chapels, these richly inscribed spaces are for offerings to statues of a named individual man, couple, or sometimes three to four individuals. The statues at the center of rituals in the chapel were located conceptually or sometimes literally above the body in the burial chamber beneath. In place of the brick chapels of previous centuries at Waset, the new monument type is part rock-cut, part more open space in front (the open parts have been less often investigated in modern excavations). In the grandest examples, the image of the official and closest family might be sculpted from the living rock; more modest chapels might have a freestanding statue of limestone or sandstone. The image is most often at the back of a long chamber; in some exceptional examples for highest officials, its place is taken by a stone door to be passed only by the spirit receiving the offerings on the Old Kingdom model. In front of the long offering chamber, a transverse chamber allowed shaded space for collecting those who would offer at festivals. Owing to the poor quality of limestone at Waset, the walls were not directly carved, but coated with two qualities of plaster, as a ground for painting inscriptions and scenes of estate life and leisure. Today, the variety and vivacity of these paintings are acclaimed in the terms of modern art history as one of the finest outpourings of Egyptian genius (Figure 7.9).

(a)

(b)

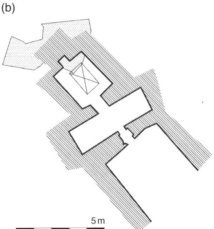

Figure 7.9   Painted plastered wall of chapel of Nakht, accountant of temple staff, Waset, about 1375 BC: (a) detail from the scenes of production on an estate. Photograph © Gianluca Miniaci. (b) plan of the chapel and shaft (crossed rectangle) leading to underground chambers for burials (dotted). Drawing © Wolfram Grajetzki.

At the entrance to the rock-cut offering chambers, the principal man of the monument is depicted facing out to the rising sun, arms raised in prayer. Over the entrance, a row of clay cones inserted into the façade incorporated rows of fired clay cones, stamped with the titles and names of the man, embedding his identity into the structure, bound into the rock face. Above, a small steep pyramid with inscribed pyramidion (capstone) reinforced this solar message with a new type of image, the stelophorous statue (from Greek *stele*," standing stone, and *phorein*, "to bear, present"): this depicts the man with arms raised, kneeling, and the words of his sun hymn inscribed on the space framed by his arms and legs. The hymns in the offering chapels and on the statues are related to the daily liturgies of hymns sung to the rising, midday, and setting sun in the temples of the sun at Iunu and, in fused form Amun-Ra, at Karnak on the east bank at Waset. In their prominence and profusion, the New Kingdom sun hymns mark an extraordinary moment in the religious literature of Egypt. From the decision, in the reign of Amenhotep I, to bury the king at Waset, the presence of the kingly body in the ground would have solarized the city terrain, as marked by the obelisks and pylons at Karnak. The strength of the sunlight permeating the tombs of officials at the site comes from that solar source. This makes Theban tomb chapels a highly localized phenomenon. No other site has preserved the same concentration of hymns to the creator sun-god; some aspects of the chapels are found across Egypt, as the pyramid form and pyramidia, while others are extremely rare elsewhere, as the stelophorous statue (one example from Sidmant). Nevertheless, the theme of sustenance remains a strong component in these monuments, from the range of subjects in the paintings (harvest and food are major themes) to the stocks of food and drink in the sealed underground chambers. A more decisive turn away from sustenance in the area of the tomb would come only in the next period.

1350–1100 BC *Underground protected space, overground devotion, provisions secondary?*

Under Akhenaten, the royal court moved to the new city Akhetaten, where rock-cut tomb chapels were cut for the dozen highest officials, in the rock face along north and south ends of the great desert bay of the city. The scenes of estate production gave way to scenes of production in the Aten temple and of the king and his wife and daughters in chariot procession to the city. Other themes continued earlier traditions, notably the sun hymns at the entrance, now facing toward the Aten temple instead of the rising sun, and the depictions of the king bestowing favor. Inscriptions indicate a continuity also in the wish to sustain the body and its ba-soul by participating in offerings at the city temples. However, at Akhetaten, this is now a daily cycle, like the circuit of the sun, with no special note of festivals. Moreover, despite the prominence of the Aten temple and kingship palaces on the offering-chapel walls, the inscriptions no longer refer to offerings coming from the altars of the deity; instead, the food and drink should come from the house and garden of the official himself (Assmann 2005, 407–408). Finally, there is the crucial missing element of transformation: Akhetaten discards the sustenance + transformation model, in place of a plainer rhythm of eternal day–night continuities.

When the court of Tutankhamun moved from Akhetaten to Mennefer, the resting place for high officials became a grand new style of temple tomb, where underground burial chambers were marked at ground level by a monumental superstructure (Martin 1992). Here, an open court surrounded by columns led to a chamber for the offerings before an image of the deceased and, usually, his wife. This may have been one focal point in the monument, but, in contrast to the layout at Waset, the statue did not mark the end, for behind it a doorway led to a second columned court. The floor of the second court concealed the mouth of the shaft leading down to the burial chamber. At the far side of the court, against westernmost wall of the whole complex, there were three chambers, the central one with an inscribed framed stone: this stone, rather than the statue, seems to have served as the innermost focus for offerings to the couple. Also unlike Waset, where painted plaster was the main medium for wall decoration, and Akhetaten, with its rock-cut offering chapels over the tombs of the wealthiest, the chosen part of the high desert plateau nearest Mennefer, at modern Saqqara, favored freestanding stone-built structures. The wall blocks are of fine northern limestone, allowing highest-quality relief sculpting. In theme, the scenes develop from Amarna a double focus: devotion to a deity and court life of the high official. However, the deities are now plural, with, alongside Ra, figures of Osiris, Isis, Thoth, Anubis, and others (Figure 7.10).

At the same period, and later, under Kings Sety I and Ramses II, monumental tombs are found now away from the kingship centers: General Sety and Vizier Parahotep at Sidmant and High Steward Nefersekheru at Zawyet el-Sultan. High officials of southern administration, including Nubia and the Amun temple, returned to the tradition of painted offering chapels at Waset, with a number of significant innovations. The themes of sustenance gave way to the same dual focus as at Mennefer: court life and devotion to deities, especially at festivals. Images and writings from the corpus of Going Out by Day become more frequent (see Centres of writing or drawing the afterlife, *Book of the Dead*). Above ground, the open court in front of the offering chapel acquires new features (Kampp-Seyfried 2003): a massive brick-built gateway; higher walls, sometimes with roofed colonnade at the sides; and a bed of earth for watering seeds in the ritual of *Khoiak*, "Ka-on-Ka," in the fourth flood month to usher in the sowing season. In this court, the body would have been consecrated on its last journey, in the ritual of Opening the Mouth (Assmann 2003). The brick-built pyramid with its pyramidion capstone is now more massive, still with niche for stelophorous *hymn-singing* statue, now on a more substantial platform. The underground burial chambers are now approached not by a steep shaft, but by a sloping passageway, sometimes winding round from mouth to burial chamber doorway, allowing annual performance of Ka-on-Ka rituals to be brought to the door of the deceased for their regeneration (Assmann 1984, 2003).

Robbers usually targeted richer burials early and often, leaving only traces of original burial equipment. Enough survives to confirm a general impression from other social levels that the theme of sustenance was no longer important in burial space. Instead, the embalmed body was wrapped with a limited set of amulets,

(a)

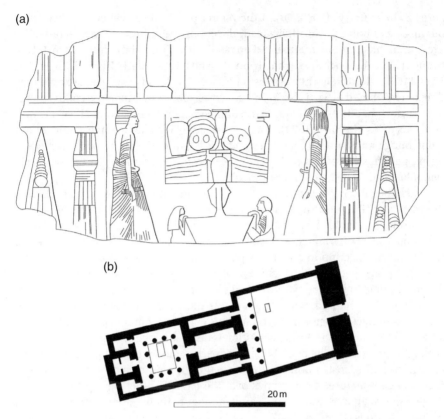

(b)

Figure 7.10 (a) The open court of a tomb chapel, as depicted on a limestone block from a chapel at Mennefer, now Petrie Museum UC408; (b) plan of the temple-sized chapel over burial place of Maya, treasurer in the court of King Tutankhamun, about 1325 BC, cemeteries of Mennefer (Saqqara). Drawing © Wolfram Grajetzki.

with focus on the heart. The large scarab over the heart is now joined by amulets in the form of the hieroglyph for the heart, sometimes with the human head, and shrine-shaped rectangular pectorals, generally in faience, with images of the deceased in adoration before funerary deities Osiris or Anubis. Three forms of amulets become particularly prominent, and inscribed examples are known for the richest individuals: the hieroglyphs *djed*, "stability," and *tiyet*, "tie" (the *knot of Isis*), and a snake head, the latter two often of red jasper or carnelian. In wealthier burials, the coffin is generally in form of wrapped body, with idealized *mask* face, and a number of *shabti* figures may be present, loose or in special boxes. Outside this scene of protective wrapping, the whole stock of household goods, as found in rich burials before 1300 BC, has disappeared. Even the pottery vessels for food and drink are gone; as a result, whoever could not afford the special amulets – the vast majority of the country – had no burial goods. Grajetzki remarks of this material revolution, "New religious beliefs seem to have affected all social levels, and many parts of the country" (2003, 90). If the poorer or middle social classes had been burying daily pottery with their dead, these pots would have been recorded by excavation directors anxious to build up typologies of material culture, such as Guy Brunton in his sweep through the region of Tjebu (Qau-Badari). Instead, the period 1350–1100 is almost absent from his reports. At Per-Bast in the Delta, excavations directed by Ahmed El Sawi also found no burial goods other than the coffins themselves, a few shabtis (9 of 210 burials), a limited range of amulets, and bead armlets and necklaces (El Sawi 1979). After Akhenaten, whether people could afford embalming or not and whether the trend was led from the top or not, across all of Egypt, people stopped supplying their dead with food, at least in the physical–symbolic form of food containers and tableware.

Sustenance did not disappear completely from the armory for the afterlife. In the corpus of Going Out by Day, sustenance remains a central theme alongside transformation (Table 5), and the corpus is present in wealthier burials as papyrus book-roll and as offering-chapel wall decoration. The theme is also relocated to the temple, as inscription on statues placed there by at least higher officials; on these, the prayers continue to include food and drink offerings at the fore of wishes for the afterlife. Nevertheless, above and below ground, afterlife space seems fundamentally restructured, with a remarkable nationwide simplification of burial space as a protected sacrosanct ground. This nationally homogenized and simplified, perhaps purified afterlife population is also more often collective on a larger scale. Far larger numbers of embalmed or partly embalmed bodies, with or without coffins and almost impossible to date in the absence of objects, are an increasingly frequent feature of cemeteries over the following thousand years, where a single tomb shaft may contain the same number of bodies as an entire graveyard of earlier periods (Grajetzki 2007).

1100–700 BC *Underground protected space, sometimes leisure, overground devotion*

After 1070 BC, kings of western nomadic origin (*Libyan*) settled at the new port city of Djanet (Tanis), in an agreed division with their relatives at Waset, generals who took the title First God's Servant of Amun (Taylor 2000). From other Delta cities, above all Per-Ramses, the Residence of Ramses II, monuments were relocated in Djanet to create a temple complex as vast as Karnak and dedicated to the same deities: Amun, Mut, and Khons. Much of our knowledge of burial practice in this period is based on the discovery of intact tombs here of three kings, a king's son, and a general of the tenth century BC (Yoyotte 1987). Otherwise, the great majority of evidence for the period comes from Waset and, less well preserved, Abdju, where many of the largest offering chapels date to this time. Probably, many burials excavated at other sites belong to the period, but without objects such as pottery, amulets, or other changing forms of burial equipment, they would not have been datable, leaving the period a substantial blank in the sources – except at Waset. There, singly, in pairs or in large groups, the wealthy were lain to rest by their survivors in a brilliantly colorful array of objects made for burial. Structures above

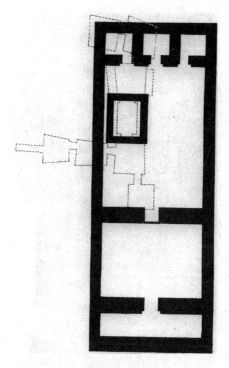

Figure 7.11   Plan of a large offering chapel with shaft in rear court leading to underground complex of burial chambers. Abdju, tomb D38, about 1200–900 BC. D. Randall-Maciver, and A. Mace, 1902. *El Amrah and Abydos.* Egypt Exploration Fund, London, 1902.

ground are less well preserved, perhaps simple brick chapels, but many groups survived intact into modern times below ground (Figure 7.11).

In the regular pattern of the richer burials at Waset, the embalmed body was equipped with heart scarab and lain in a coffin, sometimes nested within one or more outer coffins, all brightly painted with motifs from the corpus of Going Out by Day and from the Underworld Books (see Centres of writing or drawing the afterlife) which had been restricted mainly to kings in the preceding period. Embalming arts had advanced to the point where the soft internal organs could be returned to the body, each protected by the figure of a deity, often of wax. The jars previously used to hold the organs removed during embalming were still produced to guarantee survival, but these could now be solid *dummy* vases. At the foot of the coffin stood a painted round-topped wooden board, painted with image of the individual praying or offering to one of the principal deities, most often Ra-Horakhty or Osiris. Nearby stood a painted hollow wood figure of Osiris on a plinth; it contained one of two papyri written to secure the afterlife of the individual, the other being with the wrapped body in the coffin. One papyrus was from Going out by Day, and the other from Underworld Books; earlier in the period, the main source is the Litany of Ra, later the last four hours of the night journey of the sun, as depicted in the Amduat. Bright blue-glazed faience *shabti* figures with black inscriptions multiply to a kingly

(a)

Figure 7.12   Burial equipment of Nakhtefmut, at Waset: (a) cartonnage casing for the embalmed and wrapped body. (b) amulets, winged scarab, shabtis, flowers, fastening straps and protective figures of deities placed in the tomb. J. Quibell, R. Paget, A. Pirie, *The Ramesseum and The Tomb of Ptah-hetep*, Quaritch, London, 1898.

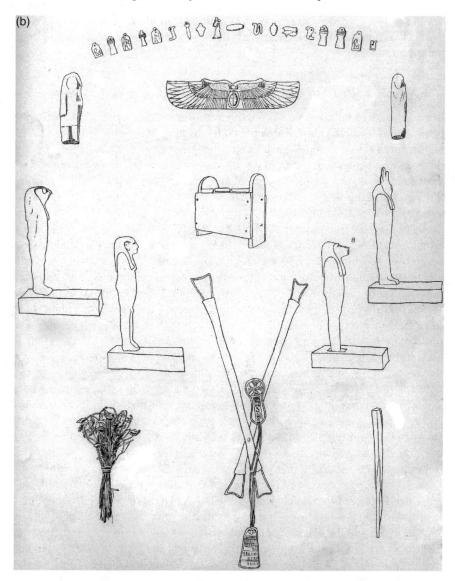

Figure 7.12   (Cont'd)

scale, giving a standard set of 401: one for every day of the of the year and one to order each group of 10, as found in accountancy documents for organizing work-forces in this life. The foremen *shabti* figures are distinguished by their short kilt and whip (Figure 7.12).

Around 850 BC, as the kingdom increasingly fragmented, coffin decoration at Waset underwent radical simplification, perhaps under the influence of northern Egyptian production (Taylor 2009). At the same time, the quality of glazed faience *shabti* production drops, and the body is no longer supplied with papyri or Osiris figure. This more austere new afterlife is harder to detect in excavations and their published reports.

700–525 BC *Underground regeneration machine, overground devotion*

During the late eighth century BC, fragmentation among *Libyan* kings was overlain by more powerful neighbors, Kush to south and Assyria to north. After about 715 BC, Kushite rulers controlled Egypt, opposing the main west Delta *Libyan* power, the governors of Sau (Sais). After fifty years, they were expelled by invading Assyrian armies; the Sau ruler Psamtek became governor for Assyria and then, gradually, independent king. In this fluid century, it is difficult to identify the source of changes between Kushite/Nubian, Egyptian, and Libyan. Much of the best-preserved evidence continues to be from Waset, now both above and below ground. As at Akhetaten and Mennefer in the fourteenth century BC, the largest seventh–sixth-century BC offering chapels over tombs at Waset give a tangible architectural index of power, showing the wealthiest core of national administration, far above the resources of the next social level (Eigner 1984). In the early seventh century BC, Harwa, high steward of the god's wife of Amun, received for his afterlife a new scale and order of architecture, a veritable temple over the underground corridors and chambers of his tomb (Aston 2003; Tiradritti 2009). Holders of two high positions, mayor and high steward, followed this example over the next century and a half, down to the abrupt end of the sequence at the Achaemenid Iranian invasion (525 BC). This *temple-tomb* type starts from the outside with a high mudbrick wall, modeled according to the palace façade motif from Early Dynastic times. A mudbrick entrance pylon gave access beneath rows of stamped title-and-name fired clay cones, as in Eighteenth Dynasty offering chapels at Waset. Beyond, a broad open court led to a second court, with the opening to the underground chambers; here in succession were a columned hall and side chambers; a second, smaller columned hall; and the burial chambers. The complex was extensively decorated in relief. Antecedents to the Harwa complex may be found nearby in the chapels over tombs of Mayor Karabasken, first pure priest Karakhamun, and the overseer of the treasuries of King Taharqo, Rames. These lie at the base of a long hill on the approach to the Deir el-Bahri cliff face, where Hathor and Amun merged in the annual Festival of the Valley, focus and setting for the grandiose architecture of Harwa as for earlier and later monuments. On its way to the Hathor sanctuary, the image of Amun in its portable boat-shrine would stop at a small way station on the line of the earlier causeway built for the temple of Queen Hatshepsut: the great tombs of Mayor Montemhat and its neighbors face toward this shrine, with imposing connecting stairways.

Where and how were families of officials working for the mayors and high stewards buried? Smaller chapels are found, but the evidence is more plentiful presumably beneath the ground. One woman at Waset, Tjesraperet with the title nurse of the daughter of King Taharqo, received, beside her coffin set, painted wood stela; Osiris figure and shabtis; and several items of cosmetic equipment (Guidotti 2008).

Figure 7.13   Amulets from early first-millennium BC burials at Lahun. Excavation archive negative PMAN 1951. © Petrie Museum of Egyptian Archaeology, UCL.

Across Egypt, there are signs of a small-scale return to the practice of burying the dead with items from life. Near Lahun, at some time between the tenth and sixth centuries BC, storage pottery is again found in tombs, along with jewelry and amulets of types worn in life (Figure 7.13). In the new range of imagery, the most prominent motifs are the eye amulet named *wedjat*, "health," and the image of nursing mother Isis with her child Horus, a still vulnerable but future divine ruler. Two other frequent amulet images are aggressive–protective forces, the lioness-headed goddess, most often named as Sekhmet and the sow sky goddess Nut, capable of devouring her own children, the stars. Some imagery may be rooted in a particular place: one rare form recorded for Lahun is the faience amulet in the form of a lyre with inward-facing gazelle heads (Petrie and Brunton 1923, 37), an instrument known from New Kingdom examples and depictions. Blue- or blue-green-glazed faience is the favorite material, often now in intricate openwork. Cowries appear in many burials, perhaps as in the Middle Kingdom mainly for young girls. At Abusir al-Malaq, across the fields from Lahun, the burial of a woman named Tadja included figurines of a standing naked woman, along with faience cosmetic vessels, openwork faience rings, and a lyre.

Starting in the mid-seventh century BC, in place of the Sekhmet figurines and jewelry worn in life, select richer burials receive only material made for the tomb, including, after almost two centuries of absence, mass-produced faience shabti figures, some exceptionally fine, and a Going Out by Day papyrus. Besides models of equipment for the Opening the Mouth ritual (below Table 7.2), there are sets of funerary amulets, gold in some burials of higher-ranking officials at Mennefer, and hard stone or faience in other contexts (Bresciani 1977). Some of these take forms known from second-millennium BC burials, but the dominant impression is of a miniature world of deities, standing or enthroned as eternal company to the deceased. The history of this new world is hard to trace, as few burials are found after 600 BC in Waset, the main source for well-preserved groups, and the dating of groups in the north remains difficult. In 525 BC, the Achaemenid Iranian conquest of Egypt seems to interrupt all production for the afterlife. However, the seventh–sixth-century BC burial equipment template is resumed after removal of Achaemenid power (404–343 BC). Despite major fourth-century BC innovations, such as the hard-stone sarcophagi inscribed with Underworld Books (see Centres of writing or drawing the afterlife), in general, the restoration is so thorough that the individual amulet, heart scarab, papyrus, shabti, painted wood stela, or coffin could belong as easily to the fourth as the sixth century BC. Time borders from political history do not easily transfer over to the afterlife.

Kingship in the technical and verbal elaboration of embalming

The historical single line traced earlier is largely the story of the most visible, and in a sense, it represents merely one of the so many possible strands from the past. However, by the factor of *prestige*, the magnetic attraction of power in a stratified society, this artery of wealth is significant also for at least a proportion of those different other strands, increasingly bound into its hegemonic weave. A major motivating factor in the success of this particular tale of increasing normative standards from the palace center is technical: at the court of the king, embalmers developed techniques for preserving the human body after death, reinforced by intricate rituals. The technical history is not unilinear and evenly progressive, and the line is frequently broken, as the richest burials most swiftly attracted robbers. Yet it is possible to write a chronology of the afterlife treatment of kings and some of those closest to them, out of the monumental architecture together with a series of finds ranging from fragments to some substantially intact burials. At Abdju, 3000–2700 BC, a series of kings were buried in large mudbrick, later stone-clad, chambers, a kilometer into the desert; closer to the fields, mudbrick enclosures were set up for the burial, perhaps also for the embalming rites, and then dismantled after the funeral (O'Connor 2011). Around the tomb and the enclosure, the courtiers were buried in small rectangular pits, with pottery and sometimes equipment from their courtly life. From 2700 to 1800 BC, in the area from Giza to Fayoum, kingship cult is at the center of far the largest building projects in the land (Lehner 2008). Massive stone pyramid structures were constructed over the place for the final, and sometimes a second, resting place for the divine mortal body. Less well preserved in most instances, temples for the offerings to the king stood east of the pyramid reliquary.

From 1475 to 1075 BC, the body of the king was laid to rest in a chamber beyond series of corridors and halls, cut from the rock in the desert valley west of Waset (Hornung 1990). The almost intact burial of king Tutankhamun indicates how kingship followed regular practice of the day, treating the underground chambers partly as a protective cocoon to project the successful embalming into eternity and partly as a storeroom for the food, clothing, jewelry, hunting and fighting equipment, and furniture of life. At this period, the temples for each ruler were separated from the tomb, along the side of the fields; longer-reigning rulers might receive more than one temple constructed along the Nile Valley in Nubia and Egypt. After 1100 BC, the pattern changes, as kings were buried in temple precincts, and their cults maintained perhaps mainly through offerings to their statues (or earlier statues reinscribed for them) in the temple forecourts. Again, in keeping with evidence for burial customs of the period, intact burials of three kings in the Amun temple complex at Djanet show a far greater focus on protection and transformation (Yoyotte 1987). Even the coffin face might take the form of a falcon, evoking the deities Ra and Horus, rather than the human face usual on coffins of both kings and others at most periods. However, the Djanet treasures also contain the silver and gold vessels of palace ceremonial and ritual life.

Amid the treasure of each period, we might expect the body of the king to be object of embalming techniques as they developed over time. Advances in burial technology would start at the palace and spread out to other centers. In a general way, this may have happened: the earliest canopic chest and jars are from the immediate circle of kingship and give the first secure evidence that soft organs were removed from the body as part of embalming. However, surviving remains do not entirely match this picture. The earliest human body part from a royal tomb is an arm of uncertain origin, concealed after removal in a crevice in the tomb of King Djer, of the First Dynasty, at Abdju (Petrie 1901, 16–17). Armlets were still around the bones, but no signs of embalming were reported. Around 1800 BC, in the cemeteries of Mennefer, the body of King Auibra Hor was buried in a fine coffin, with accompanying statue topped by outstretched arms – the hieroglyph *ka* – and a canopic chest. Unfortunately, the excavation report did not discuss embalming technique. From about 1325 BC, the body of King Tutankhamun is poorly preserved, perhaps because the embalming oils reacted badly with the atmosphere of the burial chamber or were simply applied in too great quantity. The best evidence is from the reburial of New Kingdom kings and relatives in a cache to sanctify the *Libyan* family of generals ruling from Waset after 1070 BC. Some faces are so beautifully embalmed that they seem asleep, but the success is variable and not confined to the kings. As the living would never see the face after wrapping and masking, let alone burial, perhaps these variations are not surprising; the rites of embalming may have taken precedence over the details of perfect preservation. After 1070 BC, when all kings may have been buried in low Delta sites, literal preservation may have been even less of a focus, with attention instead permanently on the transformation of the divine mortal body into an immortal.

Centers of Writing or Drawing the Afterlife: Rituals and Eternal Regeneration

From 2500 to 525 BC, images and words relating to embalming and burial are preserved on stone or painted plaster walls of offering chapels and, less often, burial chambers and on manuscripts made for the tomb or, rarely, used in rituals and then, in unknown circumstances, deposited as part of burial equipment (Assmann 2005). The earliest evidence comes from late third-millennium BC chapels of officials (Table 7.1 Burial scenes) and includes the ritual for consecrating statues, later applied to embalmed body (*Opening the Mouth*; see Table 7.2) A little later are inscriptions first found in underground chambers in pyramids of kings and their wives and so known in Egyptology as Pyramid Texts (Table 7.3). These are inscribed without any explicit overall order, and Egyptologists have debated how far they combine into longer sequences as liturgies (Hays 2012). From the end of the Old Kingdom, the compositions are attested outside the royal court (shroud of Medunefer, oasis governor, about 2200 BC; burial chambers of two high officials at Hutnennesut, perhaps a century later). During the following period, they appear alongside a developing branch of similar writing in the newer phase of the language, Middle Egyptian, and named in Egyptology Coffin Texts, because the most common medium is now the coffin. These are inscribed on the walls, lid, and floor of wood coffins or painted limestone burial chambers for regional governors and their entourages. The line between (inscribed) Pyramid Text and (handwritten)

Table 7.1 Burial scenes: The principal phases in depictions (2500–525 BC) (Altenmüller 1975)

1. Lament over the dead and procession of coffin from the house
2. Procession of coffin by boat to place of embalming
3. Offerings in the place of purification (of the body in embalming), installed as *Sais*
4. Procession of coffin to a place of meat offerings, ritually named *Sau (Sais)*
5. Procession of coffin on ox-drawn sled from *Sau* to *Pe and Dep (Buto)*
6. Ritual dancers (*muu*) receive the coffin in Pe and Dep
7. Procession of coffin to sunlit space, ritually named *Iunu (Heliopolis)*
8. Lament and purification; Opening the Mouth ritual; censing
9. Dragging the coffin into place
10. Procession of ritual crouching figure, named *tekenu*; censing
11. Procession of the canopic chest, bearing papyrus stems
12. Offering ritual
13. Delivery of burial equipment, meat offerings
14. Placing the coffin in the burial chamber
15. Circuit of the statue
16. Concluding rites

Table 7.2   *Opening the Mouth and Eyes*: The consecration ritual of images and bodies (Otto 1960)

Sources with longest series of episodes, all from Waset
1. Offering chapel of Vizier Rekhmira at Thebes (Theban Tomb 100, 1400 BC)
2. Tomb of King Sety I at Thebes (Valley of the Kings, 1300 BC)
3. Tomb of Queen Tausret (Valley of the Kings, 1225 BC)
4. Coffin of a man named Butehamun, secretary of the king's draughtsmen (Waset, now in Turin: no depictions, 1050 BC)
5. Tomb chapel of the god's wife of Amun Amenirdis at Thebes (Madinat Habu)
6. Tomb of a chief lector Padiamenipet (Theban Tomb 33)

   Those fullest versions, with eighty additional shorter sources, record seventy-five ritual episodes, around the core of rites to animate the statue, including the crucial meat offering
   - Episodes 1–9: preliminary rites
   - Episodes 10–22: sculpting and animation of the statue, including "sleep of the *sem*"
   - Episodes 23–42: meat offerings aligned with Upper Egypt
   - Episodes 43–46: meat offerings aligned with Lower Egypt
   - Episodes 47–71: funerary meal
   - Episodes 72–75: closing rites

Table 7.3   Principal *Pyramid Text* themes (for the corpus, see Allen (2005))

---

1. Meals, cleansing, clothing, and especially the great offering list (23–171) and the accompanying rituals (204–212)
2. Protection against enemies and against harmful creatures
3. Bodily integrity and revival, especially around reassembling limbs, parts of body (heart, head, and bones, opening the mouth); release from wrapping; refrain Wake!; and address to children of Horus as they lift deceased and carry
   Divine forms: star, swallow, falcon, Nut, Satet, *ka* of all gods, son of Atum/great one; kingship and rule, inheriting the throne
4. Ascension: opening door of sky, rising to sky, decree of Nun to Atum to admit deceased to sky; ferrying (with purification and ascension); knowing name of Ra and reaching him; sun hymn

---

Coffin Text is not always easy to draw, but in later periods, the Old Egyptian grammar and spelling of Pyramid Texts seem to be consciously maintained as important points of distinction, with different proportions of each copied on coffins at different periods within 2000–1800 BC (Allen 1996). Certain sequences (liturgies?) in both branches also have separate histories. Otherwise, the thematic content seems broadly similar (Tables 7.3 and 7.4).

Coffins of a dozen wealthy individuals buried at the desert cemetery east of Khemenu, 1950–1850 BC, include on the coffin floor a composition designed as a graphic journey through the afterlife (Lesko 1972). Egyptologists have named this the Book of Two Ways, from one section with a black (earth) and blue (watery) path divided by a band of red (fire). Much of the accompanying wording reappears in later periods as compositions "to make the *akh* excellent." In this period, too, the phrase "Going Out by Day" begins to emerge as technical term for the overall aims

Table 7.4   Principal *Coffin Text* themes (cf. Barguet 1986)

1. Food and clothing; not eating filth or walking upside down
2. Protection against enemies, driving off Rerek-snake, Aapep, serpent, bird; escaping the net
3. Bodily integrity and revival: power over the head, mouth, legs, limbs, heart, sexual potency, *heka*; reassembly of limbs, burial; not rotting; preventing theft of *heka*, head, heart; having property/inheritance, having family, constructing tomb; power over water, air, the four winds, breathing; not working in afterlife
    Divine forms: Ra, Atum, Ruty, Horus, Osiris, Thoth, Imsety, Isis, Nun, Shu, Reret, Nehebkau, Nile Flood, Hathor, Khentykhem, Grain, Hu, Anubis, Baba, falcon, swallow, morning star, secretary of Atum/Ra/Hathor; be beside gods
4. Free entry into next world, free movement there; opening door to heaven/underworld/ west; sailing to Iunu, landing, *uniting the riverbanks*, ferrying across winding water, river, sky; knowing paths to sky; knowing names of underworld places, knowing *ba*-souls of sacred places (Iunu, Djedu, Khemenu, Pe, Nekhen, eastern, western) ascension, tying together ladder in/to sky; going out by day

of this literature. After 1600 BC, compositions begin to be copied on shrouds for burials of women and officials at the court at Waset. Then, after 1450 BC, comes a major change in medium and formal presentation; the compositions begin to be written regularly on papyrus book-rolls and combined with polychrome illustrations that echo coffin and temple wall decoration. From these papyri, Egyptologists name the Going Out by Day corpus the *Book of the Dead* (Allen 1974). Each papyrus contains its own selection of content from a repertoire of about 150 compositions in circulation at any one time (Table 7.5).

Despite the flexibility, writers express the separateness of the corpus, when they comment that some passages are "added from another papyrus in addition to the Going out by Day" or, at Waset in the period 1000–850 BC, when they deposit with most individuals two papyri: one marked Going Out by Day and the other What Is in the Underworld (Niwiński 1989). The second papyrus draws from great compositions in the tombs of kings in the Valley of the Kings, 1450–1100 BC, dominated by images, projecting the night journey of the sun (Hornung 1990). The earliest version bears the ancient title *Book of the Hidden Chamber Which is The Underworld*, abbreviated as *imy-duat*, "What Is in the Underworld"; the night is described in a sequence of twelve hours, with individual names to the figures depicted. Accompanying this, the *Book of Adoration of Ra* celebrated in a litany the sun-god unfurled into 75 forms (in Egyptology named Litany of Ra), with passages on the mystery of the night union of Ra with Osiris as the Joined Ba-soul. During the reign of Akhenaten, the tomb of the king at Akhetaten was decorated instead with scenes of palace life and mourning and designed to include the burials of the women closest to him. After Akhenaten, new compositions proliferate in the tombs of kings at Waset, starting with a version of the *imy-duat* teeming still with images, but without the continuous naming of each feature; the first of these is the Book of Gates (ancient title unknown). The different versions cover similar themes, but

Table 7.5   Principal Going Out by Day (*Book of the Dead*) themes (cf. Barguet 1979)

---

1. Food and clothing; not eating filth or walking upside down; depiction of Marsh of Reeds with eternal miraculous harvest (tableau and accompanying writings *chapter 110*); receiving offerings as *ka*-spirit
2. Protection against enemies, driving off Rerek-snake, Aapep, crocodiles, serpents, worms, bugs, the two chant-goddesses
3. Bodily integrity and revival: power over (or preventing theft of) the head, mouth, heart, movement, name, *heka*; reassembly of limbs; not rotting; not being butchered; power over water, air, the four winds, breathing; not working in afterlife; eternally active embalming rituals (tableau *chapter 151*)
    Protection by material form of head cover (*mask*), headrest, broad collar, *tiyet*-amulet, *djed*-pillar (stability)
4. Declarations of divine identity as Ra, Atum, Ruty, Osiris, Thoth, son of Hathor; be beside gods/Thoth/Hathor
    Divine forms: *netjer*, greatest of the tribunal, living *ba*-soul, Ptah, falcon (of gold), heron, *benu*-heron, swallow, snake, lotus
5. Free movement into/in next world; opening door to heaven/underworld/*imehet*-chamber; ferrying across sky; knowing underworld place-names/*ba*-souls of sacred places (Iunu, Djedu, Khemenu, Pe, Nekhen, eastern, western); going out by day
6. Passing the judgment of the dead, with scene of weighing the heart against Right (tableau *chapter 125*)
7. Hymns to Ra and Osiris

---

without exact correspondence of contents for each segment of the night; the tenth hour of *imy-duat* depicts those marked as blessed by drowning, whereas the Book of Gates places this in the ninth (Table 7.6). Evidently, these descriptions of night cycle deploy motifs more with poetic than with literal force, even if the numerical measurements and precision of names produce an exact geographical effect. Dominant themes include the law-giving role of the sun-god (Hours 1–9), the punishment of enemies (Hours 10–12), and the life-giving light of the sun, even for the embalmed dead (Book of Gates, Hour 8).

Besides the Underworld Books, the ancient writers also kept other compositions separate from the core Going Out by Day, either never copied onto the papyrus books for the afterlife or included so rarely that they remain at the margins. This seems more a question of tradition, perhaps history of restricted use, than of theme. For example, the motif of eternal revival through the scent of the lotus flower appears in the Going Out by Day corpus as a short passage alongside the tall image of lotus flower on stem, found on dozens of papyri (1450–50 BC). On the same theme, but never included in Going Out by Day manuscripts, a longer poem is preserved on a restricted range of sources, including temples for king and gods. In the earliest version, on the miniature chapel monument of a palace keeper of baboons, Amenyseneb (1800 BC), the poem begins (Vandier 1963):

> Formula for the floral garland of every day, brought to the mound-chapel.
> This is the great one, going out from the land, crossing the sky,

Table 7.6   Twelve hours of the night journey of the sun (from Hornung (1999))

Night hour	*Imy-duat*	Book of Gates
1	Sailing 120 *iteru* to 300-*iteru* region of Wernes, sun-god as ram issues decrees	
2	Wernes, 309 × 120 *iteru*; sun-god assigns fields to underworld dwellers	
3	309-*iteru* Water of Osiris, sun-god issues decrees to the *akhu* who are with Osiris	Deities in shrines, image of the Boat of the Earth
4	Secret Cavern of West, rocky ground; sun-god as serpent	Embalmed dead in shrines; time-serpents
5	Secret Cavern of Sokar, rocky ground	Deities with field-measure cord, *ba*-souls and people
6	Waters of Underworld dwellers, sun-god assigns fields/water for offerings to deities	Judgement Hall
7	Cavern of Osiris: felling enemies	Enemies tied to jackal-head stakes, harvesters
8	Caverns of secret deities (10 sets, most with three deities)	Embalmed dead rise at approach of sun-god
9	Another secret cavern of the West, sun-god issues decrees to deities	The blessed drowned
10	Another secret cavern of the West, the blessed drowned	Netters, felling Aapep
11	Another secret cavern of the West, enemies beheaded and burnt in pits	Destruction of Aapep
12	Cavern *End of Darkness*; rebirth of the sun-god, towed through the snake Life of the Gods	Destruction of Aapep and rebirth of the sun-god

going out from heaven, great power, born of Geb,
who drives away Seth in his raging,
who pushes back against the desert-people as they journey,
the Nine Gods shrink back at the knowledge of his name,
the one who grows from the body of that noble Marshland,
the one who brings the body of the East, that assists Nemty.

In its references to deities and its poetic vocabulary, the composition that never entered the Going Out by Day corpus does not differ from the compositions that did. Thus, content alone does not explain why one composition and not another should have been included in the corpus. The reasons may lie in the place and timing of recitation, where some passages may have been confined to kingship, while others were considered more appropriate for the *book* for obtaining an afterlife. The manuscripts from each period set different boundaries of practice; for example, after 650 BC, papyri often include hymns to the sun-god and Osiris, previously found only in temple settings or in inscriptions more closely connected with the king. The focus and borders of sanctity are social constructs, changing over time.

Transforming into akh-*Being*

Among manuscripts for eternity, the title *sakhu*, "making *akh*," is found repeatedly but in specific contexts across the period preserving writing (Assmann 1990). After 2500 BC, depictions of embalming, funeral, and burial include the caption "reading *sakhu*," and the word is used as a heading for series of compositions on papyri later than the period discussed here (fourth–second century BC) but with contents already found in pyramids (2200 BC) and in the same order as found on some coffins from 2000 to 1850 BC. The word *sakh* means "to make (someone) into an *akh*" and is sometimes translated rather vaguely as "glorification." The core term *akh* in healing and afterlife papyri seems to evoke a power of impact where the cause is not immediately evident; evidently, it could refer to the successfully embalmed and securely buried body, keeping its life source beyond mortality. The *sakhu* writings envelop both the period of embalming and the offerings for the deceased into eternity.

Although they form a tradition of their own within afterlife literature, they surface within the main stream from Pyramid Texts onward. In the Going Out by Day corpus, they relate directly to the series of formulae for "making the *akh* excellent," found on most manuscripts and taken largely from the earlier Book of Two Ways. The "excellent *akh*" is the precise title given to relatives or friends on small offering stones from the village of royal artists at Waset, 1300–1100 BC. A thousand years earlier, it is found on the several Letters to the Dead, where the living invoked recently deceased relatives or friends for help with problems in daily life. Possibly, in this part of the writings for eternity, we find a shared ground for the living not only in the literate sectors of society but across different social classes. The rites and techniques of embalming to palace standards may have become the overarching goal and theme for all who could afford it, in increasing numbers over the millennia, and may have set the mold for burial practices particularly after the Amarna period. Yet a wider sense of the survival of life, anchored in a physical body, may be at the heart of the culture, expressed not in the mummified body, but in the concept of immortalized *akh*. From the written record, this would be the term and concept to test back against the record of both funerary and settlement archaeology, across the two and a half millennia considered in this book.

Hegemony and Variety: Chronological Considerations

A time line of the evidence is necessary to identify the ways one group of past people might have differed from another to avoid homogenizing the past, as in the static, dull perception of an unchanging *ancient Egypt*. However, this necessary introductory filter can offer only a simplified narrative, where regional geography and social mapping add more strands to the story. However many strands, the single line fails to capture the complexity and variety of any period, for which a more archaeological presentation of greater length would be required (as in Grajetzki 2003). According to the standard Egyptological history, between 3000 and 525 BC, increasing numbers of people at more and more places adopted practices, writings, and imagery originally developed for the body of the king as son of Ra. The strength of this narrative and its frequent repetition, as in the preceding text, recalls the linguistic dominance which Bakhtin called monoglossia – a single epic story (Chapter 1). Such force can be resisted by displacing the minority practice of the specific preservation techniques, which we call mummification, and searching instead for the majority practice at any time. Predynastic and Nubian studies lead in this area, and the principle is being extended more often now to Bronze Age and early Iron Age Egypt (e.g., Goulding 2013). Nevertheless, the trajectory of increasing *Osirification* extends beyond the theme of burial across the second and first millennia BC, entering the wider concept of the sacred; by the late first millennium BC, mainly after the period studied here, each temple precinct has separate cemeteries for Osiris figures, with prominent Osiris festivals (Raven 1978-1979). As a major phenomenon affecting a range of social settings and institutions, the attraction of mummification deserves analysis, rather than rejection, in order to understand not only its ancient significance but also its power of attraction today (Day 2006, Pringle). Besides monoglossia from Bakhtin, we might deploy the Gramscian concepts of hegemony and prestige to analyze how a particular technology of embalming practice, including the rites and materials surrounding it, achieved such overwhelming dominance that it becomes difficult to see ancient Egypt without it.

Future study may turn from the embalmed body, burial equipment, tomb chamber and chapel, and their images and words to seek explanatory contexts in the full archaeological record of all social classes of each period. The preservation of the body as an integer with sun, stars, earth, and Nile resonated with particular social groups in each period, in ways that will require careful definition and description, particularly at moments of change – the decreases in use, as well as the tide of increase. The most detailed archaeological recording across multiple types of site can provide our access to the variable patterns of attraction to, and resistance against, that persuasive millennial offer to preserve an individual body for eternity.

From Theme to Integration: Futures of Study

The focus of this and each of the preceding these chapters has been on a particular theme, and the evidence has been selected to illustrate or discuss just that thematic segment of life. The social practices for sustaining and/or transforming human life beyond the horizon of mortality can be treated as such a theme. When the same material reappears in different chapters as evidence for different topics, the recurrence may simply reflect the multifaceted character of all material objects. An item associated with healing may be defined as sacred during life, recurrent in daily offerings or activated only at an annual festival, and it may retain that value into the project to secure an eternal afterlife. Health, offering, festival, and eternity belong together but can still be studied separately. Yet the thematic divisions seem so porous and fragile that they deserve renewed scrutiny, nowhere more so than in the modern separation of funerary from nonfunerary. Particularly after separate treatment, topics need to be integrated into renewed holistic study, adequate to the complex and fuzzy practices of life in society. Returning to the house on Abu (Figure 2.16), an outline of brickwork and stones and a scatter of finds bear witness to all the range of human lived experience; the presence of the infant burial under the stones at the entrance room wall asks for our appreciation of fully rounded lives.

Comparative archaeology and anthropology build from the principle of difference, whereby the dividing lines applied in Kemet at the various periods 3000–525 BC are unlikely to coincide with those in other times and places, including the ones we would apply today. Perhaps for Kemet, the most productive aspect of the archaeological record is the degree of difference, not only between then and now but also between types of evidence within each period. In the construction of sacred space, the same architectural plan might be identified in ancient writings as *hut-netjer*, "domain of a *netjer*," or *hut-ka*, "domain for the ka," to sustain an individual for eternity (Figure 3.6). Nothing in the plan prepares you for the written evidence that the larger structure may be for an individual, not a deity, challenging the English vocabulary of temple, chapel, and tomb. The written evidence draws clear dividing lines, but at the same time, it elides the underlying similarities which the topographical plan reveals. For a wider archaeology and anthropology, each set of dividing lines is drawn in usefully different ways. Alongside the self-critique of our categories, the study of these differences may be the most important area to develop in future study.

Bibliography

Preface

Ahmad, A. 1994. *In Theory: Classes, Nations, Literatures*. Verso, New York and London.

Harris, R. 1986. *The Origin of Writing*. Duckworth, London.

Loprieno, A. 1996. *Ancient Egyptian Literature: History and Forms*. Brill, Leiden.

Said, E. 1978. *Orientalism*. Penguin, Harmondsworth.

Said, E. 1989. Representing the colonized: anthropology's interlocutors. *Critical Inquiry* 15, 205–225.

Chapter 1

Al-Sayyid Marsot, A. 1985. *A Short History of Modern Egypt*. Cambridge University Press, Cambridge.

Asad, T. 1973. *Anthropology and the Colonial Encounter*. Humanities Press, Atlantic Highlands, NJ.

Assmann, J. 2001. *The Search for God in Ancient Egypt*. Cornell University Press, Ithaca.

Belzoni, G. 1835 *Narrative of the Operations and Recent Discoveries within the Pyramids, Temples, Tombs and Excavations in Egypt and Nubia*. Remy, Brussels.

Benjamin, W. 1968 [1940]. Theses on the philosophy of history. In Benjamin, W. (ed.), *Illuminations* (translations by H. Zohn). Harcourt, Brace and World, New York, 255–265.

Budge, W. 1934. *From Fetish to God in Ancient Egypt*. Oxford University Press, London.

Butzer, K. 1974. *Early Hydraulic Civilization in Egypt*. University of Chicago Press, Chicago.

Clarysse, W., A. Schoors and H. Willems. 1998. *Egyptian Religion: The Last Thousand Years: Studies Dedicated to the Memory of Jan Quaegebeur*. Orientalia Lovaniensia Analecta 84. Peeters, Leuven.

Cole, J. 2000. *Colonialism and Revolution: Social and Cultural Origins of Egypt's `Urabi Movement*. Princeton University Press, Princeton.

Colla, E. 2007. *Conflicted Antiquities: Egyptology, Egyptomania, Egyptian Modernity*. Duke University Press, Durham.

Exploring Religion in Ancient Egypt, First Edition. Stephen Quirke.
© 2015 Stephen Quirke. Published 2015 by John Wiley & Sons, Ltd.

Collier, M. and S. Quirke, 2006. *The UCL Lahun Papyri: Accounts.* Archaeopress, Oxford.

Contardi, F. 2009. *Il Naos di Sethi da Eliopoli. Un monumento per il culto del dio Sole (CGT 7002).* Skira, Milan.

Crehan, K. 2002. *Gramsci, Culture and Anthropology.* University of California Press, Berkeley.

Cuno, K. 1988. Commercial relations between town and village in eighteenth- and early nineteenth-century Egypt. *Annales Islamologiques* 24, 111–135.

Davies, J. 2011. Believing the evidence. In Dawid, P. *et al.* (eds.), *Evidence, Inference and Enquiry.* Oxford University Press, Oxford, 395–434.

de Certeau, M. 1980. *L'invention du quotidien. Vol. 1, Arts de faire.* Gallimard, Paris.

de Ste Croix, G. 1989. *The Class Struggle in the Ancient Greek World: From the Archaic Age to the Arab Conquests.* Cornell University Press, Ithaca.

Derrida, J. and G. Vattimo (eds.), 1998. *Religion* (translations by D. Webb). Stanford University Press, Stanford.

Downes, D. 1974. *The Excavations at Esna 1905–1906.* Aris and Phillips, Warminster.

Dubiel, U. 2008. *Studien zur Typologie, Verteilung und Tragesitte der Amulette, Perlen und Siegel im Alten und Mittleren Reich anhand der Gräberfelder der Region zwischen Qau el-Kebir und Matmar.* Orbis Biblicus et Orientalis 229. Editions universitaires, and Vandenhoeck and Ruprecht, Fribourg, Göttingen.

Edwards, D. 2005. The archaeology of religion. In Díaz-Andreu, M. *et al.* (eds.), *The Archaeology of Identity.* Routledge, London and New York, 110–128.

Effland, A. and U. Effland, 2010. „Ritual Landscape" und „Sacred Space"—Überlegungen zu Kultausrichtung und Prozessionsachsen in Abydos. *MOSAIKjournal* 1, 133–167.

El Daly, O. 2004. *Egyptology, the Missing Millennium.* UCL Press, London.

El Saadawi, N. 1997. *The Nawal El Saadawi Reader.* Zed Books, New York.

Fabian, J. 1983. *Time and the Other. How Anthropology Makes its Object.* Columbia University Press, New York.

Fabian, J. 2007. *Memory against Culture: Arguments and Reminders.* Duke University Press, Durham.

Fischer, H. 1986. *L'Ecriture et l'Art de l'Egypte ancienne.* Presses universitaires de France, Paris.

Fitzenreiter, M. 2004. Bemerkungen zur Beschreibung altägyptischer Religion. *Göttinger Miszellen* 202, 19–53.

Friedman, R. (ed.) 1999. *Egypt and Nubia. Gifts of the Desert.* British Museum Press, London.

Giddy, L. 1999. The present state of Egyptian archaeology: 1997 update. In Leahy, A. and J. Tait (eds.), *Studies on Ancient Egypt in Honour of H.S. Smith.* Egypt Exploration Society, London, 109–113.

Godlewska, A. 1995. Map, text and image. The mentality of enlightened conquerors: a new look at the *description de l'Egypte. Transactions of the Institute of British Geographers,* New series 20, 5–28.

Goelet, O. 1994. Commentary. In Faulkner, R. (ed.), *The Egyptian Book of the Dead: The Book of Going Forth by Day—The Complete Papyrus of Ani Featuring Integrated Text and Full-Color Images.* Chronicle Books, San Francisco, 137–170.

Gosden, C. 1999. *Anthropology and Archaeology: A Changing Relationship.* Routledge, London and New York.

Gramsci, A. 1975. Posthumous edition In Gerratana, V. (ed.), *Quaderni del Carcere II.* Einaudi, Turin.

Hassan, F. 2007. Conserving Egyptian heritage: seizing the moment. In Brehony, N. and A. El-Desouky (eds.), *British-Egyptian Relations from Suez to the Present Day.* Saqi Books, London, 209–233.

Hayes, W. 1955. *A Papyrus of the Late Middle Kingdom in the Brooklyn Museum. Papyrus Brooklyn 35.1446.* Brooklyn Museum, Brooklyn.

Helck, W. 1974 *Die altägyptischen Gaue*. Reichert, Wiesbaden.

Hendrickx, S., D. Huyge and W. Wendrich, 2010. Worship without writing. In Wendrich, W. (ed.), *Egyptian Archaeology*. Wiley-Blackwell, Chichester, 15–35.

Hirschkop, K. 1999. *Mikhail Bakhtin: An Aesthetic for Democracy*. Oxford University Press, New York and Oxford.

Hornung, E. 1996. *Conceptions of God in Ancient Egypt: The One and the Many*. Cornell University Press, New York.

Ives, P. 2004. *Gramsci's Politics of Language: Engaging the Bakhtin Circle and the Frankfurt School*. University of Toronto Press, Toronto.

Jeffreys, D. 2010. Regionality, cultural and ritual landscapes. In Wendrich, W. (ed.), *Egyptian Archaeology*. Wiley-Blackwell, Chichester, 102–118.

Lehner, M. 2010. Villages and the old kingdom In Wendrich, W. (ed.), *Egyptian Archaeology*. Wiley-Blackwell, Chichester, 85–101.

Lepsius, R. (ed.), 1849–1859. *Denkmäler aus Aegypten und Aethiopien*, Vol. 3. Berlin.

Loprieno, A. 1996. *Ancient Egyptian Literature: History and Forms*. Brill, Leiden.

Louca, A. 2006. *L'autre Egypte, de Bonaparte à Taha Hussein*. Institut Français d'Archéologie Orientale, Cairo.

Malek, J. 1982. The original version of the Royal Canon of Turin. *Journal of Egyptian Archaeology* 68, 93–106.

Malek, J. 1992. A meeting of the old and new. Saqqara during the New Kingdom. In Lloyd, A.B. (ed.), *Studies in Pharaonic Religion and Society in Honour of J. Gwyn Griffiths*. Egypt Exploration Society, London, 57–76.

Mitchell, T. 1988. *Colonising Egypt*. University of California Press, Berkeley.

Mitchell. T. 2002. *Rule of Experts: Egypt, Techno-Politics, Modernity*. University of California Press, Berkeley.

Moreno Garcia, J.-C. 2009. From dracula to rostovtzeff, or the misadventures of economic history. In Fitzenreiter, M. (ed.), *Das Ereignis. Geschichtsschreibung zwischen Vorfall und Befund*. Gold House Publications, London, 175–198.

Morris, I. 1994. *Classical Greece: Ancient Histories and Modern Archaeologies*. Cambridge University Press, Cambridge.

Morris, I. 2000. *Archaeology as Culture History: Words and Things in Iron Age Greece*. Blackwell, Oxford and Malden.

Naville, E. 1895. *Deir el Bahri I*. Egypt Exploration Fund, London.

Naville, E. 1898. *Deir el-Bahri. Part 3*. Egypt Exploration Fund, London.

Omlin, J. 1973. *Der Papyrus 55001 und seine satirisch-erotischen Zeichnungen und Inschriften*. Catalogo del Museo egizio di Torino, Seria 1.3. Pozzo, Turin.

Petrie, W.M.F. 1890. *Kahun, Gurob, Hawara*. Kegan Paul, Trench, Trübner and Co, London.

Petrie, W.M. F. 1909. *Memphis I*. School of Archaeology in Egypt, University College, B. Quaritch, London.

Petrie, W.M.F. 1912. *Heliopolis, Kafr Ammar, Shurafa*. London.

Pinch, G. 1993. *Votive Offerings to Hathor*. Griffith Institute, Oxford.

Quirke, S. 2009–2010. Provincialising Elites: defining regions as social relations. In Moreno Garcia, J.-C. (ed.) *Elites et pouvoir en Egypte ancienne = Cahiers de Recherche de l'Institut de Papyrologie et d'Égyptologie* 28, 51–66.

Reid, D. 2002 *Whose Pharaohs? Archaeology, Museums, and Egyptian National Identity from Napoleon to World War 1*. University of California, Berkeley.

Said, E. 1978. *Orientalism*. Penguin, Harmondsworth.

Sauer, E. 2004 *Archaeology and Ancient History: Breaking Down the Boundaries*. Routledge, London and New York.

Schlott-Schwab, A. 1981. *Die Ausmasse Ägyptens nach altägyptischen Texten.* Harrassowitz, Wiesbaden.

Scott, J. 2008. Modes of power and the reconceptualisation of elites. In Savage, M. and K. Willems (eds.), *Remembering Elites.* Blackwell, Malden MA, 27–43.

Seidlmayer, S. 2001. *Historische und moderne Nilstände. Untersuchungen zu den Pegelablesungen des Nils von der Frühzeit bis zur Gegenwart.* Achet Verlag, Berlin.

Traunecker, C. 1997. Lessons from the upper Egyptian temple of el-Qal'a. In Quirke, S. (ed.), *The Temple in Ancient Egypt: New Discoveries and Recent Research,* British Museum Press, London, 168–178.

Trigger, B. 1983. The rise of Egyptian civilization. In Trigger, B. *et al., Ancient Egypt: A Social History.* Cambridge University Press, Cambridge, 1–43.

Tvedt, T. 2003. *The River Nile in the Age of the British.* I.B. Tauris, London and New York.

Waddell, W. 1940. *Manetho.* Heinemann, London.

Wendrich, W. 2010. *Egyptian Archaeology.* Wiley-Blackwell, Chichester.

Wengrow, D. 2006. *Archaeology of Early Egypt Social Transformations in North-East Africa, 10,000–2650 BC.* Cambridge University Press, Cambridge.

Chapter 2

Ashton, S.-A. 2013. *6000 Years of African Combs.* Fitzwilliam Museum, Cambridge.

Assmann, J. 1990. Egyptian mortuary liturgies. In Israelit-Groll, S. (ed.), *Studies in Egyptology Presented to Miriam Lichtheim.* Magnes Press, Jerusalem, 1–25.

Bentley, P. 1999. Report on the skeletal material. In Sowada, K., T. Callaghan and P. Bentley (eds.), *The Teti Cemetery at Saqqara. IV. Minor Burials and Other Material,* Australian Centre for Egyptology, Sydney, 94.

Berlev, O. 2000. Two suns, two kings. In Quirke, S. and O. Berlev (eds.), *Discovering Egypt from the Neva,* Achet Verlag, Berlin.

Bickel, S. 1994. *La cosmogonie égyptienne avant le Nouvel Empire.* Editions universitaires, and Vandenhoeck and Ruprecht, Fribourg, Göttingen.

Bloch, M. 1998. *How We Think They Think: Anthropological Approaches to Cognition, Memory, and Literacy.* Westview Press, Boulder, Colorado.

Bourriau, J. 1988. *Pharaohs and Mortals: Egyptian Art in the Middle Kingdom.* Cambridge University Press, Cambridge.

Brunton, G. 1927. *Qau and Badari I.* British School of Archaeology in Egypt, London.

Brunton, G. 1930. *Qau and Badari III.* British School of Archaeology in Egypt, London.

Bussmann, R. 2006. Der Kult im frühen Satet-Tempel von Elephantine. In Mylonopoulos, J. and H. Roeder (eds.), *Archäologie und Ritual. Auf der Suche nach den rituellen Handlung in den antiken Kulturen Ägyptens und Griechenlands,* Phoibos, Vienna, 25–36.

Clère, J.-J. 1995. *Les Chauves d'Hathor.* Peeters, Leuven.

Dasen, V. 1993. *Dwarfs in Ancient Egypt and Greece.* Oxford University Press, Oxford.

David, R. 2007. *The Two Brothers.* Rutherford Press, Bolton.

Dawson, W. and P. Gray, 1968. *Catalogue of Egyptian Antiquities in the British Museum. I. Mummies and Human Remains.* British Museum Press, London.

Descola, P. 2005. *Par-delà Nature et Culture.* Gallimard, Paris.

Dubiel, U. 2008. *Studien zur Typologie, Verteilung und Tragesitte der Amulette, Perlen und Siegel im Alten und Mittleren Reich anhand der Gräberfelder der Region zwischen Qau el-Kebir und Matmar.* Orbis Biblicus et Orientalis 229. Editions universitaires, and Vandenhoeck and Ruprecht, Fribourg, Göttingen.

Feucht, E. 2003. Pharaonische beschneidung. In Meyer, S. (ed.), *Ägypten, Tempel der Ganzen Welt*. Brill, Leiden, 81–94.

Fischer-Elfert, H.-W. 2005. *Abseits von Ma`at. Fallstudien zu Aussenseitern im Alten. Ägypten.* Ergon.

Friedman, R.F., W. Van Neer and V. Linseele, 2011. The elite Predynastic cemetery at Hierakonpolis: 2009-2010 update, In Friedman, R.F. and P.N. Fiske (eds.), *Egypt at its Origins 3. Orientalia Lovaniensia Analecta 205*. Peeters, Leuven, 157–191.

Gardiner, A. 1947. *Ancient Egyptian Onomastica*. Oxford University Press, London.

Geoffroy Saint-Hilaire, E. 1826. Note sur un monstre humain (anencéphale) trouvé dans les ruines de Thèbes en Egypte par M. Passalacqua. *Archives Générales de Médecine* 10, 154–126.

Geoffroy Saint-Hilaire, E.G. de 1822. *Philosophie Anatomique: des Monstruosités Humaines.* Rignoux, Paris.

Glenister, T. 1964. Fantasies, facts, and foetuses: the interplay of fantasy and reason in teratology. *Medical History* 8, 15–30.

Habachi, L. 1979. Catalogue entry on the 'ancestor bust' of Pendjerty. In *The Luxor Museum of Ancient Art*. American Research Center in Egypt, Cairo, 150.

Horváth, Z. 2009. Temple(s) and town at el-Lahun: a study of ancient toponyms in the el-Lahun papyri. In Silverman, D. and J. Wegner (eds.), *Archaism and Innovation: Studies in the Culture of Middle Kingdom Egypt*. University of Pennsylvania Museum of Archaeology and Anthropology and Department of Near Eastern Languages and Civilizations, Yale University, Philadelphia and New Haven, 171–203.

Hubert, J. 1994. Sacred beliefs and beliefs of sacredness. In Carmichael, D., J. Hubert, B. Reeves and A. Schanche (eds.), *Sacred Sites, Sacred Places*. Routledge, London and New York, 9–19.

Insoll, T. 2004. *Archaeology, Ritual, Religion*. Routledge, New York.

Joisten-Pruschke, A. 2008. *Das religiöse Leben der Juden von Elephantine in der Achämenidenzeit*. Harrassowitz, Wiesbaden.

Kemp, B. 2006. *Ancient Egypt: Anatomy of a Civilization*, 2nd edition. Routledge, New York.

Kessler, D. 1989. *Die Heiligen Tiere und der König: Beiträge zu Organisation, Kult und Theologie der spätzeitlichen Tierfriedhöfe*. Harrassowitz, Wiesbaden.

Lilyquist, C. 1979. *Ancient Egyptian Mirrors from the Earliest Times through the Middle Kingdom*. Deutscher Kunstverlag, Munich and Berlin.

McNamara, L. 2006 The revetted mound at Hierakonpolis and early kingship: a re-interpretation. In Midant-Reynes, B. and Y. Tristant (eds.), *Egypt at its Origins. II*. Peeters, Leuven.

Meskell, L. 1999 *Archaeologies of Social Life: Age, Sex, Class* et cetera *in Ancient Egypt*. Blackwell, Malden and Oxford.

Morris, E. 2011. Paddle dolls and performance. *Journal of the American Research Center in Egypt* 47, 71–103.

Nyord, R. 2009. *Breathing Flesh. Conceptions of the Body in the Ancient Egyptian Coffin Texts*. Museum Tusculanum, Copenhagen.

Petrie, W.M.F. 1891. *Illahun, Kahun, Gurob*. David Nutt, London.

Petrie, W.M.F. 1898. *Deshasheh*. Exploration Fund, London.

Petrie, W.M.F. 1900. *The Royal Tombs of the First Dynasty, 1900: Part I*. Egypt Exploration Fund, London.

von Pilgrim. C. 1996. *Elephantine XVIII. Untersuchungen in der Stadt des Mittleren Reiches und der Zweiten Zwischenzeit*. Philipp von Zabern, Mainz.

Pinch, G. 1993. *Votive Offerings to Hathor*. Griffith Institute, Oxford.

Quack, J. 1995. Dekane und gliedervergottung. Altägyptische traditionen im Apokryphon Johannis. *Jahrbuch für Antike und Christentum* 38, 97–122.

Quirke, S. 2011. Petrie's 1889 photographs of Lahun. In Aston, D. *et al.*, *Under the Potter's Tree. Studies on Ancient Egypt Presented to Janine Bourriau on the Occasion of her 70th Birthday*. Peeters, Leuven, 769–793.

Quirke, S. 2013. *Going Out in Daylight: prt m hrw—the Ancient Egyptian Book of the Dead*. Golden House Publications, London.

Ramos, A. 2012. The politics of perspectivism. *Annual Review of Anthropology* 41, 481–494.

Robins, G. 1993. *Women in Ancient Egypt*. British Museum Press, London.

Roth, A. and C. Roehrig, 2002. Magical bricks and the bricks of birth. *Journal of Egyptian Archaeology* 88, 121–139.

Spence, K. 2007. A contextual approach to Ancient Egyptian domestic cult: the case of the 'Lustration Slabs' at el-Amarna. In Barrowclough, D. and C. Malone (eds.), *Reconsidering Ritual in Archaeology*. Oxbow, Oxford, 285–292.

Steindorff, G.. 1902. *Grabfunde II. Das Grab des Sebek-o, ein Grabfund aus Gebelein*. Berlin.

Te Brake, W. 2011. The contentious politics of religious diversity. In Hanagan, M. and C. Tilly (eds.), *Contention and Trust in Cities and States*, Springer, Dordrecht, 229–248.

Tocheri, M. 2005. Roman period fetal skeletons from the East Cemetery (Kellis 2) of Kellis, Egypt. *International Journal of Osteoarchaeology* 15, 326–341.

Sweeney, D. 2006. Women growing older in Deir el-Medina. In Dorn, A. and I. Hofmann (eds.), *Living and Writing in Deir el-Medina*. Schwabe Verlag, Basel, 135–160.

Wegner, J. 2010. Tradition and innovation: the middle kingdom. In Wendrich, W. (ed.), *Egyptian Archaeology*. Blackwell, Oxford, 119–142.

Wengrow, D. 2006. *Archaeology of Early Egypt Social Transformations in North-East Africa, 10,000–2650 BC*. Cambridge University Press, Cambridge.

Westendorf, W. 1965. Beiträge aus und zu den medizinischen Texten. *Zeitschrift für Ägyptische Sprache und Altertumskunde* 92, 128–154.

Chapter 3

Assmann, J. 1990. Egyptian mortuary liturgies. In Israelit-Groll, S. (ed.), *Studies in Egyptology Presented to Miriam Lichtheim*. Magnes Press, Jerusalem, 1–25.

Assmann, J. 2001. *The Search for God in Ancient Egypt*. Cornell University Press, Ithaca.

Barta, W. 1968. *Aufbau und Bedeutung der altägyptischen Opferformel*. J.J. Augustin, Glückstadt.

Bell, L. 1997. The new kingdom "divine" temple: the example of Luxor. In Shafer, B. (ed.), *Temples of Ancient Egypt*. Cornell University Press, Ithaca, 127–184.

Berlev, O. 1972. *Trudovoe Naselenie Egipta epokhu srednego Tsarstava*. Nauk, Moscow.

Berlev, O. 2000. Two Suns, Two Kings. In Quirke, S. and O. Berlev (eds.), *Discovering Egypt from the Neva*. Achet, Berlin.

Bickel, S. 1994. *La cosmogonie égyptienne avant le Nouvel Empire*. Editions universitaires, Vandenhoeck and Ruprecht, Fribourg, Göttingen.

Blumenthal, E. 1987. Die 'Gottesvater' des Alten und Mittleren Reiches. *Zeitschrift für Ägyptische Sprache und Altertumskunde* 114, 10–35.

Brunton, G. 1927. *Qau and Badari I*. British School of Archaeology in Egypt, London.

Brunton, G. 1930. *Qau and Badari III*. British School of Archaeology in Egypt, London.

Bussmann, R. 2006. Der Kult im frühen Satet-Tempel von Elephantine. In Mylonopoulos, J. and H. Roeder (eds.), *Archäologie und Ritual. Auf der Suche nach der rituellen Handlung in den antiken Kulturen Ägyptens und Griechenlands*. Phoibos, Vienna, 25–36.

Clère, J.-J. 1995. *Les Chauves d'Hathor*. Peeters, Leuven.

Collier, M. and S. Quirke, 2006. *The UCL Lahun Papyri: Accounts*. Archaeopress, Oxford.

Coulon, L. and E.Jambon, n.d. Karnak cachette database. http://www.ifao.egnet.net/bases/cachette/about (consulted 29.30.2013).

David, R. 2007. *The Two Brothers*. Rutherford Press, Bolton.

De Morgan, J. 1903. *Fouilles à Dahchour 1894–1895*. Adolphe Holzhausen, Vienna.

Eaton, K. 2006. The festival of Osiris and Sokar in the month of Khoiak: the evidence from Nineteenth Dynasty royal monuments at Abydos. *Studien zur Altägyptischen Kultur* 35, 75–101.

Gardiner, A. and N. de Garis Davies, 1920. *The Tomb of Antefoker, Vizier of Sesostris I, and of his Wife, Senet. No.60*. The Theban Tombs Series. Egypt Exploration Society, London.

Grandet, P. 0000 Papyrus Harris.

Insoll, T. 2004. *Archaeology, Ritual, Religion*. Routledge, New York.

Jánosi, P. 1999. The tombs of officials: house of eternity. In Allen, J. *et al.*, *Egyptian Art in the Age of the Pyramids*. Metropolitan Museum of Art, New York, 27–37.

Jansen-Winkeln, K. 2006. Relative chronology of Dyn. 21. In Hornung, E., R. Krauss and D. Warburton (eds.), *Ancient Egyptian Chronology*. Brill, Leiden, 218–233.

Kemp, B. 2006. *Ancient Egypt: Anatomy of a Civilization,* 2nd edition. Routledge, New York.

Lichtheim, M. 1973. *Ancient Egyptian Literature. I. The Old and Middle Kingdoms*. University of California Press, Berkeley.

McNamara, L. 2006 The revetted mound at Hierakonpolis and early kingship: a re-interpretation. In Midant-Reynes, B. and Y. Tristant (eds.), *Egypt at its Origins. 2*. Peeters, Leuven.

Müller, V. 2006. Relikte kultischer Mahlzeiten in Auaris/Tell el-Dab'a. In Mylonopoulos, J. and H. Roeder (eds.), *Archäologie und Ritual. Auf der Suche nach der rituellen Handlung in den antiken Kulturen Ägyptens und Griechenlands*. Phoibos, Vienna, 65–83.

Nord, D. 1981. The term *hnr*: "harem" or "musical performer"? In Simpson, W. and W. Davis (eds.), *Studies in Ancient Egypt, the Aegean, and the Sudan. Essays in Honor of Dows Dunham on the Occasion of his 90th Birthday, June 1, 1980*. Museum of Fine Arts, Boston, 137–145.

Nyord, R. 2009. *Breathing Flesh. Conceptions of the Body in the Ancient Egyptian Coffin Texts*. Museum Tusculanum, Copenhagen.

Pendlebury, J. 1951. *The City of Akhenaten III*. Egypt Exploration Society, London.

Petrie, W.M.F. 1895. *Koptos*. Quaritch, London.

Petrie, W.M.F. 1900. *The Royal Tombs of the First Dynasty, 1900: Part I*. Egypt Exploration Fund, London.

Petrie, W.M.F 1905. *Ehnasya*. Egypt Exploration Fund, London.

Petrie, W. 1906. *Hyksos and Israelite Cities*. British School of Egyptian Archaeology, London.

Petrie, W. 1938. *Egyptian Architecture*. London.

Pilgrim, C. von, 1996. *Elephantine XVIII. Untersuchungen in der Stadt des Mittleren Reiches und der Zweiten Zwischenzeit*. Philipp von Zabern, Mainz.

Pinch, G. 1993. *Votive Offerings to Hathor*. Griffith Institute, Oxford.

Quack, J. 2002. Königsweihe, priesterweihe, isisweihe. In Assmann, J. and M. Bommas (eds.), *Ägyptische Mysterien?* Fink, Munich, 95–108.

Quirke, S. 1999. Women in ancient Egypt: temple titles and funerary papyri. In Tait, J. and A. Leahy (eds.), *Studies in Ancient Egypt in Honour of H.S. Smith.* Egypt Exploration Society, London, 227–235.

Redford, D. 1967. *History and Chronology of the 18th Dynasty of Egypt: Seven Studies.* University of Toronto Press, Toronto.

Ricke, H. 1935. Eine Inventartafel aus Heliopolis im Turiner Museum. *Zeitschrift für Ägyptische Sprache und Altertumskunde* 71, 111–133.

Roberts, A. 1995. *Hathor Rising: the Serpent Power of Ancient Egypt.* Northgate, Totnes.

Robins, G. 1993. *Women in Ancient Egypt.* British Museum Press, London.

Roth, A. 1991. *Egyptian Phyles in the Old Kingdom: the Evolution of a System of Social Organization.* University of Chicago Press, Chicago.

Schott, S. 1950. *Altägyptische Festdaten.* Harrassowitz, Wiesbaden.

Shaw, I. 1994. Balustrades, stairs and altars in the cult of the Aten at el-Amarna. *Journal of Egyptian Archaeology* 80, 109–127.

Spalinger, A. 1991. Some revisions of temple endowments in the New Kingdom. *Journal of the American Research Center in Egypt* 28, 21–39.

Te Brake, W. 2011. The contentious politics of religious diversity. In Hanagan, M. and C. Tilly (eds.), *Contention and Trust in Cities and States.* Springer, Dordrecht, 229–248.

Verner, M. 2002. *Abusir, Realm of Osiris.* American University in Cairo, Cairo.

Waraksa, E. 2009. *Female Figurines from the Mut Precinct: Context and Ritual Function.* Editions universitaires; Vandenhoeck and Ruprecht, Fribourg, Göttingen.

Weinstein, J. 2001. Foundation deposits. In Redford, D. (ed.), *The Oxford Encyclopedia of Ancient Egypt.* Oxford University Press, New York and Oxford, 559–561.

Zivie, A. 2009. *La tombe de Maïa, mère nourricière du roi Toutânkhamon et grande du harem (BUB. I. 20).* Caracara, Toulouse.

Chapter 4

Aldred, C. 1971. *Jewels of the Pharaohs: Egyptian Jewellery of the Dynastic Period.* Thames and Hudson, London.

Allen, T. 1974. *The Book of the Dead, or, Going forth by Day: Ideas of the Ancient Egyptians Concerning the Hereafter Expressed in Their Own Terms.* University of Chicago Press, Chicago.

Allen, J. 1988. *Genesis in Egypt: The Philosophy of Ancient Egyptian Creation Accounts.* Yale Egyptological Seminar, New Haven.

Arvidsson, S. and S. Wichmann, 2006. *Aryan Idols: Indo-European Mythology as Ideology and Science.* University of Chicago Press, Chicago.

Assmann, J. 1970. *Der König als Sonnenpriester: ein kosmographischer Begleittext zur kultischen Sonnenhymnik in thebanischen Tempeln und Gräber.* J.J. Augustin, Glückstadt.

Assmann, J. 1977a. Die Verborgenheit des Mythos im Alten Ägypten. *Göttinger Miszellen* 25, 7–43.

Assmann, J. 1977b. Das ägyptische Zweibrüdermärchen (Papyrus d'Orbiney). Eine Textanalyse auf drei Ebenen am Leitfaden der Einheitsfrage. *Zeitschrift für Ägyptische Sprache und Altertumskunde* 104, 1–25.

Assmann, J. 1992. Ein Gespräch im Goldhaus über Kunst und andere Gegenstände. In Gammer-Wallert, I. and W. Helck (eds.), *Gegengabe. Festschrift für Emma Brunner-Traut.* Attempto Verlag, Tübingen, 43–60.

Assmann, J. 2005. *Death and Salvation in Ancient Egypt.* Cornell University Press, Ithaca.

Bickel, S. 1994. *La cosmogonie égyptienne avant le Nouvel Empire.* Orbis Biblicus et Orientalis 134. Editions Universitaires, Fribourg.

Bloch, M. 1998. *How We Think They Think. Anthropological Approaches to Cognition, Memory, and Literacy.* Westview Press, Boulder.

Brunton, G. 1930. *Qau and Badari III.* British School of Archaeology in Egypt, London.

Cassirer, E. 1923–1929. *Philosophie der Symbolischen Formen.* Bruno Cassirer, Berlin. (1953–1957 English translation *Philosophy of Symbolic Forms,* Yale University Press, New Haven).

Darnell, J. 1999. Epigraphic report in R. Friedman et al., Preliminary report on field work at Hierakonpolis: 1996–1998. *Journal of the American Research Center in Egypt* 36, 1–35.

Detienne, M. 1981. *L'invention du mythe.* Gallimard, Paris.

Diakonoff, I. 1995. *Archaic Myths of the Orient and the Occident.* Orientalia Gothoburgensia 10. Acta Universitatis Gothoburgensis, Göteborg.

Dollerup, C. 1995. Translation as a creative force in literature: the birth of the European Bourgeois Fairy-Tale. *The Modern Language Review* 90, 94–102.

Dreyer, G. 1986. *Der Tempel der Satet; die Funde der Frühzeit und des Alten Reiches.* Philipp von Zabern, Mainz.

DuQuesne, T. 2009. *The Salakhana Trove: Votive Stelae and Other Objects from Asyut.* Darengo Publications, London.

Eagleton, T. 1990. *The Ideology of the Aesthetic.* Blackwell, Malden and Oxford.

Ferro, M. 1981. *Comment on raconte l'histoire aux enfants: à travers le monde entire.* Payot, Paris.

Ferro, M. 1984. *The Use and Abuse of History, or, How the Past is Taught.* Routledge and Kegan Paul, Boston.

Fischer, H. 1962. The cult and nome of the goddess Bat. *Journal of the American Research Center in Egypt* 1, 7–23.

Fischer, H. 1986. *L'écriture et l'art de l'Egypte ancienne, Essais et conference.* Collège de France, Paris.

Frandsen, P. 1986. Tabu. In *Lexikon der Ägyptologie 6.* Harrassowitz, Wiesbaden, 135-142

Garstang, J. 1902. *El Arabeh.* Quaritch, London.

Gasse, A. and V. Rondot, 2007. *Les inscriptions de Séhel.* Institut Français d'Archéologie Orientale au Caire, Cairo.

Giddy, L. 1999. The present state of Egyptian archaeology: 1997 update. In Leahy, A. and J. Tait (eds.), *Studies on Ancient Egypt in Honour of H.S. Smith.* Occasional Publication 13. Egypt Exploration Society, London, 109–113.

Gilet, P. 1998. *Vladimir Propp and the Universal Folktale. Recommissioning an old paradigm—story as initiation.* Peter Lang, New York.

Goebs, K. 2002. A functional approach to Egyptian myth and mythemes. *Journal of Ancient Near Eastern Religions* 2, 27–59.

Goodman, S. and P. Meininger (eds.), 1989. *The Birds of Egypt.* Oxford University Press, Oxford and New York.

Grajetzki, W. 2003. *Burial Customs in Ancient Egypt: Life in Death for Rich and Poor.* Duckworth, London.

Gwyn Griffiths, J. 1970. *Plutarch's De Iside et Osiride.* University of Wales, Cardiff.

Haarlem, W. van 1997. Coffins and Naoi in as votive objects in Tell Ibrahim Awad. In van Dijk, J., *Essays on Ancient Egypt in Honour of Herman te Velde.* Brill, Leiden, 167–170.

Harvey, S. 2003. Interpreting Punt: geographic, cultural and artistic landscapes. In Connor D. O' and Quirke S. (eds.), *Mysterious Lands.* UCL Press, London, 81–92.

Hassan, A. 1976. *Stöcke und Stäbe im Pharaonischen Ägypten bis zum Ende des Neuen Reiches.* Deutscher Kunstverlag, Munich and Berlin.

Hill, J. 2004. *Cylinder Seal Glyptic in Predynastic Egypt and Neighbouring Regions.* British Archaeological Reports. Archaeopress, Oxford.

Horkheimer, M. 1930. *Anfänge der bürgerlichen Geschichtsphilosophie.* Kohlhammer, Stuttgart.

Ives, P. 2004. *Gramsci's Politics of Language.* University of Toronto Press, Toronto.

Jacquet-Gordon, H. 2003. *The Graffiti on the Khonsu Temple Roof at Karnak: A Manifestation of Personal Piety.* Temple of Khonsu, Vol. 3. University of Chicago, Chicago.

James, T. G. H. 1971. *Myths and Legends of Ancient Egypt.* Grosset and Dunlap, New York.

Kemp, B. 1995. Outlying temples at Amarna. In Bomann, A. (ed.), *Amarna Reports* VI. Egypt Exploration Society, London, 411–461.

Kemp, B. 2006. *Ancient Egypt: Anatomy of a Civilization,* 2nd enlarged edition. Routledge, New York.

Leach, E. 1969. *Genesis as Myth and Other Essays.* Jonathan Cape, London.

Lichtheim, M. 1976. *Ancient Egyptian Literature. II. The New Kingdom.* University of California Press, Berkeley.

Lieven, A van 2007. *Grundriss des Laufes der Sterne: das sogenannte Nutbuch.* Museum Tusculanum, Copenhagen.

M'Closkey, K. 2002. *Swept Under the Rug: A Hidden History of Navajo Weaving.* University of New Mexico Press, Albuquerque.

Meeks, D. 2003. Locating Punt. In Connor D. O' and Quirke S. (eds.), *Mysterious Lands.* UCL Press, London, 53–80.

Meeks, D. 2008. *Mythes et légendes du Delta d'après le papyrus Brooklyn 47.218.84.* Institut Français d'Archéologie Orientale au Caire, Cairo.

Petrie, W.M.F. 1896. *Koptos.* B. Quaritch, London.

Petrie, W.M.F. 1925. *Tombs of the Courtiers and Oxyrhynchus.* British School of Archaeology in Egypt, London.

Petrie, W.M.F. 1927. *Buttons and Design Scarabs.* British School of Archaeology in Egypt, London.

Pinch, G. 1994. *Votive Offerings to Hathor.* Griffith Institute, Oxford.

Podzorski, P. 1988. Predynastic Egyptian seals of known provenience in the R. H. Lowie museum of anthropology. *Journal of Near Eastern Studies* 47, 259–268.

Propp, V. 1946. *Istoricheskie Korni Volshebnoi Skazki.* Izdatelstvo LGU, Leningrad.

Quack, J. 2009. Erzählen als Preisen. Vom Astartepapyrus zu den koptischen Märtyrerakten. In Roeder, H. (ed.), *Das Erzählen in frühen Hochkulturen. I. Der Fall Ägypten.* Wilhelm Fink, Munich, 291–312.

Quirke, S. and Z. Tajeddin, 2010. Mechanical reproduction in the age of the artwork? Faience and 5000 moulds from 14th-century BC Egypt. *Visual Communication* 9, 341–361.

Rowlands, M. 2003. The Unity of Africa. In O'Connor, D., and A. Reid (eds.), *Ancient Egypt in Africa.* UCL Press, London, 55–77.

Seipel, W. (ed.), 2001. *Gold der Pharaonen.* Skira, Milan.

Shennan, S. 1999. The development of rank societies. In Barker, G. and A. Grant (eds.), *Companion Encyclopaedia of Archaeology.* Routledge, London, 870–907.

Spalinger, A. 2007. Transformations in Egyptian folktales: the royal influence. *Revue d'Egyptologie* 58, 137–156.

Te Velde, H. 1967. *Seth God of Confusion: A Study of his Role in Egyptian Mythology and Religion.* Brill, Leiden.

Trope, B. et al. 2005. *Excavating Egypt: Great Discoveries from the Petrie Museum of Egyptian Archaeology.* Michael C. Carlos Museum, Emory.

Troy, L. 1986. *Patterns of Queenship in Ancient Egyptian Myth and History.* BOREAS 14. Acta Universitatis Upsaliensis, Uppsala.

Tvedt, T. 2003. *The River Nile in the Age of the British.* I.B. Tauris, London and New York.

Verhoeven, U. 1996. Ein historischer 'Sitz im Leben' für die Erzählung von Horus und Seth des Papyrus Chester Beatty I. In Schade-Busch, M. (ed.), *Wege öffnen: Festschrift für Rolf Gundlach.* Ägypten und Altes Testament 35. Harrassowitz, Wiesbaden, 347–363.

Westendorf, W. 1966. *Altägyptische Darstellungen des Sonnenlaufs auf der abschüssigen Himmelsbahn. Münchner Ägyptologische Studien* 10. Hessling, Berlin.

Wiese, A. 1996. *Die Anfänge der ägyptischen Stempelsiegel-Amulette. Eine typologische und religionsgeschichtliche Untersuchung zu den »Knopfsiegeln« und verwandten Objekten der 6. bis frühen 12. Dynastie.* Editions universitaires; Vandenhoeck and Ruprecht, Fribourg, Göttingen.

Willems, H. 1996. *The Coffin of Heqata (Cairo JdE 36418). A Case Study of Egyptian Funerary Culture of the Early Middle Kingdom.* Peeters, Leuven.

Zeidler, J. 1993. Zur Frage der Spätentstehung des Mythos in Ägypten. *Göttinger Miszellen* 132, 85–109.

Chapter 5

Berlev, O. 1989. Tsifrovie dannie po ugonu naselenia pokorennikh stran v Egipte (Numerical data on deportations from defeated lands in Egypt). In Dandamaev, M. (ed.), *Gosudarstvo i sotsialnie strukturi na drevnem Vostoke.* Moscow.

Beylage, P. 2003. Ich war ein Vorbild für die Kinder, ein ruhig Sprechender und Geduldiger.... In Graefe, E. *et al.* (eds.), *Ägypten-Münster: Kulturwissenschaftliche Studien zu Ägypten, dem Vorderen Orient und verwandten Gebieten.* Harrassowitz, Wiesbaden, 17–32.

Carter, H. and Earl of Carnarvon, 1912. *Five Years Exploration at Thebes.* Henry Frowde, London.

Davis, W. 1992. *Masking the Blow: The Scene of Representation in Late Prehistoric Egyptian Art.* University of California Press, Berkeley.

Deladrière, R. (ed.) 1980. *Ibn Arabi, La vie merveilleuse de Dhu-l-Nun l'Egyptien.* Sindbad, Paris.

Doyen, F. 2010. La residence d'élite: un type de structure dans l'organisation spatiale urbaine du Moyen Empire. In Bietak, M., E. Czerny, I. Forstner-Müller (eds.), *Cities and Urbanism in Ancient Egypt.* Austrian Academy of Sciences, Vienna, 81–101.

Ehrman, B. and Z. Pleše, 2011. *The Apocryphal Gospels: Texts and Translations.* Oxford University Press, Oxford and New York.

Enmarch, R. 2006. *The Dialogue of Ipuwer and the Lord of All.* Griffith Institute, Oxford.

Enmarch, R. 2011. The reception of a Middle Kingdom poem: the dialogue of Ipuwer and the lord of all. In Collier, M. and S. Snape (eds.), *Ramesside Studies in Honour of K.A. Kitchen.* Rutherford, Bolton, 169–175.

Flanagan, J. 1989. Hierarchy in simple "egalitarian" societies. *Annual Review of Anthropology* 18, 245–266.

Hendricks, J.W. 1988. Power and knowledge: discourse and ideological transformation among the Shuar. *American Ethnology* 15, 216–238.

Jones, F.W. 1908. Some lessons from ancient fractures. *British Medical Journal* 2, 455–458.

Kemp, B. 2006. *Ancient Egypt: Anatomy of a Civilization.* 2nd edition, revised. Routledge, New York.

Kemp, B. 2010. Tell el-Amarna, 2010. *Journal of Egyptian Archaeology* 97, 1–29.

Kemp, B. 2011. Tell el-Amarna, Spring 2011. *Journal of Egyptian Archaeology* 97, 1–10.

Lepsius, R. (ed.), 1849–1859. *Denkmäler aus Aegypten und Aethiopien.* Nicolaische Buchhandlung, Berlin.

Lichtheim, M. 1988 *Ancient Egyptian Autobiographies Chiefly of the Middle Kingdom: A Study and an Anthology.* Orbis Biblicus et Orientalis, Editions universitaires, and Vandenhoeck and Ruprecht, Fribourg, Göttingen.

Lorton, D. 1977. The treatment of criminals in ancient Egypt. *Journal of the Economic and Social History of the Orient* 20, 2–64.

Nunn, J. 1996. *Ancient Egyptian Medicine.* British Museum Press, London.

Petrie, W. 1908. *Memphis I.* British School of Archaeology in London, London.

Randall-Maciver, D. and A. Mace, 1902. *El Amrah and Abydos.* Egypt Exploration Fund, London.

Rose, J. 2001. *The Intellectual History of the British Working Class.* Yale University Press, Yale.

Rösing, F. 1990. *Qubbet el Hawa und Elephantine: Zur Bevölkerungsgeschichte von Ägypten.* Fischer, Stuttgart.

Seidlmayer, S. 1987. Wirtschaftliche und gesellschaftliche Entwicklung im Übergang vom Alten zum Mittleren Reich. Ein Beitrag zur Archäologie der Gräberfelder der Region Qau-Matmar in der Ersten Zwischenzeit. In Assmann, J., G. Burkard and V. Davies (eds.), *Problems and Priorities in Egyptian Archaeology.* KPI, London.

Shortland, A. 2009. The fish's tale: a foreign glassworker at Amarna? In Shortland, A., I. Freestone and T. Rehren (eds.), *From Mine to Microscope: Advances in the Study of Ancient Technology.* Oxbow, Oxford, 109–114.

Teeter, E. 1997. *The Presentation of Maat: Ritual and Legitimacy in Ancient Egypt.* Studies in Ancient Oriental Civilization 57. Oriental Institute of the University of Chicago, Chicago.

Théodoridès, A. 1971. The concept of law in ancient Egypt. In Harris, J. (ed.), *The Legacy of Egypt.* Clarendon Press, Oxford, 291–322.

Vercoutter, J. 1963. Textes exécratoires de Mirgissa. *Comptes-rendus des séances de l'Académie des Inscriptions et Belles-Lettres* 107, 97–102.

Vernus, P. 2001. *Sagesses de l'Egypte pharaonique.* Imprimerie Nationale, Paris.

Chapter 6

Aldred, C. 1971. *Jewels of the Pharaohs. Egyptian Jewellery of the Dynastic Period.* Thames and Hudson, London.

Allen, J. 2005. *The Art of Medicine in Ancient Egypt.* Metropolitan Museum of Art, New York.

Altenmüller, H. and A. Moussa, 1991. Die Inschrift Amenemhets II. aus dem Ptah-Tempel von Memphis. Ein Vorbericht. *Studien zur Altägyptischen Kultur* 18, 1–48.

Arnold, D. 1999. Three vases in the shape of mother monkeys and their young. In Arnold, D. and C. Ziegler (eds.), *Egyptian Art in the Age of the Pyramids.* Metropolitan Museum of Art, New York, 446–447.

Bardinet, T. 2010. La contrée de Ouân et son dieu. *Egypte Nilotique et Méditerranéenne* 3, 53–66.

Birzeit n. d. Web-page on items from the Tawfik Canaan collection, with images of amulets on his hand-written labels. http://virtualgallery.birzeit.edu/tour/coll_items?col_id=11091&col_title= The+Tawfiq+Canaan+Collection+of+Palestinian+Amulets (consulted March 1, 2012).

Blackman, A. 1925. Oracles in ancient Egypt I. *Journal of Egyptian Archaeology* 11, 249–255.

Blackman, W. 1927. *The fellāhīn of Upper Egypt.* Harrap, London.

Breasted, J. 1930. *The Edwin Smith Surgical Papyrus: Published in Facsimile and Hieroglyphic Transliteration with Translation and Commentary in Two Volumes.* University of Chicago Press, Chicago.

Bourriau, J. 1988. *Pharaohs and Mortals: Egyptian Art in the Middle Kingdom.* Cambridge University Press, Cambridge.

Bruyère, B. 1937. *Rapport sur les Fouilles de Deir el Médineh (1934–1935). Deuxième Partie.* Institut Français d'Archéologie Orientale, Cairo.

Capart, J. 1907. *Une rue de tombeaux à Saqqarah* 2. Vromant, Brussels.

Černý, J. 1962. Egyptian oracles. In Parker, R. (ed.), *A Saite Oracle Papyrus from Thebes*. Brown University Press, Providence, 35–48.

Coulon, L. 2011. Les *uraei* gardiens du fétiche abydénien. Un motif osirien et sa diffusion à l'époque saïte. In Devauchelle, D. (ed.), *La XXVIe Dynastie, Continuities et Rupture. Promenade Saïte Avec Jean Yoyotte.* Cybele, Paris, 85–108.

Crocker, P. 1985. Status symbols in the architecture of El-'Amarna. *Journal of Egyptian Archaeology* 71, 52–65.

Davies, T. 1907. *The Tomb of Iouiya and Touiyou.* Constable, London.

Demaree, R. 1983. *The Ax iqr n Ra-stelae: On Ancestor Worship in Ancient Egypt.* Egyptologische Uitgaven III Leiden.

Demichelis, S. 2002. La divination par l'huile à l'époque ramesside. In Koenig, Y. (ed.), *La magie en Egypte*. Musée du Louvre, Paris, 149–165.

Dominicus, B. 1994 *Gesten und Gebärden in Darstellungen des Alten und Mittleren. Reiches.* Harrassowitz, Wiesbaden.

Donnat, S. 2002. Le bol support de la Lettre au Mort: vers la mise en évidence d'un ritual magique. In Koenig, Y. (ed.), *La magie en Egypte*. Musée du Louvre, Paris.

Drummond, D., R. Janssen and J. Janssen. 1990. An ancient Egyptian rat trap. *Mitteilungen des Deutschen Archäologischen Instituts Abteilung Kairo* 46, 91–98.

DuQuesne, T. 1991. *Jackal at the Shaman's Gate. A Study of Anubis Lord of Ro-Setawe*. Oxford Communications in Egyptology, Thame.

Edwards, I. 1960. *Hieratic Papyri in the British Museum. Series IV. Oracular Amuletic Decrees of the Late New Kingdom.* British Museum, London.

Engelbach, R. 1923. *Harageh.* British School of Archaeology in Egypt and Bernard Quaritch, London.

Fischer-Elfert, H.-W. 2005a. *Abseits von Ma`at. Fallstudien zu Aussenseitern im Alten Ägypten.* Ergon, Würzburg.

Fischer-Elfert, H.-W. 2005b. "Ein Mann, der nicht gehen kann." Erste Annäherungen an das Heilritual aus dem Hypogäum von Kapelle 1190 in Deir el-Medineh (Ostr. DeM 1059 und Osrt. Berlin P.14291). In Fischer-Elfert, H.W. and T. Richter, *Literatur und Religion im Alten Ägypten*. S. Hirzel, Stuttgart and Leipzig.

Fischer-Elfert, H.-W. 2011. "Ein Mann, der nicht gehen kann." Erste Annäherungen an das Heilritual aus dem Hypogäum von Kapelle 1190 in Deir el-Medineh (Ostr. DeM 1059 und Osrt. Berlin P.14291). In Fischer-Elfert, H.W. and Richter, T. (eds.). *Literatur und Religion im Alten Ägypten*. S. Hirzel, Stuttgart and Leipzig.

Flanagan, M. 2009. *Critical Play. Radical Game Design.* MIT Press, Boston.

Gardiner, A. 1933. The Dakhleh stela. *Journal of Egyptian Archaeology* 19, 19–30.

Gestoso Singer, G. 2009. Queen Ahhotep and the golden fly. *Cahiers Caribéens d'Egyptologie* 12, 75–88.

Gnirs, A. 2009. Nilpferdstosszähne und Schlangenstäbe: zu den magischen Geräten des so genannten Ramesseumsfundes. In Kessler, D. *et al.* (eds.), *Texte-Theben-Tonfragmente. Festschrift für Günter Burkard*. ÄAT 76. Harrassowitz, Wiesbaden, 128–156.

Goedicke, H. 1984. The 'Canaanite illness'. *Studien zur Altägyptischen Kultur* 11, 91–105.

Grajetzki, W. 2014. *Tomb Treasures of the Late Middle Kingdom: The Archaeology of Female Burials.* University of Pennsylvania Press, Philadelphia.

Hutton, R. 2001. *Shamans: Siberian Spirituality and the Western Imagination.* Hambledon and London, London.

Janssen, J. 1980. Absence from work by the necropolis workmen of Thebes. *Studien zur Altägyptischen Kultur* 8, 127–152.

Jeffrey, D. 2012. Fieldschool at Memphis. In *Egyptian Archaeology*.

Ju'beh, B. al-, 2005. Magic and talismans: the Tawfiq Canaan collection of Palestinian amulets. *Jerusalem Quarterly* 22–23, 103–108.

Känel, F. von 1984. *Les prêtres-ouab de Sekhmet et les conjurateurs de Serqet*. Presses universitaires de France, Paris.

Leitz, C. 1994. *Tagewählerei: das Buch h3t nhh ph.wy d̲t und verwandte Texte*. Harrassowitz, Wiesbaden.

Meskell, L. 1999. *Archaeologies of Social Life: Age, Sex, Class* et cetera *in Ancient Egypt*. Blackwell, Oxford and Malden.

Millar, M. and S. Lane, 1988. Ethno-ophthalmology in the Egyptian Delta: an historical systems approach to ethnomedicine in the Middle East. *Social Science and Medicine* 26, 651–657.

Morris, E. 2011. Paddle dolls and performance. *Journal of the American Research Center in Egypt* 47, 71–103.

Morsy, S. 1980. Health and illness as symbols of social differentiation in an Egyptian village. *Anthropological Quarterly* 53, 153–161.

Nai, X. 1945. Ancient Egyptian Beads (PhD dissertation). University of London.

Naydler, J. 2004. *Shamanic Wisdom in the Pyramid Texts*. Inner Traditions, Rochester.

Nunn, J. 1996. *Ancient Egyptian Medicine*. British Museum Press, London.

Nyord, R. 2009. *Breathing Flesh: Conceptions of the Body in the Ancient Egyptian Coffin Texts*. Museum Tusculanum, Copenhagen.

Osing, J. and G. Rosati, 1998. *Papiri Geroglifici e Ieratici da Tebtynis*. Istituto Papirologico Italiano, Florence.

Petrie, W. 1913. *Tarkhan I and Memphis V*. British School of Archaeology in Egypt, London.

Pestman, P. 1982. Who were the owners, in the 'community of workmen' of the Chester Beatty Papyri? In Demaree, R. and J. Janssen (eds.), *Gleanings from Deir el-Medina*. Nederlands Instituut voor het Nabije Oosten, Leiden, 155–172.

Petrie, W.M.F. 1894. *Tell el Amarna*. Quaritch, London.

Petrie, W.M.F. 1914. *Tarkhan II*. British School of Archaeology in Egypt and Bernard Quaritch, London.

Petrie, W.M.F. 1931. *Seventy Years in Archaeology*. Henry Holt, New York.

Piccione, P. 1994. The gaming episode in the tale of Setne Khamwas as religious metaphor. In Silverman, D. (ed.), *For his ka: Essays Offered in Memory of Klaus Baer*. Oriental Institute, Chicago, 197–204.

Quack, J. 2006. Zur Lesung und Deutung des Dramatischen Ramesseumpapyrus. *Zeitschrift für Ägyptische Sprache und Altertumskunde* 133, 72–89.

Raven, M. 1997. Charms for protection during the epagomenal days. In van Dijk, J. (ed.), *Essays on Ancient Egypt in Honour of Herman te Velde*. STYX, Groningen, 275–279.

Roberts, A. 1995. *Hathor Rising: the Serpent Power of Ancient Egypt*. Northgate, Totnes.

Sauneron, S. 1989. *Un traité égyptien d'ophiologie. Papyrus du Brooklyn Museum Nos. 47.218.48 et 85*. Institut Français d'Archéologie Orientale, Cairo.

Sternberg-el-Hotabi, C. 1999. *Untersuchungen zur Überlieferungsgeschichte der Horusstelen: ein Beitrag zur Religionsgeschichte Ägyptens im 1. Jahrtausend v. Chr.* Harrassowitz, Wiesbaden.

Sweeney, D. 2006. Women growing older in Deir el-Medina. In Dorn, A. and I. Hofmann (eds.), *Living and Writing in Deir el-Medina*. Schwabe Verlag, Basel, 135–160.

Szpakowska, K. 2003a. *Behind Closed Eyes: Dreams and Nightmares in Ancient Egypt*. Swansea University Press, Swansea.

Szpakowska, K. 2003b. Playing with fire: initial observations on the religious uses of clay cobras from Amarna. *Journal of the American Research Center in Egypt* 40, 43–53.

Toivari-Viitala, J. 2001. *Women at Deir el-Medina. A Study of the Status and Roles of the Female Inhabitants in the Workmen's Community during the Ramesside Period.* *Egyptologische Uitgaven XV.* Brill, Leiden.

Vernus, P. 1986. Traum. In Helck, W., E. Otto and W. Westendorf, *Lexikon der Ägyptologie VI,* Harrassowitz, Wiesbaden.

Vernus, P. 1995. *Essai sur la Conception de l'histoire dans l'Egypte Pharaonique.* Champion, Paris.

Weiss, L. 2009. Personal religious practice: house altars at Deir el-Medina. *Journal of Egyptian Archaeology* 95, 193–208.

Wente, E. 1990. *Letters from Ancient Egypt.* Scholars Press, Atlanta.

Wiese, A. 1996. *Die Anfänge der ägyptischen Stempelsiegel-Amulette: eine typologische und religionsgeschichtliche Untersuchung zu den "Knopfsiegeln" und verwandten Objekten der 6. bis frühen 12. Dynastie.* Orbis Biblicus et Orientalis, Series Archaeologica 12. Editions universitaires, and Vandenhoeck and Ruprecht, Fribourg, Göttingen.

Winlock, H. 1942. *Excavations at Deir el-Bahri 1911–1931.* Metropolitan Museum of Art, New York.

Yamazaki, N. 2003. *Zaubersprüche für Mutter und Kind: Papyrus Berlin 3027.* Achet Verlag, Berlin.

Chapter 7

Allen, J. 1996. Coffin texts from Lisht. In Willems, H.O. (ed.), *The World of the Coffin Texts: Proceedings of the Symposium held on the Occasion of the 100th Birthday of Adriaan de Buck.* Peeters, Leuven, 1–15.

Allen, J. 2005. *The Ancient Egyptian Pyramid Texts.* Society of Biblical Literature, Atlanta.

Allen, T. 1974. *The Book of the Dead, or, Going Forth by Day: Ideas of the Ancient Egyptians Concerning the Hereafter Expressed in their Own Terms.* University of Chicago Press, Chicago.

Altenmüller, H. 1975. Bestattungsritual. In *Lexikon der Ägyptologie* 1 Harrassowitz, Wiesbaden, 745–765.

Arnold, D. 2008. *Middle Kingdom Tomb Architecture at Lisht.* Metropolitan Museum of Art, New York.

Assmann, J. 1990. Egyptian mortuary liturgies. In Israelit-Groll, S. (ed.), *Studies in Egyptology Presented to Miriam Lichtheim.* Magnes Press, Jerusalem, 1–25.

Assmann, J. 2003. The Ramesside tomb of Nebsumenu (TT183) and the ritual of Opening the Mouth. In Strudwick, N. and J. Taylor (eds.), *The Theban Necropolis: Past, Present and Future.* British Museum Press, London, 53–60.

Assmann, J. 2005. *Death and Salvation in Ancient Egypt.* Cornell University Press, Ithaca.

Assmann, J., M. Bommas and A. Kucharek, 2005. *Altägyptische Totenliturgien 2. Totenliturgien und Totensprüche in Grabinschriften des Neuen Reiches.* Universitätsverlag Winter, Heidelberg.

Aston, D. 2003. The Theban west bank from the twenty-fifth dynasty to the Ptolemaic period. In Strudwick, N. and Taylor, J. (eds.). *The Theban Necropolis. Past, Present and Future.* British Museum Press, London, 138–166.

Barguet, P. 1979. *Le Livre des Morts des anciens Egyptiens.* Le Cerf, Paris.

Barguet, P. 1986. *Textes des sarcophages égyptiens du Moyen Empire.* Le Cerf, Paris.

Bentley, P. 1999. Report on the skeletal material. In Sowada, K., T. Callaghan and P. Bentley (eds.), *The Teti Cemetery at Saqqara. IV. Minor Burials and Other Material.* Australian Centre for Egyptology, Sydney, 94.

Bickel, S. 1994. *La cosmogonie égyptienne avant le Nouvel Empire.* Editions universitaires, Fribourg, and Vandenhoeck and Ruprecht, Göttingen.

Bourriau, J. 1991. Patterns of change in burial customs during the Middle Kingdom. In Quirke, S. (ed.), *Middle Kingdom Studies.* SIA, New Malden, 3–20.

Bourriau, J. 2001. Change of body position in Egyptian burials from the mid XIIth Dynasty until the early XVIIIth Dynasty. In Willems, H. (ed.), *Social Aspects of Funerary Culture in the Egyptian Old and Middle Kingdoms: Proceedings of the International Symposium Held at Leiden University, 6–7 June, 1996.* Peeters, Leuven, 1–20.

Bresciani, E. 1977. *La tomba di Ciennehebu, capo della flotta del re.* Giardini, Pisa.

Brunton, G. 1927. *Qau and Badari I.* British School of Archaeology in Egypt, London.

Brunton, G. 1930. *Qau and Badari III.* British School of Archaeology in Egypt, London.

Day, J. 2006. *The Mummy's Curse: Mummymania in the English Speaking World.* Routledge, New York.

Dubiel, U. 2008. *Studien zur Typologie, Verteilung und Tragesitte der Amulette, Perlen und Siegel im Alten und Mittleren Reich anhand der Gräberfelder der Region zwischen Qau el-Kebir und Matmar.* Orbis Biblicus et Orientalis 229. Editions universitaires, and Vandenhoeck and Ruprecht, Fribourg, Göttingen.

Eigner, D. 1984. *Die monumentalen Grabbauten der Spätzeit in der thebanischen Nekropole.* Österreichische Akademie der Wissenschaften, Vienna.

El Sawi, A. 1979. *Excavations at Tell Basta: Report of Seasons 1967–1971 and Catalogue of Finds.* Charles University, Prague.

Emery, W. 1961. *Archaic Egypt.* Penguin, Harmondsworth.

Garstang, J. 1907. *The Burial Customs of Ancient Egypt: As Illustrated by Tombs of the Middle Kingdom: A Report of Excavations Made in the Necropolis of Beni Hassan During 1902-3-4.* University of Liverpool, Institute of Archaeology, London.

Goulding, E. 2013. *What did the Poor Take with Them? An Investigation into Ancient Egyptian Eighteenth and Nineteenth Dynasty Grave Assemblages of the Non-Elite from Qau, Badari, Matmar and Gurob.* Golden House Publications, London.

Grajetzki, W. 1998. Bemerkungen zu einigen Spruchtypen auf Särgen des späten Mittleren Reiches. *Göttinger Miszellen* 166, 29–37.

Grajetzki, W. 2003. *Burial Customs in Ancient Egypt: Life in Death for Rich and Poor.* Duckworth, London.

Grajetzki, W. 2004. *Tarkhan: A Cemetery at the Time of Egyptian State Formation.* Golden House Publications, London.

Grajetzki, W. 2007. Multiple burials in ancient Egypt to the end of the Middle Kingdom. In Grallert, S. and W. Grajetzki (eds.), *Life and Afterlife in Ancient Egypt during the Middle Kingdom and Second Intermediate Period,* Golden House Publications, London, 16–34.

Grajetzki, W. 2008. The architecture and the significance of the Tarkhan mastabas. *Archéo-Nil* 18, 103–112.

Guidotti, M. 2008. The burial furniture of Tjes-ra-peret, wet nurse of Taharqo's daughter. In Tiradritti, F. (ed.), *Pharaonic Renaissance: Archaism and the Sense of History in Ancient Egypt.* Museum of Fine Arts, Budapest, 103–105.

Harpur, Y. 1987. *Decoration in Egyptian Tombs of the Old Kingdom: Studies in Orientation and Scene Content.* KPI, London.

Hays, H. 2012. *The Organization of the Pyramid Texts: Typology and Disposition.* Probleme der Ägyptologie 31. Brill, Leiden.

Hirsch, E. 2004. *Kultpolitik und Tempelbauprogramme der 12. Dynastie. Untersuchungen zu den Göttertempeln im Alten Ägypten.* Achet Verlag, Berlin.

Hornung, E. 1990. *The Valley of the Kings: Horizon of Eternity*. Timken Publishers, New York.

Hornung, E. 1999. *The Ancient Egyptian Books of the Afterlife*. Cornell University Press, Ithaca.

Kampp-Seyfried, F. 2003. The Theban necropolis: an overview of topography and tomb development from the middle kingdom to the Ramesside period. In Strudwick, N. and J. Taylor (eds.), *The Theban Necropolis: Past, Present and Future*. British Museum Press, London, 2–10.

Lehner, M. 2008. *The Complete Pyramids*. Thames and Hudson, New York and London.

Lesko, L. 1972. *The Ancient Egyptian Book of Two Ways*. University of California Press, Berkeley.

Lichtheim, M. 1988. *Ancient Egyptian Autobiographies Chiefly of the Middle Kingdom: A Study and an Anthology*. Editions Universitaires, and Vandenhoeck and Ruprecht, Fribourg, Göttingen.

Manuelian, P. Der, 2003. *Slab Stelae of the Giza Necropolis*. Peabody Museum of Natural History and University of Pennsylvania Museum of Archaeology and Anthropology, New Haven.

Martin, G. 1992. *Hidden Tombs of Memphis: New Discoveries from the Time of Tutankhamun and Ramesses the Great*. Thames and Hudson, London.

Messiha, K. and H. Messiha. 1964. A new concept about the implements found in the excavations at Gîza. *Annales du Service des Antiquités d'Egypte* 58, 209–225.

Miniaci, G. and S. Quirke. 2009. Reconceiving the tomb in the late Middle Kingdom: the burial of the accountant of the main enclosure Neferhotep at Dra Abu al-Naga. *Bulletin de l'Institut Français d'Archéologie Orientale* 109, 339–383.

Niwiński, A. 1989. *Studies on the Illustrated Theban Funerary Papyri of the 11th and 10th Centuries B.C.* Editions Universitaires, and Vandenhoeck and Ruprecht, Fribourg, Göttingen.

Nyord, R. 2009. *Breathing Flesh. Conceptions of the Body in the Ancient Egyptian Coffin Texts*. Museum Tusculanum, Copenhagen.

O'Connor, D. 1974. Political systems and archaeological data in Egypt. 2600–1780 B.C. *World Archaeology* 6, 15–38.

O'Connor, D. 1985. The 'cenotaphs' of the middle kingdom at Abydos. In Posener-Kriéger, P. (ed.), *Mélanges Gamal Eddin Mokhtar*. Institut Français d'Archéologie Orientale, Cairo, 161–177.

O'Connor, D. 2011. *Abydos: Egypt's First Pharaohs and the Cult of Osiris*. Thames and Hudson, New York and London.

Otto, E. 1960. *Das Ägyptische Mundöffnungsritual*. Harrassowitz, Wiesbaden.

Petrie, W. 1891. *Illahun, Kahun, Gurob*. Quaritch, London.

Petrie, W.M.F. 1901. *Royal Tombs of the Earliest Dynasties. II*. Egypt Exploration Fund, London.

Petrie, W.M.F. 1913. *Tarkhan I and Memphis V*. British School of Archaeology in Egypt, London.

Petrie, W.M.F. 1914. *Tarkhan II*. British School of Archaeology in Egypt, London.

Petrie, W.M.F. and G. Brunton, 1923. *Lahun II*. British School of Archaeology in Egypt, London.

Pilgrim, C. von 1996. *Elephantine XVIII. Untersuchungen in der Stadt des Mittleren Reiches und der Zweiten Zwischenzeit*. Philipp von Zabern, Mainz.

Pinch, G. 2003. Redefining funerary objects. In Hawass, Z., and L. Pinch Brock (eds.), *Egyptology at the Dawn of the Twenty-first Century: Proceedings of the Eighth International Congress of Egyptologists, Cairo, 2000*, Vol. 2. American University in Cairo Press, Cairo, 443–447.

Quibell, J., R. Paget and A. Pirie, 1898. *The Ramesseum and The Tomb of Ptah-hetep*. Quaritch, London.

Quibell, J. 1908. *Excavations at Saqqara, 1906–1907*. Institut français d'archéologie orientale, Cairo.

Reisner, G. 1936. *The Development of the Egyptian Tomb Down to the Accession of Cheops.* Harvard University Press, Cambridge.

Richards, J. 2002. Text and context in late old kingdom Egypt: the archaeology and historiography of Weni the elder. *Journal of the American Research Center in Egypt* 39, 75–102.

Roth, A.M. 2006. Little women: gender and hierarchic proportion in Old Kingdom mastaba chapels. In Bárta, M. (ed.), *The Old Kingdom Art and Archaeology: Proceedings of the Conference Held in Prague, May 31–June 4, 2004.* Czech Institute of Egyptology, Prague, 281–296.

Seidlmayer, S. 2007. People at Beni Hasan: contributions to a model of ancient Egyptian rural society. In Hawass, Z. and J. Richards (eds.), *The Archaeology and Art of Ancient Egypt: Essays in Honor of David B. O'Connor,* Vol. 2. Supreme Council of Antiquities, Cairo, 351–368.

Simpson, W. 1974. *Terrace of the Great God at Abydos. The Offering Chapels of Dynasties 12 and 13.* Peabody Museum of Natural History, New Haven.

Smith, S. 1992. Intact tombs of the 17th and 18th dynasties from Thebes and the new kingdom burial system. *Mitteilungen des Deutschen Archäologischen Instituts, Abteilung Kairo* 48, 193–231.

Taylor, J. 2000. The third intermediate period (1069–664 BC). In Shaw, I. (ed.), *The Oxford History of Ancient Egypt.* Oxford University Press, Oxford, 324–363.

Taylor, J. 2009. Coffins as evidence for a "north-south divide" in the 22nd–25th Dynasties. In Broekman, G., R. Demarée, and O. Kaper (eds.), *The Libyan Period in Egypt: Historical and Cultural Studies into the 21st–24th Dynasties. Proceedings of a Conference at Leiden University, 25–27 October 2007.* Peeters, Leuven, 375–416.

Tiradritti, F. 2009. La tombe de Haroua à Louqsor: un chef-d'œuvre de la renaissance pharaonique. *Égypte, Afrique et Orient* 54, 25–40.

Tooley, A. 1995. *Egyptian Models and Scenes.* Shire Egyptology, Princes Risborough.

Ucko, P. 1969. Ethnography and archaeological interpretation of funerary remains. *World Archaeology* 1 (2), 262–280.

Vandier, J. 1963. Un curieux monument funéraire du Moyen Empire. *Revue du Louvre. La revue des musées de France* 13, 1–10.

Verbovsek, A. 2004. *"Als Gunsterweis des Königs in den Tempel gegeben": Private Tempelstatuen des Alten und Mittleren Reiches.* Harrassowitz, Wiesbaden.

Wendrich, W. 2010. *Egyptian Archaeology.* Wiley-Blackwell, Chichester.

Wengrow, D. 2006. *Archaeology of Early Egypt Social Transformations in North-East Africa, 10,000–2650 BC.* Cambridge University Press, Cambridge.

Willems, H. 1996. *The Coffin of Heqata (Cairo JdE 36418): A Case Study of Egyptian Funerary Culture of the Early Middle Kingdom.* Orientalia Lovaniensia Analecta 70. Peeters, Leuven.

Winlock, H. 1955. *Models of Daily Life in Ancient Egypt: from the Tomb of Meket-Rē' at Thebes.* Harvard University Press, Cambridge.

Woods, T.J. 2007. Death in contemporary western culture. *Islam and Christian-Muslim Relations* 18 (3), 333–343.

Yoyotte, J. 1987. *Tanis. L'or des Pharaons.* Association Française d'Action Artistique, Paris.

Index

Exploring Religion in Ancient Egypt, First Edition. Stephen Quirke.
© 2015 Stephen Quirke. Published 2015 by John Wiley & Sons, Ltd.

superstition, modern concept of, 2, 25, 36
Susa, 18
sustenance of body after death, 201–202,
    215, 219, 221
swallow, 231–233
Sweeney, Deborah, 182
sycamore, 31
syncretism *see* fusing of names
Syria, 203

tabu (*buwt*), 118
Tadja, 227
Taharqo, 226
Tale of a Shipwrecked Sailor, 196
Tale of Khuninpu, 168–169
Tale of Neferty, 168
Tale of Two Brothers, 114
Tale of Woe see Literary Letter, from Hiba
Tamiyt, 44
Tanis *see* Djanet
Tarkhan *see* Semenuhor
Tasenetnefret, 34
Tashereteniah, 196
tattooing, 49
Tausret, 231
Taweret *see* Ipy
Teaching for King Merykara, 162–163
Teaching of a man to his son, 165
Teaching of Amenemipet, 48, 170–171,
    174–175
Teaching of Any, 79, 169–170
Teaching of Kaires, 165–166
Teaching of Khety (Satire of Trades), 153,
    166–167
Teaching of King Amenemhat, 163–164
Teaching of Ptahhotep, 57, 164–165
Teachings (literary genre), 8, 153, 161–171,
    173
Tebtunis, 138
Tefnut, 79, 137, 143
Tekh (*drunkenness*) festival, 99
Tell el-Daba *see* Hutwaret
Tell el-Yahudiya *see* Natahut
Tell Ibrahim Awad, 126
temple architecture, 5–6, 11, 19–23, 36–37,
    62–67, 80–88, 95, 106–108, 134, 137,
    210, 236–237 *see also* foundation rituals
temple offerings *see* daily cult; votive
    offerings

temple staff, 36, 126 *see also* watch (*sa*) of
    temple staff rota
Tepihu, 20
terraced temple, 87
Teti, 55
textiles, beaded, 106
Thebes *see* Waset
theft, 154, 171
theology, university discipline, 6
theory, role in study, 7–8
Thoth (Djehuty), 20–21, 28, 32, 47–48, 56,
    101, 103, 129, 133, 137, 143, 145–146,
    198, 220, 232–233
thunder (role of Seth), 147
Thutmes, sculptor, 154
Thutmes III, 34, 100–101, 162
Thutmes IV, 159
Tihna, 84, 208
Timia, 46
Tiy, queen, 123
tiyet amulet, 58–59, 221, 233
Tjanefer, third god's servant of Amun, 162
Tjaru, 21
Tjebnetjer (Sebennytos), 18, 21
Tjebu (Qau), 13, 20, 58, 62–64, 86, 129–130,
    207, 222
Tjemehu *see* Libyans, ancient
tomb robbery papyri, 155
tombs, 37, 84, 204, 206, 211, 216–218, 220,
    223, 230, 237 *see also* sloping passage,
    tombs with; stairway tombs
tombs, superstructure (offering chapels),
    49–50, 56, 60–61, 79, 82–83, 88–89,
    100–101, 117, 130, 178, 204, 206–212,
    217–223, 226, 230, 233, 237 *see also*
    funerary cones, inscribed; mastaba;
    stone door, solid
tools, miniature, in burials, 207
total history, concept of, 12
totemism, 39
towns, ancient, 14–15, 153–154, 178–179,
    203 *see also* Abu; Akhetaten; Hutwaret;
    Lahun
transfigured dead *see* akh
transformation of person after death,
    201–202, 219–220, 230 *see also* akh
transformations (forms, *kheperu*), 60,
    232–233
Traunecker, Claude, 33–34